BIRNBAUM'S

2017

W9-BGP-294

Disneyland®
RESORT

Expert Advice from the Inside Source

Wendy Lefkon EDITORIAL DIRECTOR

Jill Safro EDITOR

Pam Brandon CONTRIBUTING EDITOR

Clark Wakabayashi DESIGNER

Alexandra Mayes Birnbaum CONSULTING EDITOR

THE OFFICIAL GUIDE

Stephen Birnbaum FOUNDING EDITOR

DISNEP
EDITIONS
LOS ANGELES • NEW YORK

For Steve, who merely made this all possible.

ISBN 978-1-4847-3776-7
FAC-038091-16218
First Edition, September 2016
10 9 8 7 6 5 4 3 2 1

D23
The Official Disney Fan Club
D23.com

Printed in the United States of America

Other 2017 Birnbaum's Official Disney Guides:
Walt Disney World
Walt Disney World For Kids

SUSTAINABLE FORESTRY INITIATIVE   Certified Sourcing
www.sfiprogram.org
SFI-00993
This Label Applies to Text Stock Only

Contents

What's New?

To spotlight shops, attractions, shows, and restaurants making their debut, some listings are marked with the stamp shown here. Look for it throughout the book. Here are a few highlights:

- ❦ Frozen—Live at the Hyperion (page 99)
- ❦ Jedi Training—Trials of the Temple (page 79)
- ❦ Luigi's Rollickin' Roadsters (page 103)
- ❦ Soarin' Around the World (page 100)
- ❦ Star Wars Launch Bay (page 79)

A Word from the Editor

Walt Disney, the man who pioneered the realm of family entertainment, was at once an artist, entrepreneur, and creative visionary. He was also a dad. And, like many of the folks who visit Disneyland each year, Walt treasured the time he spent with his children. In fact, while his two daughters were growing up, Walt accompanied them to carnivals, zoos, and local amusement parks. It was something of a Saturday tradition for the Disney family. During these outings he'd often make the same observation: The youngsters were happily entertained, but the adults didn't have much to do. It didn't seem right that he'd be stuck sitting on a bench while the kids had all the fun. To his way of thinking, a park should appeal to the sense of wonder and exploration in guests of all ages. His bold vision became a reality on July 17, 1955, when Disneyland opened in Anaheim, California.

Now, six decades after welcoming its first visitors, Walt's original park is as beloved as ever—and it continues to grow. As Imagineers lovingly construct the much-anticipated Star Wars Land, guests can get an immediate fix of the Force at Star Wars Launch Bay and Jedi Training—Trials of the Temple, both in Disneyland park's Tomorrowland. While this land of enchantment is wonderfully familiar, Disney California Adventure is a newer playing ground, and finding the best ways to take it in has been an exciting adventure in itself. Attractions such as California Screamin', Tower of Terror, and Toy Story Midway Mania! helped put this place on the map, but they're just the tip of the iceberg. Guests are treated to new attractions and entertainment bearing that distinctive Disney stamp. Among them: a peppy musical stage show dubbed Frozen—Live at the Hyperion; the zippy new Cars Land attraction, Luigi's Rollickin' Roadsters; and the recently relaunched, high-flying fan favorite, Soarin' Around the World.

When Steve Birnbaum launched this guide, he made it clear what was expected of anyone who worked on it. The book would be meticulously revised each year, leaving no attraction untested, no meal untasted, no hotel untried. First-hand experiences like these, accumulated over the years, make this book the most authoritative guide to the Disneyland Resort. Our expertise, however, was not achieved by being escorted through back doors of attractions. Instead, we've waited in lines with everyone else, always hoping to have a Disney experience like any other guest.

Of course, there's more to the Disneyland Resort than the theme parks. There's also a dining, shopping, and entertainment district known as Downtown Disney, and three Disney hotels. It all adds up to a total that is truly greater than the sum of its parts. And, though it has more than a half century of history under its belt, this is just the beginning—as per its founder's wishes: "Disneyland will never be completed. It will continue to grow as long as there is imagination left in the world."

Take Our Advice

In creating this book, we have considered every possible aspect of your trip, from planning it to plotting day-to-day activities. We realize that even the most meticulous vacation planner needs detailed, accurate, and objective information to prepare a successful itinerary. To achieve that goal, we encourage the submission of factual information and insight from Disneyland staffers—but the decision to use such information is entirely at the discretion of the editor.

We have also packaged handy bits of advice in the form of "Hot Tips" throughout the book. These helpful hints come directly from the copious notes we've taken during our countless trips to the Disneyland Resort and the surrounding Anaheim area. We've also used our "Birnbaum's Best" stamp of approval wherever we deemed it appropriate, highlighting our favorite attractions and restaurants—the crowd-pleasers we feel stand head, shoulders, and ears above the rest.

You, the reader, benefit from the combination of years of experience—and access to up-to-date inside information from the Disneyland staff—that makes this guide unique. We like to think it's indispensable, but you be the judge of that 134 pages from now.

Credit Where Credit Is Due

We hope we are not omitting any names in thanking Karen McClintock, Heather Reed Guay, Paula Wheeler, Keyu Shah, Melanie Braunstein, Nick Filippone, Scott Bristow, Claudia Erdogan, Michelle Harker, Susan McRaven, Vayshali Bhakta, Jessica Saffran, Loretta Gordon, Julianna Alley, Carolyn Randolph, and Erin Glover, Laura Schaeffell, Kathy Crummey, John McClintock, and Chris Ostrander for helping us ensure the factual accuracy of *Birnbaum's Official Guide to Disneyland 2017*.

Kudos to Michelle Olveira for her outstanding fact-checking, and to copy editor extraordinaire Diane Hodges. We'd also like to tip our hats to Dushawn Ward, Jennifer Eastwood, Jerry Gonzalez, Mike Carroll, Jessica Ward, Tracey Randinelli, and Christina Fontana for their editorial support and production panache.

Of course, no list of acknowledgments would be complete without mentioning our founding editor, Steve Birnbaum, whose spirit, wisdom, and humor still infuse these pages, as well as Alexandra Mayes Birnbaum, who continues to be a guiding light—to say nothing of a careful reader of every word.

The Last Word

Finally, it's important to remember that every worthwhile travel guide is a living enterprise; the book you hold in your hands is our best effort at explaining how to enjoy the Disneyland Resort at the moment, but its text is not etched in stone. Disneyland is always changing and growing, and in each annual edition we refine and expand our material to serve your needs better. Just before the grand opening of Disneyland, Walt Disney remarked that the main attraction was still missing—people. That's where you come in.

Don't Forget to Write!

No contribution is of greater value to us in preparing the next edition of this book than your comments on its usefulness and your own experiences at the Disneyland Resort. Drop us a postcard or send a letter to the address on the right.

Jill Safro
Birnbaum's Disneyland 2017
Disney Editions
125 West End Avenue, 3rd Floor
New York, NY 10023

Have a wonderful time!

—JILL SAFRO, EDITOR

Getting Ready to Go

T O ALL THAT COME TO THIS HAPPY PLACE: *WELCOME. DISNEYLAND IS YOUR LAND.* So said Walt Disney on June 17, 1955. Fast-forward more than 60 years, and the "Happiest Place on Earth" is as welcoming as ever, hosting millions of visitors from around the globe every year. The 500-acre Disneyland Resort has evolved a bit over time, but Walt Disney's original theme park, Disneyland, is still at its heart. Besides this magical kingdom, guests will find the Disney California Adventure theme park; the Downtown Disney District; a trio of on-property hotels: Disney's Grand Californian Resort & Spa, the Disneyland Hotel, and Disney's Pacific Pier Hotel; and dozens of decidedly Disney dining and shopping destinations. Of course, you'll want to do and see it all, but where should you start? When should you go? And then there are the all-important questions of how to get there and where to stay. Maybe you want to extend your vacation—perhaps you'll include a visit to (or a stay at) the beach or one of the other nearby attractions.

That's a lot to think about. But don't worry: By the time you've read this chapter, you'll have the information you need to make smart decisions. So read on, and remember—a little advance planning goes a long way.

When to Go

When you weigh the best times to visit the Disneyland Resort, the most obvious possibilities seem to be weekends, Christmas, Easter, and summer vacation—particularly if there are children in the family. But there are a few good reasons to avoid these periods—the major one being that almost everybody else wants to go then, too. (The pedestrian traffic at Disney California Adventure is occasionally lighter than it is at Disneyland Park, but it is much busier than it used to be.)

If you can only visit during one of these busy times and worry that the crowds might spoil your fun, there are some tactics for making optimum use of every minute and avoiding the longest of lines—notably, go to the park early to get a jump on the day (and on the crowds), use the free Fastpass system whenever possible, and remember that Disney keeps the parks open later during busy seasons. Note that "early entry" (aka "Extra Magic Hour" or "Magic Mornings") is offered on select days to guests staying at Disneyland hotels, Walt Disney Travel Company guests, and day guests with a pre-purchased 3-day (or more) Park Hopper.

On the other hand, choosing to visit when the parks are least crowded may mean that you miss some of the most entertaining parades and special events. For instance, Disneyland Park's fireworks show and Paint the Night parade might not be listed on the entertainment schedule, and certain attractions may be closed for annual refurbishment.

A lovely time to visit Disneyland—when it's not too crowded but everything is still open—is the period between Thanksgiving until about a week before Christmas, when the Christmas parade takes place and carolers add festive music to the mix. Other good times to visit are the periods after summer—September through early October—and after New Year's Day.

When Not to Go: If crowds make you queasy, keep in mind that Saturday is the busiest day year-round. In summer, Sunday, Monday, and Friday are the next busiest. If you decide to visit Disneyland Park during a weekend, opt for Sunday. And remember that the week before Christmas through New Year's Day, Easter week, and the period from early July through Labor Day are packed.

Crowd Patterns

Least Crowded

- Second week in January to Presidents' week
- Two weeks after Easter Sunday to Memorial Day week
- End of Labor Day week to Columbus Day
- End of Thanksgiving weekend to mid-December

Average Attendance

- Period just after Presidents' week until about two weeks before Easter
- Sundays in spring, autumn, and winter, except holiday weekends
- Memorial Day week to beginning of summer vacation
- Week after Labor Day weekend
- Columbus Day to day before Thanksgiving

Most Crowded

- Any Saturday
- Sundays during summer and holiday weekends
- Presidents' week
- Weeks before through weeks after Easter Sunday
- Beginning of summer through Labor Day weekend
- Thanksgiving weekend (Thursday through Sunday)
- Week before Christmas through first week of January

Keeping Disney Hours

Operating hours tend to fluctuate according to the season, so call 714-781-4565 or 714-781-7290, or visit *www.disneyland.com* for updates.

DISNEYLAND PARK: This park is typically open from about 10 A.M. to 8 P.M. Monday–Thursday, 9 A.M. to 10 P.M. on Friday and Sunday, and 8 A.M. to 11 P.M. on Saturday. Hours are often extended in the summer and during holiday seasons. "Magic Morning" hour is offered on Tuesday, Thursday, and Saturday. This allows guests staying at Disneyland Resort hotels to enter the park one hour early. Those bearing multi-day park passes that include Magic Mornings (it is stated on the ticket) may enter the park one hour early on Tuesday, Thursday, and Saturday mornings.

DISNEY CALIFORNIA ADVENTURE: The park generally opens at 9 or 10 A.M. and closes at about 9 or 10 P.M. on weekdays, sometimes later on weekends and during the summer. Call 714-781-4565 for specifics. Disneyland Resort hotel guests may enter the park one hour early on "Extra Magic Hour" days: Sunday, Monday, Wednesday, and Friday.

DOWNTOWN DISNEY: Some spots in this shopping, dining, and entertainment district open as early as the theme parks do, but many stick to the following hours: 10 A.M. to 10 P.M. Sunday–Thursday, 10 A.M. to midnight on Friday and Saturday.

TRANSPORTATION: The monorail begins making its 2.5-mile loop about the time Disneyland opens (including early-entry Magic Mornings), and runs until about 15 minutes before the park closes. Trams transporting guests between parking lots and the parks begin picking up guests about an hour before the first park opens, and continue transporting guests back to parking areas until about an hour or so after the last park closes. If you miss the last tram, ask a cast member about alternate transportation to the Mickey and Friends parking structure (usually in the form of a van).

Disneyland Weather

If dry, sunny weather is your ideal, Anaheim may seem like a dream come true. Rainy days are few and far between and generally occur between the months of November and April, which is also the coolest time of year. During this season, Santa Ana winds sometimes produce short periods of dry, warm desert weather and sparkling-clear skies that unveil distant mountains usually hidden by smog. In summer, thin, low morning clouds make it prudent to plan expeditions to the beach for the afternoon, when the haze burns off and the mercury rises. Mornings and nights are generally cool. The average daytime year-round temperature is about 73 degrees.

	Temperature AVERAGE HIGH	Temperature AVERAGE LOW	Rainfall AVERAGE (INCHES)
January	71	48	2.86
February	71	48	3.07
March	73	51	1.90
April	76	53	0.80
May	78	57	0.28
June	81	61	0.10
July	87	65	0.03
August	89	65	0.01
September	87	63	0.25
October	82	58	0.72
November	76	52	1.38
December	70	47	2.02

Holidays & Special Events

The Disneyland Resort sponsors special events during the year. Here are a few highlights. Find out about specific events by calling 714-781-7290 or visiting *www.disneyland.com.*

JANUARY–FEBRUARY

Valentine's Day: Sweethearts will swoon over the romantic backdrop that Disneyland Park provides on this love-struck holiday.

Mardi Gras: With its Cajun and Creole cuisine and boutiques, Disneyland's New Orleans Square offers a festive Mardi Gras setting. The Big Easy really comes to life at this time of year—especially during a weekend-long party featuring jazzy music, fancy food, and Disney characters. Ralph Brennan's Jazz Kitchen (Downtown Disney) is hopping, too.

MARCH–MAY

Easter: The parks remain open late the week before and the week after Easter, making this a popular time to visit.

JUNE–AUGUST

All-American College Band: Disney's All-American College Band performs for nine weeks during the summer (usually beginning in mid-June), Tuesday through Sunday. Performances take place throughout the park.

Fourth of July: This is one of the busiest days of the year—and one to avoid if you're easily overwhelmed by crowds. The more-patriotic-than-usual day features exceptionally festive fireworks at Disneyland Park.

LATE SEPTEMBER–OCTOBER

Halloween Festivities: At Disneyland park, Halloween Time lets guests celebrate in not-so-scary ways. In addition to the fall color decor, the Disneyland Band and Dapper Dans celebrate with seasonal tunes. The Haunted Mansion holiday transformation gives this spooky spot a Tim Burton's *The Nightmare Before Christmas* motif. Jack Skellington hosts the fireworks, too—as part of the special-ticket event known as Mickey's Halloween Party. At that popular Disneyland soiree, costumes (for kids under age 14) and trick-or-treating (for all ages) are encouraged on select September and October evenings. Note that policies regarding guests Halloween costumes are subject to change: visit *www.disneyland.com* for updates.

NOVEMBER–DECEMBER

Thanksgiving Weekend: The four days of this holiday weekend are filled with musical entertainment and the early installments of Disneyland's Christmas Fantasy Parade and It's a Small World Holiday, and the holiday transformations of Cars Land and Buena Vista Street, all of which kick off in mid-November. The parks observe extended hours. At the Disneyland Hotel, the characters host A Disney Family Thanksgiving buffet in the grand ballroom. Reserve up to two months in advance (714-781-3463)—seating is limited and in high demand for this perennial favorite.

Christmas Festivities: By early November, Main Street in Disneyland Park is festooned with greenery and poinsettias, while more than 200,000 lights create a holiday wonderland that glistens from the Town Square Christmas Tree to Sleeping Beauty's Winter Castle. On two festive evenings in December, a massive choir walks down Main Street in a Candlelight Ceremony and Procession. It features a live orchestra and guest narrator who reads the story of the Nativity. There is also a special holiday-themed fireworks show, Believe In Holiday Magic. It is not to be missed.

In Fantasyland, It's a Small World is transformed into a world of holiday magic and music. Adventureland gets in on the act with a holiday version of the Jungle Cruise—the aptly named Jingle Cruise. A Christmas Fantasy Parade also takes place. Haunted Mansion Holiday extends through the Christmas festivities. Disney California Adventure gets into the act with a holiday version of World of Color and ¡Viva Navidad!, an energetic street party hosted by the Three Caballeros (and featuring appearances by beloved mice and one very jolly old elf).

Magical Milestones

Walt Disney once said, "Disneyland will never be completed. It will continue to grow as long as there is imagination left in the world." Truer words were never spoken. Here's a sampling of major milestones and important dates in Disney history.

1901
Walter Elias Disney is born on December 5 in Chicago, Illinois. He spends part of his childhood in Marceline, Missouri.

1922
Walt and collaborator Ub Iwerks start Laugh-O-Gram Films, an animation studio located in Kansas City, Missouri. (The business lasts one year.)

1923
Walt and his brother Roy open the Disney Bros. Studio in Hollywood, California.

1928

Disney's studio introduces the world to the immortal Mickey Mouse with *Steamboat Willie*, the world's first cartoon with a synchronized soundtrack. (Walt Disney himself provides the voice for Mickey.)

1932
Flowers and Trees wins the Disney Studio its first Academy Award.

1937
Disney releases *Snow White and the Seven Dwarfs*, the world's first feature-length animated movie.

1940
Great works of classical music meet Disney animation with the release of *Fantasia*.

1955
Disneyland opens its doors in Anaheim, while television's original *Mickey Mouse Club* begins a four-year run.

1967
Disneyland debuts Pirates of the Caribbean—one of the most popular and beloved attractions of all time.

1971
Walt Disney World opens near Orlando, Florida.

1989
Disney animation experiences a renaissance of sorts with the release of the Studio's 28th animated film, *The Little Mermaid*.

2001
For the first time since its opening, the Disneyland Resort gets a new theme park: Disney California Adventure.

2003
The Many Adventures of Winnie the Pooh makes its debut in Disneyland Park.

2004
The Twilight Zone™ Tower of Terror starts shaking up guests at Disney California Adventure.

2006
Captain Jack Sparrow joins the merry marauders in the Pirates of the Caribbean.

2008
Toy Story Mania! opens at Disney California Adventure—and becomes an instant classic.

2011
The Little Mermaid—Ariel's Undersea Adventure makes a splashy debut.

2012
Cars Land races onto the scene with brand-new attractions, including Radiator Springs Racers and Mater's Junkyard Jamboree.

2016
Up, up, and away! A newly re-imagined attraction known as Soarin' Around the World takes off at Disney California Adventure, joining another new addition to the park: Luigi's Rollickin' Roadsters.

Weddings & Celebrations

The Disneyland Resort's customized Fairy Tale Weddings program lets brides and grooms create an affair to remember in the parks or at one of the Disneyland Resort hotels—either indoors or out. Couples may go the traditional route or plan a themed event with invitations, decorations, souvenirs, napkins, and thank-you notes emblazoned with their favorite Disney character couples, including Cinderella and her Prince, and Mickey and Minnie Mouse.

One spot for tying the knot is the rose garden gazebo at the Disneyland Hotel, in a picturesque garden setting where the bride or couple may arrive in Cinderella's crystal coach. Another choice is the courtyard area at Disney's Grand Californian. A fantasy reception may follow (in any of these hotels), at which the fanfare of trumpets greets the happy couple. Mickey Mouse and Minnie Mouse may arrive to help the newlyweds with the cake-cutting moment.

A Disney wedding coordinator assists with the arrangements for the wedding and reception—everything, that is, except providing a guest's very own Prince or Princess Charming.

The bridal salon (at the Disneyland Resort Center, between the Disneyland Hotel and Paradise Pier Hotel) helps guests through the planning and preparation stages, and even through those pre-ceremony jitters.

For more information about creating a happy occasion in a happy location, contact the Disneyland Fairy Tale Weddings department, which coordinates events at all three hotels and in Disneyland: 714-956-6527. To learn more about Disneyland honeymoons, contact Disneyland Resort Travel Sales at 800-854-3104.

Quinceañeras

Along with the wedding program, the Disneyland Resort also offers customized Quinceañera celebrations for young ladies who are coming of age. These family-oriented milestone events invite the birthday girl to become a "princess for a day" and step into the fairy-tale realms of Cinderella or Beauty and the Beast. Held in a ballroom, the celebration features dinner, dancing, and time-honored Quinceañera traditions. For more information, call 714-520-7079.

Planning Ahead

Collect as much information as you can about the attractions you're interested in from the sources listed below (and this book, of course!). Then consider all the possibilities before making definite travel plans.

Information

For up-to-the-minute information about special events and performance times, the latest ticket prices, operating hours, rides under refurbishment, and other Disneyland Resort specifics, contact:

Disneyland Resort Guest Relations;
Box 3232, Anaheim, CA 92803; 714-781-4565; *www.disneyland.com*.

If you are staying at one of the Disneyland Resort hotels (see the *Accommodations* chapter), contact Guest Services at the hotel for help in planning your visit to both the parks and the surrounding area.

www.disneyland.com

For up-to-date Disneyland Resort information, visit *www.disneyland.com*, the official Disneyland Resort website. It can help you plan your vacation, learn about the three Disneyland Resort hotels, book travel packages, and order theme park tickets, plus check park hours and show schedules. You can also book your Disneyland Resort vacation through *www.disneytravel.com*.

Fun on the Run

The Disneyland Half Marathon Weekend, which usually takes place in early September, features races and games for the whole family. Events include the half marathon, a 5K Family Fun Run, kids races (including the ever-popular "Diaper Dash"), and a Health and Fitness Expo. For details or to register for an event, call 714-781-7290 or visit *www.rundisney.com*. Entrance fees range from about $20 to $200. The *Star Wars* Half Marathon Weekend (in January) is popular, too—register as early as possible.

Inside the Disneyland Resort: Cast members (the folks who work at Disneyland) can answer many questions. Information stations in Disneyland Park include City Hall in Town Square and the Information Board on the west side of Central Plaza, at the far end of Main Street. In Disney California Adventure, the Chamber of Commerce is on the east side of the Entry Plaza, and the Information Board is at the far end of Buena Vista Street, adjacent to the Red Car Trolley stop. At any Disneyland Resort hotel, visit the lobby for assistance.

For other area information, contact these bureaus of tourism:

Anaheim/Orange County Visitor & Convention Bureau; Call 855-405-5020 during business hours to reach a representative, or go to *www.visitanaheim.org*. You can visit them in the Convention Center at 800 W. Katella Ave., Anaheim, CA 92802.

Long Beach Area Convention & Visitors Bureau; 301 E. Ocean Blvd., Ste. 1900, Long Beach, CA 90802; 562-436-3645 or 800-452-7829; *www.visitlongbeach.com*.

Los Angeles Convention & Visitors Bureau; There are two walk-in Visitor Information Centers: Union Station, 800 N. Alameda St., Los Angeles, CA 90012; and 6801 Hollywood Blvd., Hollywood, CA 90028; 323-467-6412; *www.discoverlosangeles.com*.

Orange Chamber of Commerce; 1940 N. Tustin St., Orange, CA 92865; 714-538-3581; *www.orangechamber.com*.

Reservations

Given the popularity of the Disneyland Resort, advance planning is essential. To get your choice of accommodations, especially for visits during the busy spring and summer seasons, make lodging reservations as far in advance as possible—at least six months ahead, if you can, since area hotels fill up rather quickly during these months. For visits at other times of the year, check with the Anaheim/Orange County Visitor & Convention Bureau (855-405-5020) to see if any conventions are scheduled when you want to travel. Some of these events can crowd facilities enough to warrant altering your travel plans.

Travel Packages

The biggest advantage to purchasing a travel package is that it almost always saves you money over what you'd pay separately for the individual elements of your vacation, or it offers special options not available if you simply buy a ticket at the ticket booth. This is especially true the longer you stay. And there is the convenience of having all the details arranged in advance by someone else.

Finding the best package for yourself means deciding what sort of vacation you want and studying what's available. Don't choose a package that includes elements that don't interest you—remember, you're paying for them. And if it's Disney theming and "extras" you want, consider a Walt Disney Travel Company package.

The Walt Disney Travel Company offers packages that include a stay at a Disney hotel and a Park Hopper ticket. It's possible to add extras, such as a character breakfast in the park or a guided tour of Disneyland, as well as admission to another Southern California attraction, such as Sea World or Legoland. Purchase extras separately.

Besides booking guests into an official Disneyland Resort hotel, the Walt Disney Travel Company also works closely with dozens of Good Neighbor hotels and motels (see pages 45–50 for details), and they are included in its packages as well. To book a vacation package at the Disneyland Resort, contact a travel agent, or call the Walt Disney Travel Company at 714-520-5060.

The Disneyland Resort is also featured in a wide variety of non-Disney-run package tours, including those sponsored by individual hotels,

airlines (United Vacations, Alaska Airlines Vacations, Southwest Vacations, and jetBlue Vacations offer packages, for instance), and organizations. AAA Vacations (888-780-5185) offers packages to the traveling public, too.

This book's selective guide to Anaheim-area hotels and motels can help you decide initially which property best suits your travel style, needs, and budget (refer to the *Accommodations* chapter of this book). Pick one, then contact a travel agent or the desired hotel directly to make a reservation or book a Disneyland Resort package. Be sure to inquire about deposit requirements, cancellation policies, and trip insurance (we highly recommend insuring your trip). Happy hunting!

What to Pack

Southern California isn't so laid-back that you only need to pack a few pairs of shorts and a T-shirt. Nor is it a place that demands formal attire. Casual wear will suffice in all but the fanciest restaurants, and, even there, men can usually wear sports jackets without ties. Bathing suits are an obvious must if you plan to take advantage of your hotel's swimming pool or go for a walk on a long, surf-pounded Pacific beach. It's also a good idea to bring along a bathing suit cover-up and sunglasses (and don't forget the sunscreen). Tennis togs or golf gear may be necessary if you plan to hit the courts or the course. The weather in summer can be quite warm, but because Southern California air-conditioning is extremely efficient, you should take a lightweight sweater or jacket to wear indoors.

In winter, warm clothing is a must for evening; during nighttime visits to the parks, a heavy jacket may be a godsend. Whatever the time of year, come prepared for the unexpected: Pack an umbrella, a light shirt, and a jacket—just in case.

Making a Budget

Vacation expenses tend to fall into five major categories: (1) transportation (which may include costs for airfare, airport transfers, train tickets, car rental, gas, parking, and taxi service); (2) lodging; (3) theme park tickets; (4) meals; and (5) miscellaneous (recreational activities, souvenirs, toiletries, forgotten items, and expenses such as pet boarding, etc.).

When budgeting, first consider what level of service suits your needs. Some prefer to spend fewer days at the Disneyland Resort, but stay at a deluxe hotel like the Grand Californian or dine at pricier restaurants. Others want a longer vacation with a value-priced Good

Neighbor hotel and less expensive meals. The choice is up to you. (Having said that, we do feel that a great deal of the Disney experience comes from staying on-property and recommend at least making room in your budget for accommodations at the somewhat more moderately priced Disneyland Hotel or Paradise Pier Hotel.)

Once you've established your spending priorities, it's time to determine your price limit. Then make sure you don't exceed it when approximating your expenses—without a ballpark figure to work around, it's easy to get carried away.

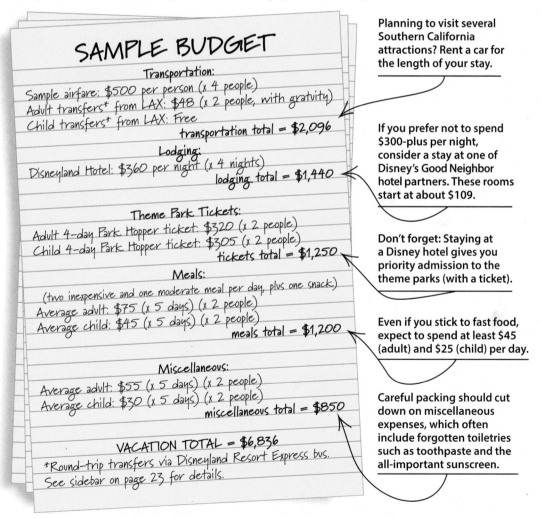

SAMPLE BUDGET

Transportation:
Sample airfare: $500 per person (x 4 people)
Adult transfers* from LAX: $48 (x 2 people, with gratuity)
Child transfers* from LAX: Free
transportation total = $2,096

Lodging:
Disneyland Hotel: $360 per night (x 4 nights)
lodging total = $1,440

Theme Park Tickets:
Adult 4-day Park Hopper ticket: $320 (x 2 people)
Child 4-day Park Hopper ticket: $305 (x 2 people)
tickets total = $1,250

Meals:
(two inexpensive and one moderate meal per day, plus one snack)
Average adult: $75 (x 5 days) (x 2 people)
Average child: $45 (x 5 days) (x 2 people)
meals total = $1,200

Miscellaneous:
Average adult: $55 (x 5 days) (x 2 people)
Average child: $30 (x 5 days) (x 2 people)
miscellaneous total = $850

VACATION TOTAL = $6,836
*Round-trip transfers via Disneyland Resort Express bus.
See sidebar on page 23 for details.

Planning to visit several Southern California attractions? Rent a car for the length of your stay.

If you prefer not to spend $300-plus per night, consider a stay at one of Disney's Good Neighbor hotel partners. These rooms start at about $109.

Don't forget: Staying at a Disney hotel gives you priority admission to the theme parks (with a ticket).

Even if you stick to fast food, expect to spend at least $45 (adult) and $25 (child) per day.

Careful packing should cut down on miscellaneous expenses, which often include forgotten toiletries such as toothpaste and the all-important sunscreen.

This is an example of a moderately priced budget for a family of four (two adults and two kids staying at the Disneyland Resort for four nights and five days during "off-peak" times). Theme park admission prices are likely to increase in 2017.

Money-Saving Strategies

Cost-Cutting Tips

LODGING: The most important rule is not to pay for more than you need. Budget chains don't offer many frills, but they are usually clean and provide the essentials; many even have a swimming pool, albeit a small one.

You can also save by checking the cutoff age at which kids can no longer share their parents' room for free. Many hotels and motels allow children under age 18 to stay free. A few places have a cutoff age of 15 or 17, so it's good to find out before making a reservation. And ask about special rates or discounts, especially if you are a California resident, Disney Vacation Club or AARP member, or are in the military.

Hostels and RV parks also offer lower-priced lodging alternatives. Contact the Anaheim/Orange County Visitor & Convention Bureau at 855-405-5020 for a listing of those areas closest to the Disneyland Resort.

FOOD: The budget-minded (and who isn't?) should plan to have meals in coffee shops or fast-food restaurants, or save your splurges for the buffets to get your fill and your money's worth. If you want to try an upscale place, go for lunch; the entrées are often the same as those at dinnertime, but usually cost less.

Pack a picnic and enjoy meals outside. There's a small picnic area just to the left of Disneyland's entrance. (It's surrounded by trees—so it's easy to miss—but last we checked it was still there.) Vending machines dispense soft drinks. Snacks may be brought into the parks, but not glass bottles, knives, or beverages containing alcohol. Refillable plastic or metal cups and bottles are permitted. You can also save on meals by choosing lodging with kitchen facilities and opting to eat in some of the time. The savings on food may more than cover the additional cost of accommodations. Don't forget to pack snack items, too—especially if traveling with kids.

In the Anaheim area, a number of places offer refrigerators or kitchen facilities (look for suite hotels); some provide breakfast.

TRANSPORTATION: When calculating the cost of driving to the Disneyland Resort, consider your car's gas mileage, the price of gasoline, and the expense of the accommodations and food en route. If you are planning to fly, don't forget about the cost of getting from home to the airport and later to the hotel. Also factor in the cost of renting a car at your destination, if that's part of your plan. Remember to ask if your hotel charges for parking (the rates tend to vary) or shuttle transportation to the Disneyland Resort—these daily charges can tack quite a bit onto a family's room bill.

> ## HOT TIP!
> For information on special offers for many of Anaheim's hotels, restaurants, and attractions, visit *www.visitanaheim.org* (click on the "deals" tab), or contact via telephone: 855-405-5020.

Disney Discounts

ANNUAL PASSPORT: Annual Pass–bearers may net savings on Disneyland Resort hotel rooms, Disneyland restaurants, select merchandise throughout the parks and Downtown Disney, and select guided tours. Signature and Signature Plus Annual Passholders enjoy up to 20% discounts on merchandise at many Disneyland resort locations, 10% to 15% discounts at many dining spots, unlimited free PhotoPass downloads (see page 85), and free parking. Note that the option of adding parking to a Deluxe Annual Passport is no longer offered. Current annual passholders may net a savings when they renew, too.

DISNEY VISA® CARDS: Cardmembers who pay with their Disney Visa Card enjoy savings on merchandise, dining, and guided tours. Cardmembers can use the Disney Visa Card wherever Visa is accepted. Specifics are subject to change. Visit *DisneyRewards.com* or *DisneyDebit.com* for additional details.

AUTOMOBILE ASSOCIATION OF AMERICA (AAA): You don't have to be a member of the Automobile Association of Club to order a vacation package through AAA. Contact your local AAA office for details.

BIRNBAUM COUPONS: The coupons at the back of this book will net you savings at several Downtown Disney spots.

Theme Park Tickets

Admission media (except for annual passes) are also known as tickets. A one-day park ticket lets you visit just that: one park. Park Hopper tickets allow you unlimited park-hopping between Disneyland Park and Disney California Adventure. Admission tickets include use of all attractions (except arcades) once inside.

Ticket Options

One- through Five-Day Tickets without the park-hopping feature allow admission to one Disneyland Resort theme park per day, while One- to Five-Day Park Hopper tickets allow admission to both parks and allow you to "hop" between the two parks. Theme park tickets generally expire 13 days after first use.

The three main types of annual passports are known as the Deluxe, Signature, and Signature Plus versions. All passes afford the bearer shopping and dining discounts, as well as park-hopping—that is, visiting both theme parks on the same day. The biggest difference between types of annual passes are block-out dates (select dates when the passholder may not enter the theme parks).

The Signature Plus Annual Passport is valid for a year, includes parking, and has no block-out dates. The Signature Annual Passport is valid 350 days of the year with block-out periods such as December holidays, Saturdays from March through June, and other peak times. The Deluxe Annual Passport is valid 320 days of the year. Premier passes allow entry to all Disney theme parks within the United States and come with all the benefits of a Signature Plus pass.

Annual passes are sold at the ticket booths and via www.disneyland.com and processed at the main ticket booths. There are usually special passes available for purchase by Southern California residents. Offers change from time, so inquire before you visit. Call 714-781-4565, or visit www.disneyland.com for details.

Purchasing Tickets

Long lines often form at the Disney ticket booths—especially in the morning. Avoid the wait and purchase the tickets with the "Extra Magic" option (allowing early access to a park on select days of the week) ahead of time.

Where to Buy Tickets: All tickets are sold at park ticket booths. Some Disney Stores sell tickets, too (they do not offer one-day tickets).

Tickets by Mail: Send check or money order and ticket request (plus a $10 fee for orders over $200) to Disneyland Ticket Mail Order Services, Box 61061, Anaheim, CA 92803. It's also possible to order by calling Ticketing & Reservations at 714-781-4400 (up to 30 days ahead). Allow 10 business days for processing.

Tickets Online: Select tickets are available at www.disneyland.com. (You can print them, have them mailed, or pick them up at Will Call. The latter two options come with a fee.) There may be special offers—be sure to inquire.

Tickets by Phone: Call 714-781-4565 and have a credit card handy. Allow seven days for delivery, ten during busy times of the year.

How to Pay for Tickets: Cash, traveler's checks, personal checks, Disney gift cards, Disney Dollars, American Express, Visa, MasterCard, JCB Card, and Discover Card are accepted. Personal checks must be imprinted with name and address, and accompanied by a valid government-issued photo ID.

Note that ticket structure and pricing are apt to change. For updates, visit www.disneyland.com.

Ticket Prices

Although prices† will likely increase, the following should give you an idea of what you'll pay for tickets in 2017. For updates, call 714-781-4565, or visit www.disneyland.com.

	ADULTS	CHILDREN*
1-Day Ticket (1 park)	$95/105/119	$89/99/113
1-Day Ticket (hopper)	$155/160/169	$149/154/163
2-Day Ticket (hopper)	$235	$223
3-Day Ticket (hopper)**	$295	$283
4-Day Ticket (hopper)**	$320	$305
5-Day Ticket (hopper)**	$335	$320
2-Park Deluxe Annual Passport		$599
2-Park Signature Annual Passport		$899
2-Park Signature Plus Annual Passport		$1,049
Premier Annual Passport		$1,439

† One-day prices are quoted in Value/Regular/Peak order. For dates visit www.disneyland.com.
*3 through 9 years of age; children under 3 free
**Includes "Magic Morning" early park admission with select attractions on Tuesday, Thursday, or Saturday.
Note that there is a single price (for adults and children) for annual passports.

Customized Travel Tips

Traveling with Children

When you tell your kids that a Disney vacation is in the works, the challenge is keeping them relatively calm until you actually arrive at the Disneyland Resort.

PLANNING: Get youngsters involved in plotting a Disneyland trip from the outset, putting each child in charge of a small part of the vacation preparation—such as visiting *www.disneyland.com*, choosing which attractions to see and in what order to see them, and investigating which other activities to include in your Southern California visit.

EN ROUTE: Certain resources can stave off the "Are we there yet?" chorus, such as travel games, books and magazines, and snacks to quiet rumbling stomachs. If you drive, take plenty of breaks along the way. If you fly, try to time your departure and return flights for off-peak hours and during the off-season, when chances are better that an empty seat or two will be available. During takeoffs and landings, encourage toddlers to suck on bottles or pacifiers to keep ears clear, and supply older kids with chewing gum or water.

IN THE HOTELS: During the summer and select periods, several hotels offer special kids' programs. Some offer baby-sitting services or baby-sitting referrals year-round. Pinocchio's Workshop at Disney's Grand Californian is available to take requests for "day of" child activity services for hotel guests. There is a charge for these services.

IN THE THEME PARKS: The smiles that light up your kids' faces as they enter a Disney theme park should repay you a thousandfold for any fuss en route. No place in the world is more aware of the needs of children—or their parents—than this one.

Favorite Attractions: Fantasyland and Mickey's Toontown in Disneyland Park are great places to start with small kids, who delight in the bright colors and familiar characters. In Disney California Adventure, A Bug's Land, Cars Land, Disney Junior—Live on Stage!, and Monsters, Inc.—Mike and Sulley to the Rescue! have big kid appeal. If you have children of different ages in your party, you may have to do some juggling or split the group up for a few hours so that older kids won't have to spend their whole vacation waiting in line for Dumbo. Some rides, like Snow White's Scary Adventures, may be too scary for some youngsters. If they're afraid of the witch, skip the attraction.

Strollers: They can be rented for $15 ($25 for two) at the Stroller Shop, located to the right of the main entrance of Disneyland Park. This is the only place to rent a stroller for either park. If you leave the parks, but plan to return later that day, keep the receipt and get another stroller at no additional charge.

Baby Care: Baby Care Centers feature toddler-size flush toilets that are quite cute—and completely functional. In addition, there are changing tables, a limited selection of formulas, strained baby foods, and diapers for sale, plus facilities for warming baby bottles (you can wash out your bottles here, too). A special room with comfortable chairs is available for nursing mothers.

The decor is soothing, and a stop here for diaper changing or feeding is a tranquil break for parent and child alike. The Baby Care Centers are located in Central Plaza, at the Castle end of Main Street in Disneyland, and near Ghirardelli Soda Fountain & Chocolate Shop in Disney California Adventure.

Changing tables and diaper machines are also available in many restrooms.

Note: Parents of toddlers should pack a supply of swim diapers. They'll come in handy for children who want to spend time splashing in the parks' interactive fountains.

Where to Buy Baby Care Items: Disposable diapers, baby bottles, formula, etc. are sold at the Baby Care Centers in the parks. Pack as much of your own as possible—prices can be steep and the selection is small.

Lost Children: Youngsters should carry the mobile phone number for the parent or guardian who accompanies them to the parks. But even without it, when a child gets separated from his or her family or fails to show up on time, trained cast members and Disneyland Resort's security force follow specific procedures when they encounter a lost child.

Kids up to age 10 may be escorted (by a Disney cast member) to Child Services, adjacent to First Aid, where Disney movies and books provide amusement—while a parent is contacted via mobile phone or otherwise directed to the Child Services location. The child's name is registered in the lost children's logbook there. Kids 11 and older may have their parents reached on their cell phones, leave messages with Guest Services attendants, and check in often at City Hall in Disneyland Park, or the Chamber of Commerce in the entrance area of California Adventure.

Traveling Without Children

Disneyland is as enjoyable for solo travelers and couples as it is for families for several reasons: Its ambience encourages interaction, and the attractions are naturally shared events.

PLANNING: Read Disney literature carefully before you arrive to familiarize yourself with the Resort's layout and activities. Also, search the Internet for info about other places in Southern California that you intend to visit.

Food for Thought: Sightseeing takes lots of energy, and only healthy meals can provide it at a consistent level. Don't attempt to save money by skipping meals. Prices at the parks and nearby "off-property" eateries are relatively reasonable, and there are healthful options, even in the fast-food restaurants. And don't forget to stay hydrated—running around theme parks all day is a lot of work.

Health Matters: If you visit in summer, avoid getting overheated. Protect yourself from the sun with a hat and plenty of sunscreen, rest in the shade often, and beat the midafternoon heat with a cold drink or a snack in an air-conditioned spot.

If you feel ill, speak to a Disney cast member or go to First Aid and ask to see a nurse. *In case of emergency, call 911.* Above all, heed attraction warnings. If you have a back problem, heart condition, or other physical ailment, suffer from motion sickness, or are pregnant, skip rough rides. Restrictions are noted at attraction entrances, as well on park guidemaps.

Lost Companions: Traveling companions can get separated. If someone in your party wanders off or fails to show up at an appointed meeting spot and cell phone communication is thwarted, head for City Hall in Disneyland or Chamber of Commerce in California Adventure. Guests can leave and receive messages for one another during the day.

MEETING OTHER ADULTS: Downtown Disney, with its mix of restaurants and clubs, is a nice spot to mingle. While each of Disney's hotels has lounges worth visiting, Trader Sam's at the Disneyland Hotel is exceptionally engaging.

Travelers with Disabilities

The Disneyland Resort is quite accessible to guests with disabilities, and, as a result, it makes a good choice as a vacation destination. But planning is still essential.

GETTING TO ANAHEIM

Probably the most effective means of ensuring a smooth trip is to make as many advance contacts as possible for every phase of your journey. It's important to make phone calls regarding transportation well before your departure date to arrange for any special facilities or services you may need en route.

The Society for Accessible Travel & Hospitality (SATH, 347 Fifth Ave., Suite 605, New York, NY 10016; 212-447-7284; *www.sath.org*) has member travel agents who book trips for travelers with disabilities, keeping special needs in mind. Membership costs $49, or $29 for students and seniors age 63 and older.

Height Ho!

At attractions with age and/or height restrictions, a parent who waits with a child too young or too small to ride while the other parent goes on the attraction may stay at the front of the line and take a turn as soon as the first parent comes off. This is called the "rider switch" policy, and if lines are long, it can save a lot of time. Be sure to ask the attendant, and he or she will explain what to do.

The following agencies specialize in booking trips for travelers with physical disabilities: Accessible Journeys (35 W. Sellers Ave., Ridley Park, PA 19078; *www.accessiblejourneys.com*; 610-521-0339 or 800-846-4537) and Flying Wheels Travel (143 W. Bridge St., Owatonna, MN 55060; 877-451-5006 or 507-451-5005; *www.flyingwheelstravel.com*).

Hertz (800-654-3131), Alamo (800-651-1223), and National (888-273-5262) rent hand-controlled cars at the airports in Southern California. Order your car at least 48 hours in advance and confirm it before you arrive.

Though less convenient, it is also possible to access the area by public transportation. All buses operated by Anaheim Resort Transportation (call 714-563-5287, or visit *www.rideart.org*) and the Orange County Transportation Authority (714-560-6282 or *www.octa.net*), the public bus company that serves Orange County, are outfitted with lifts so that travelers using wheelchairs can board them easily. Many of the routes pass by the Disneyland Resort.

Sightseeing tour buses are another option. Though only a few of them are wheelchair accessible, all have storage facilities for collapsible chairs, making this a possibility for travelers who have a companion to help them on and off the bus. Coach USA is wheelchair accessible. It offers tours to many Disneyland-area attractions. Make reservations (at least 48 hours ahead if a wheelchair lift will be needed) by calling 714-978-8855 or 800-828-6699; *www.graylineanaheim.com*.

Scootaround rents standard and electric wheelchairs, as well as scooters. Pick-up and delivery is available to all hotels in the Disneyland Resort area. Call 888-441-7575, or visit *www.scootaround.com*. Wheelchair Getaways of California rents wheelchair accessible vans and has pick-up and delivery options for most hotels in the area. Call 800-642-2042, or visit *www.wheelchairgetaways.com*.

LODGING

Most hotels and motels in Orange County have rooms equipped for guests with disabilities, with extra-wide doorways, grab bars in the bathroom for shower or bath and toilet, and sinks at wheelchair height, along with ramps at curbs and steps to allow wheelchair access. Unless otherwise indicated, all the lodging described in the *Accommodations* chapter (page 39) provide guestrooms for travelers with disabilities.

INSIDE THE DISNEYLAND RESORT

Cars displaying a "disability" placard will be directed to a section of each Disney parking lot, next to the tram pick-up and drop-off area.

Wheelchairs and Electric Conveyance Vehicles (ECVs) can be rented at the Stroller Shop just outside the main entrance at Disneyland Park. This is the only rental location for both theme parks. The price is $12 per day for wheelchairs, and $50 for ECVs. A few wheelchairs may be available to borrow from Disney's three hotels; inquire at the front desk. Quantities are very limited. We recommend you bring your own wheelchair whenever possible.

Most waiting areas are accessible, but some attractions have auxiliary entrances for guests using wheelchairs or other mobility devices; guests may be accompanied by up to five party members using the special entry point. The Main Street train station is not wheelchair accessible. However, guests using wheelchairs may access the train in New Orleans Square, Mickey's Toontown, or Tomorrowland.

Accessibility information is provided in special brochures (see Park Resources, below). In all cases, guests with mobility disabilities should be escorted by someone in their party who can assist as needed.

In some theme park attractions, guests may remain in their wheelchair or Electric Conveyance Vehicle; in others, they must be able to transfer in and out of their wheelchair or ECV. In a few attractions, they must be able to leave their wheelchair or ECV and remain ambulatory during the majority of the attraction experience.

For Guests with Visual Disabilities: An audio tour, along with the *Braille Guidebook*, are available upon request at City Hall in Disneyland and at Chamber of Commerce in California Adventure. Both are free, but require a $100 and $20 refundable deposit, respectively.

Park Resources

Contact Guest Relations at 714-781-7290 for details on *Services for Guests with Visual Disabilities* and *Hearing Disabilities; Services for Guests with Service Animals;* and *Attraction Access for Guests Using Wheelchairs and Electric Conveyance Vehicles (ECVs),* or visit *www.disneyland.com*. Information is also available at City Hall inside Disneyland and at Chamber of Commerce in Disney California Adventure.

Service animals are permitted almost everywhere, except on attractions that involve a great deal of motion. In such instances, the service animal may wait in a crate provided by the attraction while the guest rides.

For Guests with Hearing Disabilities: Dozens of attractions provide a written story line for guests to follow. For details, check at City Hall in Disneyland Park or Chamber of Commerce inside California Adventure.

Closed captioning is available in the pre-show areas of select attractions—inquire at the attraction entrance; contact Guest Relations for the use of a handheld closed-captioning unit (free with refundable deposit). Reflective captioning and audio descriptions are available at several shows as well; inquire at each attraction. Quantities are limited.

Text typewriters (TTYs) are located in between the main entrance to Disneyland and the kennel, and at the pay phones near the exit from Space Mountain. In Disney California Adventure, TTYs can be found in the area beside King Triton's Carousel and inside the Guest Relations Lobby.

Sign language interpretation is available for select shows and attractions in both Disneyland Resort theme parks. Reservations must be made at least seven days in advance. To make this arrangement, contact Resort Tour Services at 714-817-2229.

Assistive-listening devices may be borrowed at City Hall in Disneyland and Chamber of Commerce in Disney California Adventure (with a $25 refundable deposit).

DISNEYLAND RESORT TOURS

The following guided tours provide guests with an opportunity to explore Disneyland Park and Disney California Adventure in entertaining and informative ways. Annual Passholders and Disney Visa® Cardmembers receive a discount on select guided tours. Tours may be booked up to 30 days in advance. Availability is limited. For details or to book a tour, call 714-781-8687 or visit *www.disneyland.com*, or stop by City Hall (in Disneyland Park) or Chamber Commerce at Disney California Adventure. Theme park admission is required (but not included) for all tours:

• *Welcome to the Disneyland Resort* (Friday–Monday): A 2½-hour journey that takes you through Disneyland and California Adventure, with stops at attractions, shows, and more. It costs about $25 per person.

• *Cultivating the Magic* (Saturday–Monday): A 2-hour exploration of the intricate horticultural theming and planning that went into converting an orange grove into Disneyland park. Includes a collectible pin and souvenir seed pack. Cost is $49 per person.

PHOTO BY JILL SAFRO

• *Walk in Walt's Disneyland Footsteps* (9:30 A.M. daily and select afternoons): Led by a knowledgeable guide, the tour covers the whole park. If you already have a park ticket, you pay an extra $109 (per person, all ages) for the 3-hour tour. Guests travel through Walt's original Magic Kingdom, while hearing stories of the challenges, inspiration, and fun associated with all of his creations. The tour includes a meal on Main Street, a collectible pin, and a visit to two classic Disneyland attractions.

• *Disney California Story* (Daily): Explore the Golden State history that inspired a young Walt Disney to embark on his magical journey from new kid on the block to the man behind the Mouse. The journey just might inspire *you*, too. Participants enjoy a meal on Buena Vista Street, a collectible pin, and select attractions. This Disney California Adventure experience costs about $109 per person.

• *Disney's Happiest Haunts Tour* (Seasonal): Journey though both parks at dusk and prepare for a night of chilling tales and eerie sights on this 3-hour walking tour. Cost is about $80 per person and includes a souvenir keepsake and a Halloween treat. Guests should be at least 40 inches tall. The tour is not recommended for guests using wheelchairs or strollers. Guests ride Haunted Mansion, Big Thunder Mountain, and Tower of Terror (subject to change).

• *Holiday Time at the Disneyland Resort* (Seasonal): This tour shares the history of Disneyland's holiday traditions and enchanting tales of holidays from around the world, includes visits to attractions that have had holiday makeovers, and offers special seating for the holiday parade, A Christmas Fantasy. Cost is about $80 per person and includes a pin, a warm beverage, and a gingerbread cookie.

How to Get There

Most visitors to the Disneyland Resort arrive by car. Many who live nearby own an annual pass and drive there frequently to spend a day or weekend at the resort. But for those traveling any significant distance, it tends to cost less to fly than to drive, and can save time. During your days at the Disneyland Resort, you won't need a vehicle. Rent a car for the days you plan to venture off-property, or rely on local tours to see the area sights. If you prefer to leave the driving to someone else, traveling to Disneyland by bus or train are alternatives.

HOT TIP!

Driving to Disneyland and looking for an address for the GPS? Look no further: 1313 S. Harbor Blvd., Anaheim, CA 92802.

By Car

SOUTHERN CALIFORNIA FREEWAYS: Driving almost anywhere in Orange County, or farther afield, requires negotiating a number of freeways and surface streets. But once you familiarize yourself with a few names and numbers, navigating becomes much more manageable.

The freeways are well marked and fast, barring (common) traffic snags. That said, they can be rather frenetic. Major thoroughfares may merge with little or no notice. Monstrous traffic jams are common during morning and evening rush hours. And proper names of most roads change, depending on where you are. I-5, for instance, is called the Santa Ana Freeway in Orange County; in the Los Angeles area, it becomes the Golden State Freeway; to the south, it's the San Diego Freeway. It's a good idea to learn both the name and the route number of any freeway on which you plan to

travel. Exit signs list a route number and either a direction or city name (but not always both).

It's also useful to have an idea of the overall layout of the freeways. Several run parallel to the Pacific coast and are intersected by others running east and west. While this scheme is fairly straightforward, it is complicated by a couple of freeways that squiggle across the map.

CALIFORNIA DRIVING LAWS: Under state law, seat belts are required for *all* passengers; right turns at red lights are legal unless otherwise posted, as are U-turns at intersections; and pedestrians have the right-of-way at crosswalks. By law, kids must be in car or booster seats until they reach the age of 8 or a height of 4 feet, 9 inches. And keep that phone in your pocket— it is illegal to use it while driving in California.

AUTOMOBILE CLUBS: Any one of the nation's leading automobile clubs will come to your aid in the event of a breakdown en route (be sure to bring your membership card with you), as well as provide insurance covering accidents, arrest, bail bond, lawyers' fees for defense of contested traffic cases, and personal injury. They also offer trip-planning services—not merely advice, but also complimentary maps and route-mapping assistance.

MAPS/GPS: If you don't have a GPS app on your smartphone, know that many car rental agencies provide GPS systems and maps. Of course, it's still wise to familiarize yourself with the route beforehand. Routes can be plotted in advance through *http://maps.yahoo.com*; *www.mapquest.com*; or *http://maps.google.com*.

By Air

Anaheim lies about 45 to 100 minutes southeast of Los Angeles by car. Most Disneyland Resort guests who arrive by plane disembark at Los Angeles International Airport (LAX), one of the world's busiest. It handles approximately 1,500 departures and arrivals daily of more than 75 commercial airlines. Major carriers serving Los Angeles include American, Delta, and United airlines.

Much closer to Anaheim, Orange County's John Wayne Airport, in Santa Ana, is less than a half-hour drive from Disney and is served by 9

commercial airlines and more than 250 flights a day. It is sometimes possible to find the same fare to John Wayne/Orange County Airport (SNA) as to LAX, and if it's a nonstop flight, so much the better. There aren't as many direct flights available, but given the proximity to the Disneyland Resort, it's worth considering. Another airport vying for attention is the Long Beach Airport (LGB). It is also near Anaheim, but few airlines serve it on a nonstop basis.

HOW TO GET THE BEST AIRFARE: Airfares seem to be forever in flux, changing often. That makes it important to shop around—or have your travel agent do so. It pays (literally) to keep these suggestions in mind:

• Check into all airlines serving your destination. See if you can get a lower fare by slightly altering the dates of your trip, the hour of departure, or the duration of your stay—or, if you live halfway between two airports, by leaving from one rather than the other or by flying into a different area airport.

• Fly weekends on routes heavily used by business travelers, or midweek on routes more commonly patronized by vacationers.

• Purchase your tickets online. Airlines often offer lower fares or waive transaction fees when customers use their websites.

• Keep an eye on websites and newspapers for ads announcing new or special fares.

AIRPORT TRANSPORTATION: Friendly, reasonably-priced, scheduled bus service is offered by Disneyland Resort Express (visit *www.graylineanaheim.com,* or call 714-978-8855 or 800-828-6699). It not only goes to the Disneyland Resort hotels and the properties in Anaheim, but also several hotels in Buena Park (7 miles away). Pre-paid round-trip service is offered at a small discount. The standard-size bus stops at each LAX airline terminal, outside baggage claim; look for the green bus stop signs on the center island and for DISNEYLAND RESORT EXPRESS above the windshield (the Disney theming makes the buses easy to spot!). Note that this bus stops airport pickups at about 6 P.M. (possibly earlier).

Those who fly into John Wayne Airport (named after one of Orange County's most famous residents), 16 miles from Disneyland, have an easier time of it. The ride into town takes half the time than from LAX. From baggage claim, head to the Ground Transportation Center. The coaches pick up from the ticket booth located to the left. Look for the full-size motor coach that has DISNEYLAND RESORT EXPRESS displayed above the windshield.

SuperShuttle (call 800-258-3826, or visit *www.supershuttle.com*) also serves area airports. At Los Angeles International Airport, claim your luggage, then head to the SHARED RIDE VAN sign on the outer island and contact a blue-uniformed guest service rep for details. A van should arrive within 15 to 30 minutes.

At John Wayne, proceed to the transportation center across the street and look for the island marked VAN SHUTTLE SERVICE. A van should arrive within 15 to 30 minutes. Advance reservations are required for pick-up at Long

To Anaheim from the Airports

	Disneyland Resort Express Bus	SuperShuttle
Los Angeles Int'l Airport	$30 ($48 round-trip) per adult; $22 ($36 round-trip) per child ages 3–11.* It runs until about 6 P.M.	$20 per person (one way)
John Wayne Airport	$20 ($35 round-trip) per adult; $15 ($26 round-trip) per child ages 3–11.*	$14 per person (one way)
Long Beach Airport	Resort Express service is not available, but it's possible to take a Yellow Cab for about $52–$60 each way.	$38 for the first guest in the party, about $9 for each additional guest.

*For each paying adult, one child may ride for free. Children under 3 ride free. Prices are subject to change. SuperShuttle customers net a small discount if they book round-trip fares online: *www.supershuttle.com.*

Beach. Here, vans collect passengers across from the main terminal in the car rental return lot. To return to any airport without an existing reservation, check with your hotel front desk the day before the departure for bus schedules and reservation information.

HOT TIP!
If you take a taxi, note whether or not the trip is metered or if there is a flat fee to your destination—and make sure you are charged accordingly.

CAR RENTALS: Several major car rental agencies have locations at LAX, John Wayne, and Long Beach airports; in Union Station; at many hotels; and elsewhere in Anaheim. Expect to pay between $117 and $270 a week for an intermediate car (plus tax and insurance fees), and $24 to $54 for a 3-day weekend, with unlimited mileage. Some rental companies to choose from are Avis (800-331-1212), Budget (800-527-0700), Dollar (800-800-4000), Hertz (800-654-3131), Alamo (800-327-9633), and National (800-227-7368).

It pays to call all the agencies and check websites to get the best available deals. Be sure to ask about any special promotions or discounts. Loss Damage Waiver (LDW) coverage is essential for your protection in case of an accident, but it can add a lot to your bill (usually at least $9 a day). Most packages that include a rental car do not include LDW. If you have your own car insurance, check with your carrier to see what is covered.

An increasing number of major credit card companies offer free collision damage coverage for charging the rental to their card, and some may provide primary coverage. That means your credit card company may deal with the rental company directly in the event of an accident, rather than compensate you after your insurance has kicked in. It's worth a phone call to find out.

If you're renting a car at Los Angeles International Airport (LAX), the drive to the Disneyland Resort is only 31 miles, but it will take at least 45 minutes with light traffic, or up to two hours if the roads are congested. From John Wayne Airport (SNA), the drive takes about 25 minutes (without traffic). Expect a drive of about a half hour from Long Beach Airport (LGB)—again, that estimate does not factor in that tricky wild card known as Southern California traffic.

PHOTO BY JILL SAFRO

By Train

It's possible to get to Anaheim by rail from L.A.'s Union Station using Amtrak's Pacific Surfliner train (*www.amtrak.com*; 800-872-7245) or L.A.'s Metrolink Orange County light-rail (*www.metrolinktrains.com*; 800-371-5465). Union Station is in downtown Los Angeles and is served by trains from all over the country.

You can get to Union Station from L.A. International Airport (LAX) by cab, by bus (LAX FlyAway Bus; *www.lawa.org/flyaway*; 866-435-9529), or by L.A.'s Metro subway (323-466-3876; *www.metro.net*; the system also serves Long Beach Airport). Hertz and Budget rental agencies have counters at Union Station; call companies directly for rates and hours.

The Anaheim train station is adjacent to Angel Stadium in Anaheim, which is about two miles from the Disneyland Resort. Yellow Cabs can be called from the station (714-535-2211). In addition, Hertz and Budget car rental agencies will pick up customers from the Anaheim train station; contact the companies directly for rates and hours.

By Bus

Buses make sense if you're traveling a short distance, if you have plenty of time to spend in transit, if there are only two or three people in your party, and/or if cost-control is key.

Buses make the trip from Los Angeles and San Diego, though they usually make a few stops along the way. Travel from most other destinations usually requires a change of vehicle in L.A. Transfers are usually made at 1716 E. 7th St. at Alameda in downtown L.A.

The Anaheim Greyhound bus terminal is at 2626 E. Katella Ave; *www.greyhound.com*; 800-231-2222. Yellow Cabs can get you to Disneyland from the bus terminal for about $12; 714-535-2211.

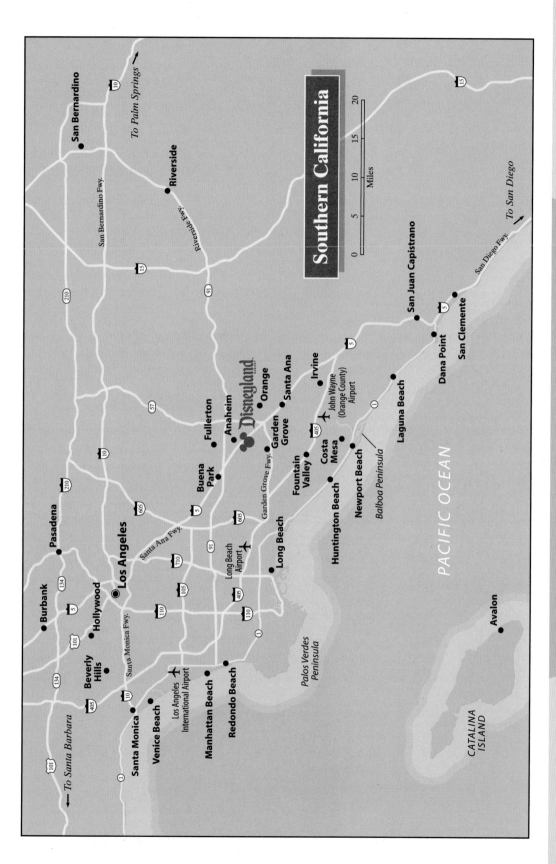

Southern California

Miles
0　5　10　15　20

To Santa Barbara
To Palm Springs
To San Diego

San Bernardino
Riverside
Pasadena
Burbank
Hollywood
Los Angeles
Beverly Hills
Santa Monica
Venice Beach
Manhattan Beach
Redondo Beach
Los Angeles International Airport
Buena Park
Fullerton
Anaheim
Disneyland
Orange
Santa Ana
Garden Grove
Irvine
Fountain Valley
Costa Mesa
Huntington Beach
Newport Beach
Long Beach
Long Beach Airport
John Wayne (Orange County) Airport
Laguna Beach
Dana Point
San Juan Capistrano
San Clemente
Avalon

San Bernardino Fwy.
Riverside Fwy.
Santa Ana Fwy.
Santa Monica Fwy.
Garden Grove Fwy.
San Diego Fwy.
Balboa Peninsula
Palos Verdes Peninsula

PACIFIC OCEAN
CATALINA ISLAND

Getting Oriented

Southern California's patchwork of small communities has undeniably blurred borders. The Disneyland Resort is in Anaheim, but you might not know if you were in that city or one of its immediate neighbors except for the signs. Buena Park lies to the northwest, Garden Grove to the south, Santa Ana to the southeast, and Orange to the east.

Farther south—in Huntington Beach, Newport Beach, Laguna Beach, and San Juan Capistrano—there's a bit more breathing room between communities. Heading northwest from Anaheim, you'll come to Los Angeles International Airport.

Continuing northwest into L.A., you'll find Santa Monica to the west, and, to the east, Beverly Hills, West Hollywood, and Hollywood. On the beach farther north and west is Malibu, and inland to the east are Burbank (home of the Walt Disney Studios) and Glendale. The San Fernando Valley lies farther north and a bit inland from Los Angeles proper, while Santa Barbara, Southern California's northern boundary, is on the coast, about two hours to the north.

North–South Freeways: There are two: I-5 (the Santa Ana Freeway in the Anaheim area) runs from Vancouver, Canada, to San Diego, and is the main inland route in Southern California, linking Los Angeles and San Diego; I-405 (the San Diego Freeway) sprouts from I-5 north of Hollywood, veers south toward the coast, then rejoins I-5 at Irvine, a bit south of Anaheim.

East–West Freeways: Of the roads that intersect the two principal north-south arteries, one of the closest to the Disneyland Resort is Route 22, also known as the Garden Grove Freeway; it begins near the ocean in Long Beach and runs beyond the southern border of Anaheim. Route 91, called the Artesia Freeway on the west side of I-5 and the Riverside Freeway on the east, lies about eight miles north of Route 22.

Farther north you'll reach I-10, called the Santa Monica Freeway from its beginning point near the Pacific shore in Santa Monica to just east of downtown Los Angeles. At this juncture, it jogs north and then turns east again, becoming the San Bernardino Freeway. I-10 is located approximately 12 miles north of Route 91.

North of I-10 (anywhere from two to eight miles, depending on your location) is U.S. 101, which heads south from Ventura and then due east, crossing I-405. It is known as the Ventura Freeway until a few miles east of I-405, at which point it angles south and becomes the Hollywood Freeway, and eventually merges into I-5.

HOW TO GET THERE: Disneyland Resort is on Harbor Boulevard between Katella Avenue, Disneyland Drive, and Ball Road, 31 miles

Travel Times

To/From the Resort	Approx. Distance	Drive Time
Balboa	30 miles	40 min.
Buena Park	7 miles	12 min.
Carlsbad	50 miles	60 min.
Costa Mesa	20 miles	30 min.
Dana Point	30 miles	40 min.
Garden Grove	5 miles	10 min.
Huntington Beach	15 miles	25 min.
John Wayne Airport	16 miles	25 min.
Laguna Beach	30 miles	45 min.
Las Vegas	280 miles	5–6 hrs.
Long Beach	20 miles	30 min.
Los Angeles (downtown and airport)	31 miles	45–90 min.
Newport Beach	20 miles	30 min.
Palm Springs	180 miles	3–4 hrs.
San Diego	87 miles	90 min.
San Juan Capistrano	32 miles	45 min.
San Simeon	270 miles	5–6 hrs.
Santa Ana	5 miles	10 min.
Santa Barbara	110 miles	2–3 hrs.

Drive times are under optimal conditions; rain or rush-hour traffic will increase or even double the time.

south of downtown Los Angeles and 87 miles north of San Diego. Many visitors drive to Disneyland from elsewhere in Southern California, while those who come from farther away fly into one of the area airports, rent a car, and drive from there. Once at their hotel, guests may prefer to use the hotel's shuttle or Anaheim Resort Transit (ART) to and from Disneyland.

Southbound I-5 Exit: To get to Disneyland, southbound I-5 (the Santa Ana Freeway) travelers should exit at Disneyland Drive, turn left, cross Ball Road, and follow signs to the most convenient parking area.

Northbound I-5 Exit: Northbound travelers should exit I-5 at Katella Ave., proceed straight to Disney Way, and then follow signs to the most convenient parking area.

From John Wayne/Orange County Airport: Take I-405 north to CA-55 north to I-5 north. Watch carefully for highway signs once out of the airport. Exit at Katella Ave., head straight to Disney Way, then follow signs to the most convenient parking area.

From Los Angeles International Airport: Take I-105 east to I-605 north to I-5 south. Take Disneyland Drive exit toward Ball Road. Merge onto Disneyland Drive, and proceed to the most convenient parking area.

Exit off Orange Freeway: Travelers on the 57 freeway should exit on Katella Ave. and proceed west. Turn right on Harbor Blvd., and follow signs to the parking area.

ANAHEIM SURFACE STREETS: Disneyland is in the center of the Anaheim Resort, a 1,100-acre district. Disneyland is bounded by Harbor Boulevard on the east, Disneyland Drive (a segment of West Street) on the west, Ball Road on the north, and Katella Avenue on the south.

Harbor Boulevard, near Ball Road, is the most convenient place to pick up I-5 (Santa Ana Freeway) going north to Los Angeles. Katella Avenue, past Anaheim Boulevard, is the most convenient entrance to southbound I-5 going to Newport Beach and points south.

Note: Be sure to park in a designated lot, or feed the parking meter often: Parking fines can run between $32 and $282 in Anaheim.

LOCAL TRANSPORTATION: The Orange County Transportation Authority (OCTA; 714-560-6282; *www.octa.net*) provides daily bus service throughout the area, with limited weekend service. Several different lines stop

> ## HOT TIP!
> Guests getting picked up or dropped off by car should go to the drop-off/loading area on Harbor Boulevard between the East Shuttle Entry and Disney Way, or to the Downtown Disney parking area, between the ESPN Zone and Rainforest Cafe. (Parking at Downtown Disney is free for the first two hours.)

at the Disneyland Resort, but note that public transportation, while cost-efficient, may involve considerable waiting and transferring. At press time, the fare was $3 one way or $6 for a one-day unlimited pass. Seniors (age 65 and older) and people with disabilities pay $1.50 one way or $3 for a one-day pass. Exact change is required; pennies are not accepted.

If you have wanderlust but lack wheels, your best bet is to sign up for a bus tour, such as one of those offered by Gray Line of Anaheim (*www.graylineanaheim.com*; 800-828-6699). Hotel and motel desks provide information on tour schedules and prices, and even arrange to have you picked up at the hotel.

Anaheim Resort Transportation (888-364-2787; *www.rideart.org*) is a multi-route guest transit system serving the Anaheim Resort area. Passes may be purchased online and from many area hotels, public sales outlets, and various kiosk locations. Drivers do not sell passes. Adult fares are $5 for a one-day pass, $12 for three days, and $20 for a five-day pass. Kids ages 3 to 9 pay $2 for one day, $3 for three days, and $5 for five-day passes. There is no charge for baby passengers.

The Met serves L.A. County and the major attractions of Orange County (323-466-3876; *www.metro.net*). Cost is about $1.75 each way (75 cents for seniors). Exact change or a token is required. Tokens may be bought in bags of ten ($17.50) at locations throughout the L.A. area.

TAXIS: The only licensed taxi company that's officially authorized to serve the Disneyland Resort is the Anaheim Yellow Cab Company (714-999-9999 *www.yellowcab.com*). Cab fare to John Wayne Airport from the Disneyland Hotel runs about $50, plus tip; if you're going to LAX, figure at least $105 (or more, depending on the traffic); Long Beach Airport runs approximately $62, plus gratuity. Prices for town cars are slightly higher. Taxis can be called to pick you up at train and bus stations.

Planning Your Itinerary

For those lucky enough to live in the Los Angeles/Orange County area, the Disneyland Resort offers the opportunity to return frequently. Seasoned visitors and first-timers alike will do well to plan each step of their visit far in advance—make the travel arrangements as soon as vacation dates are set (refer to the Trip Planning Timeline below to make sure you don't miss any crucial steps), and then study the following chapters of this book to decide how you'd like to spend each day of the trip.

How many days should you spend with the Mouse? Well, that's up to you, but to experience the Disneyland Resort at its best, we recommend a stay of at least four full days—you will have enough time to see every attraction, parade, and show (plus revisit all of your favorites), lounge by your hotel's pool, enjoy a character meal, shop for souvenirs, and dance the night away. If you'd like to visit other area attractions, add on one day for each excursion. But don't try to cram too much into one visit; this is a vacation, after all.

Once you've decided how many days you're going to dedicate to Disney, it's time to decide how you'll split up your time on-property. We suggest that you begin with a day at Disneyland Park (for the original and quintessential Disney experience), followed by a visit to Disney California Adventure (to sample the attractions and shows). On the third day, return to Disneyland and hit the park's highlights, plus any attractions you missed on the first day, and save time for souvenir shopping. Day four should be dedicated to your preferred park and some downtime by the pool or in Downtown Disney's shopping plaza. Evenings can be spent in the park, if it's open late, or in Downtown Disney's restaurants, lounges, and movie theaters. The options are plentiful.

On the following pages, we've provided full-day schedules to guide you through four days in the theme parks (with special tips for families with young children and priorities for days when the lines are at their longest). The schedules are meant to be flexible and fun (not Disney boot camp), so take them at your own pace and plan breaks to relax: Have a Mickey Mouse ice cream bar, browse through the shops, smell the flowers, or just pick a bench and watch the crowds rush by.

Trip Planning Timeline

First Things First
★ Make hotel and transportation reservations as far ahead as possible. Call 714-520-5050 to purchase theme park tickets and to book Disney hotel accommodations (see pages 14 and 40 for details); remember that a deposit must be paid within 21 days of the reservation. Log all confirmation numbers in a notebook, and call to confirm before you leave home.
★ Decide where you will be on each day of your vacation, and create a simple schedule.

6 Months
★ Unless you opted for a vacation package that includes theme park admission, it's time to purchase your Disney park tickets (see page 17 for ticket options and ordering methods).

Up to 2 Months
★ Find out park hours, the attraction refurbishment schedule, and details on any special events by calling 714-781-4565 or by visiting *www.disneyland.com*; add this information to your day-by-day schedule.

★ Make dining reservations (they're necessary at certain table-service Disney restaurants; call 714-781-3463), and add the information to your day-by-day schedule. Refer to the *Good Meals, Great Times* chapter for details on Disneyland Resort eateries.

2 Weeks
★ Airline confirmation and travel vouchers should have arrived by now. Contact your travel agent or the travel company if they haven't shown up yet.

1 Week
★ Reconfirm all reservations and finalize your day-by-day vacation schedule.
★ Add all your important telephone numbers (doctor, family members, house sitter) to your trip planning notebook, and be sure to bring it and your day-by-day schedule with you.

1 Day
★ Place any tickets you may have purchased (and a valid, government-issued photo ID) into a carry-on bag.

Disneyland Park

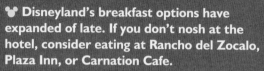

One-Day Schedule

❤ Disneyland's breakfast options have expanded of late. If you don't nosh at the hotel, consider eating at Rancho del Zocalo, Plaza Inn, or Carnation Cafe.

❤ Take in the sights as you walk down Main Street, but don't stop to shop or snack now (you'll have time for that later). Instead, head straight to Adventureland's Indiana Jones* and Jungle Cruise before making your way to Splash Mountain* and The Many Adventures of Winnie the Pooh in Critter Country. (If you plan to dine at the Blue Bayou, be sure to make a reservation in advance by calling 714-781-3463.)

❤ Backtrack to New Orleans Square, and visit the Haunted Mansion* and Pirates of the Caribbean before breaking for lunch.

❤ Next, see the show at the Golden Horseshoe Saloon, then tackle Big Thunder Mountain Railroad* in Frontierland. (Don't ride Big Thunder on a full stomach.)

❤ Explore Fantasy Faire. Then walk through the Castle into Fantasyland and visit Snow White, Pinocchio, Peter Pan, and Mr. Toad. Be sure to see Alice, the Mad Tea Party, the Matterhorn, and It's a Small World, too.

❤ Keep an eye on the time and try to fit the afternoon parade into your schedule.

❤ Make your way to Mickey's Toontown and see as many of this land's attractions as you can, making Roger Rabbit's Car Toon Spin* a top priority.

* Fastpass is available for this ride. Retrieve your time-saving Fastpass before visiting the land's remaining attractions. To learn how the system works, see page 58.

Continued on page 30 . . .

LINE BUSTERS

When the park is packed, the following attractions may have shorter waits: Enchanted Tiki Room, Tarzan's Treehouse, The Many Adventures of Winnie the Pooh, and The Disneyland Story—Presenting Great Moments with Mr. Lincoln.

IF YOU HAVE YOUNG CHILDREN

• First, head to Fantasyland and visit each area attraction (note that some are scary for small children) before heading to Mickey's Toontown. Then visit Critter Country to enjoy The Many Adventures of Winnie the Pooh.

• Scope out a spot on a Main Street curb up to an hour before the parade. For smaller crowds, watch the parade from the viewing area near It's a Small World.

• Take tykes to It's a Small World and King Arthur Carrousel. If you need cooling off, backtrack to Toontown and splash around at Donald's Boat.

• Ride the Jungle Cruise, then sing with the Tiki Birds in Adventureland and climb Tarzan's Treehouse before returning to your favorite rides.

DISNEYLAND DELIGHTS

These attractions form the quintessential Disneyland experience:

Indiana Jones Adventure	Star Tours—The Adventures Continue
Pirates of the Caribbean	Jungle Cruise
Haunted Mansion	The Many Adventures of Winnie the Pooh
Big Thunder Mountain Railroad	Buzz Lightyear Astro Blasters
Splash Mountain	Space Mountain
Peter Pan's Flight	Paint the Night (evening parade)
Matterhorn Bobsleds	
It's a Small World	Mr. Toad's Wild Ride

Disneyland Park
One-Day Schedule

. . . Continued from page 29

MEET THE CHARACTERS

There are lots of places to mix and mingle with Disney characters in this park. Some of the better spots include Toontown (Mickey, Minnie, Donald, Goofy, and more), Critter Country (Pooh and pals), and Fantasyland's Fantasy Faire (princesses). Check a park Times Guide for the schedule. And don't forget your camera!

TOP SHOPS

Whether you're browsing or buying, Disneyland is a shopper's paradise. Here are a few of the spots where wallets get a workout:

Candy Palace

Disneyana

Emporium

Main Street Magic Shop

Pieces of Eight

Pioneer Mercantile

South Seas Traders

The Star Trader

❤ Head to Tomorrowland. Hit the Finding Nemo Submarine Voyage, Buzz Lightyear Astro Blasters, and Space Mountain* before heading to dinner.

Note: If the park is open late, you can board the monorail in Tomorrowland and dine in Downtown Disney before returning to the park.

❤ After dinner, take the wheel of a snazzy hotrod at Autopia,* then take flight at Star Tours—The Adventures Continue,* and/or Astro Orbitor.

❤ Take little ones back to Mickey's Toontown before it closes for the day—it closes earlier than the rest of the park when there is a fireworks presentation (generally one hour before the show starts).

❤ On nights when Paint the Night is presented, make a point of getting to New Orleans Square and the Rivers of America in plenty of time to see it. (Check a park Entertainment Times Guide for the schedule.) If there is more than one performance scheduled, the later one is usually less crowded.

❤ Stroll back to Main Street. Shop, stop for dessert, see the Disneyland Story, and watch the fireworks burst over the Castle.

❤ If there's time, take a second spin on your favorite attractions.

* Fastpass is available for this ride. Retrieve your *free* time-saving Fastpass before visiting the land's remaining attractions.

HOT TIP!

If you'd like to meet Mickey Mouse, make a beeline for his Toontown house—the Big Cheese greets guests in the movie barn out back. For the shortest wait, get there as soon as Toontown opens.

Disney California Adventure

One-Day Schedule

❦ Begin your California adventure by snagging a Fastpass for a high-flying ride on Soarin' Around the World* (it tends to run out of Fastpass assignments early, as do Tower of Terror and Radiator Springs Racers). Then head directly to Toy Story Midway Mania! followed by a visit to The Little Mermaid—Ariel's Undersea Adventure. If you plan to stay until the park closes, get a Fastpass for World of Color.*

❦ Depart from Paradise Pier and head to Cars Land. Do not miss Radiator Springs Racers*! If possible, visit Mater's Junkyard Jamboree before moving on to Hollywood Land. Enjoy a thrilling trip at the Twilight Zone™ Tower of Terror.* Refer to a park guidemap for the next performance of the new Frozen-themed musical stage show, and plan to arrive at the theater at least 20 minutes before the show. In the meantime, enjoy Monsters, Inc.—Mike & Sulley to the Rescue!, Disney Animation (be sure to meet Anna and Elsa [with a Fastpass] and see Turtle Talk with Crush). Take tots to the inter-active Disney Junior—Live on Stage!

❦ Head to A Bug's Land and don your insect eyes for a creepy-crawly screening of It's Tough to be a Bug! (though it may scare little ones).

* Fastpass is available for this ride. Retrieve your *free* time-saving Fastpass before visiting the area's remaining attractions. To learn how the system works, turn to page 58.

Continued on page 32 . . .

MEET THE CHARACTERS

Guests have many opportunities to catch up with characters at Disney California Adventure. Among the best spots are Buena Vista Street (Mickey, Goofy, Donald, Oswald, Chip, and Dale), Hollywood Land (Anna, Elsa, and Olaf), Cars Land (Mater, McQueen, and Red the Fire Engine), Redwood Creek Challenge Trail (Russell and Dug), and Paradise Pier (Woody, Buzz, Jessie, and more). Check a park Times Guide for the schedule.

IF YOU HAVE YOUNG CHILDREN

• Head straight to the Hollywood Land section of the park. Stop in to visit with Anna & Elsa before experiencing Monsters, Inc.—Mike & Sulley to the Rescue! Head over to Animation for Turtle Talk and Sorcerer's Workshop. Next, pay a visit to Disney Junior—Live on Stage. Then maneuver young water lovers through the sprinkler maze and rides in A Bug's Land. Note that It's Tough to be a Bug! often frightens young children.

• Try the kid-friendly obstacle course on the Redwood Creek Challenge Trail and visit Russell and Dug (from the film *Up*).

• Take a spin on the carousel and go to Toy Story Mania! before hitting The Little Mermaid—Ariel's Undersea Adventure.

• Finally, treat night-owl tots to the World of Color water show. (The noisy water jets might spook some.) Warn kids that they might get a little wet.

Disney California Adventure

One-Day Schedule

. . . Continued from page 31

ADVENTURE ACES

If you're short on time, be sure to catch as many of the following four-star attractions at Disney California Adventure as possible:

Turtle Talk with Crush	It's Tough to be a Bug!
Radiator Springs Racers	California Screamin'
Frozen—Live at the Hyperion	**Monsters, Inc. —Mike & Sulley to the Rescue!**
Mater's Junkyard Jamboree	The Twilight Zone™ Tower of Terror
World of Color	**Luigi's Rollickin' Roadsters**
Soarin' Around the World	The Little Mermaid— Ariel's Undersea Adventure
Toy Story Midway Mania!	

❦ Make your way over to Grizzly Peak, and get set to get wet on the drenching **Grizzly River Run*** white-water raft ride. If you're up for it (and properly shoed), then visit the Redwood Creek Challenge Trail.

❦ Pick up some wine-pairing tips or sample California's finest at the Golden Vine Winery.

❦ Explore the Pacific Wharf area before proceeding on to Paradise Pier's daredevil rides (don't ride on a full stomach!).

❦ Work your way around Paradise Bay, making sure **California Screamin'*** and **The Little Mermaid—Ariel's Undersea Adventure** are top priorities.

❦ Be sure to catch the delightful nighttime extravaganza **World of Color.*** Line up for a waterside viewing spot at least 45 minutes before showtime—and know that you might get a little wet if you are up close.

* Fastpass is available for this ride. Retrieve your *free*, time-saving Fastpass before visiting the area's remaining attractions. See page 58 for details.

TOP SHOPS

Shopping at this park can be an adventure in and of itself! These are some of the spots that belong in the spotlight:

Big Top Toys

Elias & Co.

Off the Page

Rushin' River Outfitters

Sarge's Surplus Hut

Tower Hotel Gifts

Trolley Treats

Wandering Oaken's Trading Post

LINE BUSTERS

When lines abound at Disney California Adventure, we suggest heading to the following attractions: Redwood Creek Challenge Trail, Disney Animation, King Triton's Carousel, and Monsters, Inc.—Mike & Sulley to the Rescue!

A Second Day in
Disneyland Park

Returning for a second or third day in each of the theme parks means more time to savor the atmosphere, try any attractions you missed the first day, and revisit all the old and new favorites. Knowing that there will be a second day to play also makes for a much less harried pace on day one.

❦ Start the morning with a character breakfast at the Plaza Inn (you can also share a morning meal with the characters outside the park at Goofy's Kitchen in the Disneyland Hotel, the Grand Californian's Storytellers Cafe, or PCH Grill in Disney's Paradise Pier Hotel).

❦ Head to Tomorrowland and ride Space Mountain,* Star Tours—The Adventures Continue,* Buzz Lightyear Astro Blasters, and visit other favorites.

❦ Stroll over to Mickey's Toontown. See the sights and spend some time mingling with resident Disney characters.

❦ Visit It's a Small World, enjoy the fanfare at the nearby show, Mickey and the Magical Map, and then tour Fantasyland.

❦ Stroll, shop, and take a lunch break on (or on the way to) Main Street, U.S.A.

❦ Watch the afternoon parade from the Main Street Railroad depot, or secure a curbside spot.

❦ Ride a Main Street Vehicle up to Town Square and continue on foot toward Adventureland.

❦ Stop at the Enchanted Tiki Room and Tarzan's Treehouse before heading on to New Orleans Square. Here, the priorities are the Haunted Mansion* and Pirates of the Caribbean. Visit them and move on to Splash Mountain* in Critter Country.

❦ Meander through the shops of New Orleans Square, and then stop for a leisurely dinner at a nearby eatery. River Belle Terrace, the French Market, and the full-service Blue Bayou and Cafe Orleans are all excellent options.

❦ Select a viewing spot about 45 minutes ahead for the evening's performance of Paint the Night (if it is scheduled).

❦ Wait for the crowds to disperse at show's end and make your way to Big Thunder Mountain Railroad* for one last ride before the park closes.

* Fastpass is available for this ride. To learn how the system works, refer to page 58.

Disney California Adventure

🐚 If you don't have a reservation for Ariel's Princess Celebration Breakfast at Ariel's Grotto, grab breakfast at Fiddler, Fifer & Practical Cafe (aka Starbucks Coffee).

🐚 Cut through Hollywood Land and head straight for the Twilight Zone™ Tower of Terror.* Then move over to Cars Land, followed by Paradise Pier.

🐚 Thrill seekers will flip for California Screamin',* and gamers will swoon over Toy Story Midway Mania!

🐚 Take a lunch break at Award Wieners, Cocina Cucamonga, or Pacific Wharf Cafe; or, if the park is open late, head back to your hotel to relax or splash in the pool (get your hand stamped before exiting, so that you can return later in the day). Another option is to spend the afternoon in Downtown Disney—the restaurants and shops open by noon.

🐚 Your California Adventure picks up again with Soarin'* (in Grizzly Peak Air-field), followed by a trip to It's Tough to be a Bug!, a visit to The Little Mermaid—Ariel's Undersea Adventure, then on to Grizzly River Run* (if you don't mind the likelihood of getting a tad soggy).

🐚 Stop for the parade if you haven't seen it already, and then make your way over toward Hollywood Land.

🐚 Wander through the backlot, enjoying the impromptu entertainment, take in Turtle Talk with Crush, and meet Anna and Elsa* inside Disney Animation (a Fastpass is a must). Olaf may greet guests in Holly-wood Land, too. Take little ones for a tour of Monstropolis on Monsters, Inc.—Mike and Sulley to the Rescue!

🐚 Plan to line up at least 30 minutes early for the new, musical stage show known as Frozen—Live at the Hyperion.

🐚 If time permits after the show, revisit some of your favorite attractions or search for last-minute souvenirs at the shops on Buena Vista Street.

🐚 Don't miss World of Color*—it's an extremely popular show. (Guests up front may get spritzed.)

* Fastpass is available for this ride.

Fingertip Reference Guide

BARBERS AND SALONS

One nearby spot at which hair may be cut or coiffed is Marika's Hair Salon at the Hilton Anaheim Hotel (777 Convention Way; 714-703-1367).

CAR CARE

The Anaheim office of the Automobile Club of Southern California is located at 420 N. Euclid Street; 714-774-2392; *www.calif.aaa.com*. For emergency roadside service, call 800-400-4222.

DRINKING POLICIES

While there's a strict no-alcohol policy at Disneyland Park, imbibing is an option at many of the dining spots at Disney California Adventure and at Downtown Disney, as well as at all three Disneyland Resort hotels. Alcohol may also be purchased in the lounges and restaurants of the three Disney hotels. The legal drinking age in California is 21.

LOCKERS

Lockers of various sizes are available just outside the main entrance of the parks (our preferred location), inside Disneyland on Main Street (behind the Market House), and inside Disney California Adventure (DCA) across from Guest Relations. Prices are $7, $10, $12, or $15 per day, depending on the locker's size. These storage facilities make it convenient to intersperse frolicking on the attractions with shopping; just make your purchases and stash them in a locker. Availability is limited, and during busy periods all the space can be taken well before noon. Disney California Adventure guests may stash items in lockers for free while they ride Grizzly River Run. The lockers are off to the side of the attraction's entrance.

HOT TIP!
To avoid the sometimes maddening congestion at the Main Street locker location, consider stowing your stuff at the lockers near the picnic area, just outside Disneyland Park's turnstiles. (They are on the left side as you face the park.)

LOST AND FOUND

Lost and Found is located to the left of the entrance to Disneyland Park. At any given time, a survey of the shelves might turn up cameras, umbrellas, strollers, handbags, lens caps, sunglasses, radios, jewelry, and even a few crutches, false teeth, and hubcaps. (Once, a wallet containing $1,700 in cash was turned in.) The Disneyland Resort will return lost items to guests who fill out a report.

If you find a lost item, you may be asked to fill out a card with your name and address; if the object isn't claimed by the owner, you may have the option of claiming it. This system encourages honesty, so if you lose something in the parks, check at Lost and Found. If you lose something at a hotel, contact the front desk.

MAIL

Postcards are sold in gift shops throughout Anaheim, in many shops and souvenir stands on Disneyland Resort property, and at the three Disneyland Resort hotels. Stamps are sold at all Disney hotels, too.

Cards that are deposited in the mailboxes in the Disney theme parks are picked up and delivered to the U.S. Post Office once a day, early in the morning. All items are postmarked Anaheim, not Disneyland. (By the way, don't forget to arrange for your own mail to be held by the post office or picked up by a neighbor while you're on vacation.) Due to the heavy volume, expect delivery to take much longer than usual—don't mail your rent from here.

Post Office: The U.S. Post Office closest to Disneyland is Holiday Station, a half-mile away (1180 W. Ball Rd., Anaheim; 714-533-8182). It's open from 9 A.M. to 5 P.M. weekdays only.

MEDICAL MATTERS

Blisters are the most common complaint received by Disney's First Aid departments, located at the north end of Main Street, next to Lost Children in Disneyland, and at the Chamber of Commerce near the entrance of Disney California Adventure. So be forewarned, and wear comfortable, broken-in shoes (bring a backup pair, too)—and pack Band-Aids, just in case.

If you have a serious medical problem while on-property, call 911 and contact any Disney cast member (aka employee). He or she will get in touch with First Aid to make further arrangements. First Aid, staffed with registered nurses, will supply breathing machines and crutches for guests. It will not dispense medication to anyone under 18 without the consent of a parent or chaperone.

It's a good idea to carry an insurance card and any other pertinent medical information. Those with chronic health problems should carry copies of all their prescriptions, along with their doctor's telephone number.

Prescriptions: The pharmacy at CVS, about a mile from Disneyland Resort, is open 24 hours a day, seven days a week (480 South Main St.; 714-938-1200). On Katella near Euclid Street is a Walgreens, with a drive-thru pharmacy that is open Monday through Friday from about 8 A.M. until about 9 P.M., Saturdays from 9 A.M. to 6 P.M., and Sundays from 10 A.M. until 6 P.M. (10840 Katella Ave., Anaheim; 714-808-0126).

Refrigerator Facilities: In the parks, insulin and antibiotics that must be refrigerated can be stored for the day at First Aid. (It does not store breast milk for nursing mothers.) Outside the parks, there are refrigerators in many of the area's hotels and motels. If your room doesn't have one, a fridge can usually be supplied for a nominal charge, or the hotel or motel may be able to store insulin in its own refrigerator. Inquire in advance.

MONEY

Cash, traveler's checks, Disney Dollars, Visa, American Express, MasterCard, JCB, Discover Card, Diner's Club, and Disney gift cards are accepted as payment for admission to the theme parks, for merchandise purchased in shops, and for meals (except at select souvenir and food carts, where it's strictly cash or Disney Dollars). Personal checks may be used to pay for park admission. Checks must be imprinted with the guest's name and address, drawn on a U.S. bank, and accompanied by proper ID—that is, a valid driver's license or passport. Department store charge cards are

not acceptable identification for check-writing purposes. Disney hotel guests who have left a credit card number at check-in can charge most expenses in the parks to their hotel bill.

Disney Dollars: First introduced by the Walt Disney Company in 1987, Disney Dollars were discontinued in 2016. However, those already in circulation are still accepted as cash at most Disneyland Resort, Walt Disney World, and Disney Store locations. So if you have Disney Dollars burning a hole in your pocket, rest assured you can still use that colorful cash. Note that change is provided in U.S. currency, not Mickey money.

Disney Gift Cards: Available for purchase at many merchandise locations, these may be redeemed throughout the Disneyland Resort (though there are some exceptions at Downtown Disney and vendors not equipped to accept credit cards).

Financial Services: Automated Teller Machines (ATMs) are located at each park's main entrance; in Disneyland at The Disney Gallery on Main Street, by the Fantasyland Theatre, by the Frontierland Stockade, and in Tomorrowland; in California Adventure at the Entry Plaza, in the Pacific Wharf region, at the restrooms near Goofy's Sky School, and by Embarcadero Gifts; in Downtown Disney by Häagen-Dazs; and in all Disneyland Resort hotels. For details, inquire at Guest Relations.

Personal checks are not accepted. The ATMs at the main entrance accept credit cards for cash advances. Note that the presence of a bank on Main Street is a tad deceiving: The bank offers no financial services.

American Express Cardmember Services: Cardholders can purchase American Express Travelers Cheques, American Express Gift Cheques, and American Express gift cards, and exchange foreign currency (for a fee) at the Altour/American Express Travel Representative Office: 240 Newport Centre Dr., Suite 116, Newport Beach, CA; 714-541-3318. This office is open Monday through Friday from 9 A.M. to 5:30 P.M. and on Saturday from 9 A.M. to 4 P.M.

Many Anaheim banks sell American Express traveler's checks, usually for a one percent fee.

Foreign Currency Exchange: Foreign currency may be exchanged (at the current exchange rate) at City Hall in Disneyland, Chamber of Commerce at Disney California Adventure, and at the front desk at each of the three Disneyland Resort Hotels. Paper currency only (no coins).

PETS

Except for service animals, pets are not allowed in Disneyland or Disney California Adventure. However, nonpoisonous creatures may be boarded in the Disneyland Pet Care Kennel, which is located by the entrance to Disneyland Park. Reservations are not necessary (the kennel rarely reaches capacity). Pets may be boarded for the day (no overnight stays). In addition to proof of rabies and distemper vaccinations, guests have to show proof of hepatitis and leptospirosis vaccinations for dogs over four months of age. Without proof of all four vaccinations, the dog will not be permitted entrance to the kennel. At press time, it cost about $20 per day, per pet. Cash only. To ask about the kennel rates during your visit, call 714-781-7290.

Disney personnel do not handle the animals, so the pet owners themselves must put their animals into the cages and take them out again. Guests are encouraged to drop by to visit with and walk their pets several times a day. Kennel attendants are not responsible for walking any animals in their care.

Note: During busy seasons, there may be a morning rush, starting about 30 minutes before the theme parks open, so you may encounter some delay in arranging your pet's stay.

Outside the Disneyland Resort: If you want to board your pet nearby, contact Animal Inns of America, 10852 Garden Grove Blvd., Garden Grove, CA 92843; 714-702-1745; *www.animalinns.com.*

Some hotels and motels in the Disneyland area accept well-behaved (preferably small) pets, but most do not allow guests to leave animals in the room unattended.

To find out about other possibilities for pets, contact the Anaheim/Orange County Visitor & Convention Bureau; 855-405-5020; or search "pets" at *www.visitanaheim.org.*

PHOTOGRAPHIC NEEDS

The Main Street Photo Supply Co. inside Disneyland can answer questions and recharge most batteries (or you can bring your own charger and plug it in there). Disney California Adventure offers similar services. For anything more serious, rent a camera and have a factory-authorized shop do the work on your camera when you return home. If you've lost your lens cover, it's worth checking at Lost and Found (see page 35); they may not have your cap, but they often have extras.

Try not to take your camera on wet, rough, or bumpy rides. Stash it in a locker or with a non-riding member of your party.

HOT TIP!
Disneyland Resort offers a one-day PhotoPass package for $39. It includes unlimited downloads of pictures taken by Disney photographers. It's a great way to get shots of your entire party. For details, refer to page 85.

RELIGIOUS SERVICES

Catholic: St. Justin Martyr; 2050 W. Ball Rd., Anaheim, about two miles from Disneyland; *www.saintjustin.org*; 714-774-2595. Masses are in English and Spanish; call or check the website for times.

Episcopal: St. Michael's Episcopal Church; 311 W. South St., Anaheim; 714-535-4654; *http://stmichaels.ladiocese.org*; about seven blocks from Disneyland. Sunday services are at 7:30 A.M. and 11:15 A.M. (English). Call for mass time in Spanish.

Jewish: Temple Beth Emet; 1770 W. Cerritos Ave., Anaheim; 714-772-4720; *www.tbe-oc.org*; a few blocks from Disneyland. Services are held on Fridays at 6:30 P.M., the fourth Friday of each month at 8 P.M., and 9 A.M. Saturdays.

Lutheran: Prince of Peace Lutheran Church; 1421 W. Ball Rd., Anaheim; 714-774-0993; *www.princeofpeaceanaheim.org*; about one mile from the Disneyland Resort. Sunday services are at 8:30 A.M. (traditional) and 10 A.M. (praise).

Non-denominational: The Kindred Community Church; 8712 E. Santa Ana Canyon Rd., Anaheim; 714-282-9941. Services are held on Sundays at 8:45 A.M. and 10:30 A.M. The church is about 11 miles from Disneyland; *www.kindredchurch.org*.

United Methodist: West Anaheim United Methodist Church; 2045 W. Ball Rd., Anaheim; 714-772-6030; Sunday morning services are held at 11 A.M. (traditional); approximately two miles from the Disneyland Resort.

SHOPPING FOR NECESSITIES

It's a rare vacationer who doesn't leave some essential at home or run out of it mid-trip. Gift shops in almost all the hotels stock items no traveler should be without, but they usually cost more than in conventional retail shops. One good source is CVS Pharmacy at 480 S. Main St.; 714-938-1200.

Inside the theme parks, aspirin, bandages, suntan lotions, and other sundries are sold at a variety of shops; just ask a cast member to direct you to the closest one. Some items are also available at each park's First Aid location and Baby Care Center.

SMOKING POLICIES

State law bans smoking (including electronic cigarettes) anywhere inside restaurants, bars, and lounges, but many places provide patios for puffing and often heat them on chilly evenings. At the Disney parks, smoking is allowed in designated smoking areas. Check a park guidemap for exact locations. All hotels at the Disneyland Resort are smoke-free.

TELEPHONES

If you don't have your wireless phone handy, know that local calls from most pay phones in Southern California cost 50 cents. Most hotels in the area charge an average of a dollar or more for local, toll-free, and credit-card calls made from your room.

For long-distance calls, policies vary from hotel to hotel, but charges are always higher than they would be for direct-dial calls made from a pay phone. It makes the most sense to use a calling card when dialing long-distance from a room phone.

Phone Cards: Disney offers AT&T prepaid phone cards in values of $10 and $20. They can be purchased at select locations at the Disneyland resort hotels.

Weather Hotlines: For weather info, visit *www.weather.gov; www.weather.com;* or *www.wunderground.com.*

Wireless Phones: To ensure a dose of uninterrupted magic for you and those around you, stick to texting while visiting the parks and silence your ringer. You'll be glad you did. Note that selfie sticks are not permitted.

TIPPING

The standard gratuities around Anaheim are about the same as in any other city of its size. Expect to tip bellhops about $1 per bag. Generally, tip cabdrivers 15 percent; outstanding shuttle or tour bus drivers, $1. Valets usually get $1 to $2 when you pick up the car. In restaurants, a 15 to 20 percent gratuity is the norm. If you are pleased with the condition of your room, it is customary to leave a gratuity of $2 to $5 per day for the housekeeper (leave a note with the tip to avoid confusion). Note that room service bills often include a gratuity.

Accommodations

The welcome sign is always out at the three Disneyland Resort hotels, where themed meals, amenities, and decor are definitely in character and add to the fun of a Disneyland vacation. And the resort's Disneyland Hotel and Grand Californian Hotel & Spa take staying at Disneyland to a lovely level of luxury.

In addition to the three hotels within the Disneyland Resort, there are dozens of properties in Orange County, known as Disneyland Good Neighbor hotels, that the Walt Disney Travel Company has handpicked to round out the Disney lodging options. We've selected a bunch of these recommended hotels, based on services and proximity to Disneyland, to highlight in this chapter.

If the sole purpose of your trip is to visit Disney, plan to stay in Anaheim, either on Disneyland property or at one of the surrounding hotels. Once you arrive and check in, you won't need your car again until you leave. Transportation to and from the parks is provided by monorails and trams serving the Disneyland Resort, and by buses serving neighboring hotels, motels, and inns. If struck with a bit of wanderlust, know that Anaheim is within range of a host of Southern California destinations, including movie studios, museums, beaches, and more. Whatever your vacation goals, we've provided a variety of options in Anaheim, from old-fashioned to contemporary, simple to sublime.

Disneyland Resort Hotels

Fans of the Disneyland Resort are faced with a difficult decision. It isn't whether or not to stay on-property (that's recommended if it's within the budget), but which of the three hotels to choose. Some factors to consider:

The whimsical pool area and character meals make the classic Disneyland Hotel appeal to the kids in the family (and the kid in us all).

Meanwhile, Disney's Paradise Pier Hotel boasts a sunny facade to complement Disney California Adventure. Inside, Disney's influence is subtle, but it is possible to dine with characters.

The design team has really outdone itself with the Grand Californian Hotel & Spa. Located inside Disney California Adventure, the hotel's theming and style touch every detail, right down to the floorboards.

Whichever hotel you choose, one thing is certain—a stay on-property is sure to complete the overall Disney experience. From a resort information TV channel to wake-up calls from Mickey Mouse himself, every detail reminds you that you're in Disney's land.

Exclusive Benefits: Some perks are reserved for guests staying at a Disneyland Resort Hotel. Perhaps the most significant of these is "Extra Magic Hour," which allows early entry

HOT TIP!
Rooms equipped for guests with disabilities are available at the three Disney hotels, all of which are completely non-smoking. No exceptions.

into the parks (at no extra cost) on each morning of their stay (with a ticket). There's also preferred admission (with ticket) to a park if it reaches capacity. There's even an exclusive entrance to Disney California Adventure park, available only to guests staying at a Disneyland Resort hotel (ID is required).

One of the most convenient perks is the ability to charge most expenses incurred at a Disney park back to the hotel room, if a credit card imprint was taken at check-in. Purchases can be charged to the room from the time of check-in until 11 A.M. on the day of departure.

Shoppers may also enjoy the benefit of having purchases delivered to their hotel's Bell Services Desk, where they can pick up their packages the next day—rather than having to carry them through the parks all day.

Other on-property perks include in-lobby screenings of Disney's animated classics (at all Disneyland Resort hotels), in-room light shows

(Disneyland Hotel only), and wake-up calls from Mickey. Courtesy pick-up is available for guests with disabilities to and from Paradise Pier in Disney California Adventure park.

Check-in and Check-out: Check-in begins at 3 P.M. (4 P.M. for the villas at Disney's Grand Californian), but guests who arrive early can check in, store their luggage at the Bell Desk, and go have fun. A photo ID is required at check-in. Check-out is at 11 A.M., and, again, bags can be stored until guests are ready to depart. Express check-out is available by leaving a credit card imprint at check-in.

Prices: Rates for standard guest rooms range from about $269 to $705. Concierge-level rooms start at about $380. Suites range from about $662 to $8,270. They vary based on hotel, view, and season. Note that it costs $18 per day to park at a Disneyland Resort hotel. Local calls, weekday newspaper, fitness center access, and unlimited high-speed wireless Internet access are now available to all hotel guests.

Deposit Requirements: A deposit equal to one night's lodging (plus tax) is required at time of booking when making a "room only" reservation. Packages require a $200 deposit, due within 38 days of booking. Final payment is due 45 days prior to arrival. Packages booked within 30 days prior to final payment due date (45 days before arrival) don't require a deposit. If you prefer not to use a credit card to pay the deposit, call 714-520-5050.

Cancellation Policy: For a room-only booking, the deposit will be refunded if the reservation is canceled at least 5 days before the scheduled arrival. If you need to cancel a package, expect to be charged a $200 cancel fee, plus insurance cost (where applicable), if the package is canceled 29 days or less prior to arrival.

Additional Costs: Sleeping bags and cribs are free. Self-parking costs $18 per day, while valet parking is available for $28 per day. Note that there is no longer an additional fee for extra guests (up to room capacity).

Discounts: Annual Passholders may get special discounts throughout the Disneyland Resort. There may be discounts available to California residents, members of the military, and teachers, too—ask when you make your reservation. Disney Visa® Cardmembers can reap savings on merchandise, guided tours, and dining at the Disneyland Resort. For more information, visit *DisneyRewards.com*.

Packages: The Walt Disney Travel Company offers packages that feature a stay at one of the Disneyland hotels. Call 714-520-5050.

PHOTO BY MIKE CARROLL

DISNEYLAND HOTEL: This fanciful resort adjacent to the Downtown Disney District was the first hotel erected at Disneyland Resort—way back in 1955. It has had many looks over the years, and the newest one proves the old adage: Everything old is new again! While the new motif is a tribute to yesteryear and highlights the original mid-20th-century style of the hotel, there are some decidedly 21st-century touches, such as fiber-optic "fireworks" on many guest room headboards.

Some of the most noticeable changes have taken place in the pool area. With a nod to iconic park signage, "Disneyland" is spelled out in familiar blocks atop a platform supporting two water slides. Reminiscent of the original monorail station at the Disneyland Hotel, at each slide's entrance sits a replica monorail car that guests glide through as they twist and turn toward the water below. The largest of the slides sits 26 feet high and stretches 187 feet. The area also has a two-lane, mini slide for younger guests, as well as bubble jets in which to play. There are two hot tub spas and six poolside cabanas, too (there's a fee for cabana use).

The hotel has nearly 1,000 rooms, including 60 or so suites, located in three towers. Most tower rooms have two queen beds, and many rooms can accommodate up to five people (one of them on a daybed). The 11-story Adventure Tower looks toward Downtown

PHOTO BY JILL SAFRO

Disney and Disney California Adventure on one side and the main pool on the other. The 11-story Fantasy Tower offers rooms with pool views, but only on one side; guests on the other side look out over city rooftops, with Disneyland to the right, and the best view of the fireworks. The 14-story Frontier Tower's rooms provide city and courtyard views.

A monorail stop is a short walk away in neighboring Downtown Disney, which means extremely easy access to Disneyland (it drops guests off in Tomorrowland)—a nice convenience for guests who relish a break in their park-going with a trip to one of the hotel pools, the Mandara Spa, or the Fitness Center (a gym that features weight machines and aerobic exercise equipment). The workout room may be used by all resort guests and is accessed with a room key.

In the lobby of the Fantasy Tower, a large shop called Fantasia sells Disney souvenirs. Goofy's Kitchen, hosted by Chef Goofy and his Disney pals, is an extremely popular buffet open for brunch and dinner; Steakhouse 55 offers breakfast and dinner in an elegant setting; The Coffee House provides snacks and quick meals for guests on the go. Room service is available; and Tangaroa Terrace, a tiki-inspired casual dining spot, serves up three meals a day with a South Seas flair, as well as grab-and-go items. The adjoining bar, Trader Sam's, is a nice spot for drinks and appetizers. (For more information about dining, see *Good Meals, Great Times*, beginning on page 109.)

The convention and meetings area, adjacent to Goofy's Kitchen and linked to the lobby via a photo-lined passageway, deserves a look for its Disney-related artwork, including a floor-to-ceiling collage of Disney collectibles and milestones. Created entirely from old toys, souvenirs, name tags, and other assorted memorabilia, it commemorates the colorful and unique history of Disneyland.

The hotel can provide safe-deposit boxes, currency exchange, and child-care referrals. An ATM is on the premises. Airport buses bound for Orange County and Los Angeles airports stop at the nearby Disneyland Resort transportation area on Harbor Boulevard (aka West Shuttle Area), as do tour buses, city, and county buses.

Standard room rates run from about $360 to $558, depending on the view and season; no charge for rollaways or cribs. Concierge-level rooms start at about $586. Suites range from $722 to $4,719. (The higher amount is for the Pirates of the Caribbean Suite and the Mickey Mouse Penthouse Suite.)

Self-parking costs $18 per day; valet parking runs $28 a day. Non-resort guests visiting the hotel pay $28 for the first hour and $9 for each extra hour to self-park (with a $58 maximum for 24 hours); $28 for the first hour and $9 for each additional hour of valet parking (with a $100 max). High-speed Internet access is included, too. Note that all prices were correct at press time but are likely to change in 2017.

Disneyland Hotel, 1150 Magic Way, Anaheim, CA 92802; 714-956-6425 (to make reservations) or 714-778-6600 (front desk); *www.disneyland.com.*

DISNEY'S GRAND CALIFORNIAN HOTEL & SPA: This hotel is in a prime location—right in the middle of the Disneyland Resort. And, thanks to the Disney Vacation Club, the resort includes about 200 more studio rooms, 44 suites, 50 villas, and a swimming pool. The resort has its own private entrance to Disney California Adventure park and easy access to the Downtown Disney District.

A border of trees surrounds the six-story hotel, built as a tribute to the American Craftsman tradition of the early 1900s. Cedar and redwood paneling decorates the cavernous lobby, where display cabinets filled with original art and reproductions introduce guests to that rich period of art. The lobby's great hearth has a perennially lit fire. Furnishings throughout the hotel have warm colors and intricate textures.

Each deluxe guestroom and suite features a 32-inch flat-panel TV, DVD player, small safe, 24-hour room service, desk with two-line telephone, high-speed Internet access

(no charge), iron, and small (unstocked) refrigerator. The bathroom has a makeup mirror and hair dryer.

Most of the guestrooms in the hotel feature two queen beds, though 80 have a king bed, and 160 have one queen bed, plus a bunk bed with a trundle (these rooms sleep five). The carved wooden headboards are designed to resemble vines on a trellis, and Bambi appears subtly in the shower curtain pattern.

The Disney Vacation Club villas reflect the same design as the hotel and are available to all guests when not occupied by DVC members. Each studio has a queen-size bed and queen-size sleeper sofa, plus a kitchenette with microwave, coffeemaker, and mini fridge. Larger (one-, two-, and three-bedroom) villas sleep 5 to 12 and offer dining areas, kitchens, laundry facilities, master baths with hot tub spas, and DVD players. They include a king-size bed in the master bedroom, a living room with queen-size sleeper sofa (and a sleeper chair in the one- and two-bedroom villas), and either two queen-size beds or a queen bed and a double sleeper sofa in extra bedrooms.

Guest services include 24-hour room service, laundry and dry cleaning, and a full-service business center. The concierge level offers upgraded amenities and services. Guests can relax at the Fountain Pool or frolic in the Redwood Pool (the two are adjacent); or they can enjoy the kids' pool, gift shop, and a licensed child-care center known as Pinocchio's Workshop. (Guests staying at the Paradise Pier and Disneyland Hotels may also use this service.) The luxurious Mandara Spa features treatment rooms and a couples suite accented with Balinese-inspired art and textiles. The spa includes a modern fitness center, steam rooms, and a nail salon.

Among the dining options are the award-winning Napa Rose, which features California cuisine and wines, and Storytellers Cafe, open for three meals in an Old California setting and the backdrop for a character-hosted breakfast. A quick-service eatery, White Water Snacks, supplies coffee, fast food, and baked goods; the poolside bar is good for a quick meal or snack. The Hearthstone Lounge doubles as a breakfast spot, dispensing coffee and pastries to guests heading into the park.

The hotel can provide safe-deposit boxes and currency exchange. An ATM is on the premises. Airport buses bound for Orange

County and Los Angeles airports stop at the hotel's main entrance, as do tour buses, and city and county buses. City and County buses stop at the nearby Disneyland Resort transportation center (aka East Shuttle Area).

Rates for standard rooms run about $417 to $705, depending on the view and season. Concierge rooms start at about $694; suites range from about $983 to $8,270. There are no rollaway beds, but a themed sleeping bag with a pad can be supplied; no charge for cribs. Self-parking costs $18 a day; valet parking is $28. Non-resort guests pay $18 for the first hour of self-parking and $9 for each additional hour (with a $58-dollar maximum); $28 for the first hour of valet parking, and $9 for each additional hour (with a $100 max).

Disney's Grand Californian, 1600 S. Disneyland Drive, Anaheim, CA 92803; 714-956-6425 (for reservations) or 714-635-2300 (front desk); *www.disneyland.com.*

or two queen beds, plus a twin daybed in the sitting area (a particular convenience for families). The rooms on the cabana level open onto a large recreation area that includes a sundeck, swimming pool, slide, hot tub spa, children's play area, and snack bar. If you plan to spend a lot of time in or beside the pool, consider a concierge-level room on the third floor for direct access.

The Mickey in Paradise shop, a coffee bar, and a restaurant are on the ground level of the hotel. Disney's PCH Grill offers lunch, dinner, and a character breakfast, Surf's Up Breakfast with Mickey and friends. Room service offers PCH Grill specialties. The hotel also has an exercise room, guest laundry service, a small concierge lounge, and an ATM. A glass-enclosed elevator provides a bird's-eye view of the lobby and Disney California Adventure.

Guests staying here have exclusive access to the hotel's entrance into Disney California Adventure. The hotel is also connected to the Disneyland Resort and Downtown Disney by a landscaped walkway. Guests (with tickets) can get to Disneyland by taking the monorail from the Downtown Disney station. Both Disneyland and Disney California Adventure theme parks are within a 10- to 15-minute walk.

Standard rooms accommodate up to five guests. Rates run from about $269 to $401, depending on the view and the season (no charge for kids under 18 sharing their parents' room); no charge for rollaways or cribs. Concierge rooms start at about $380. Suites range from about $662 to $2,967. Self-parking costs $18 a day; valet parking is $28.

Disney's Paradise Pier Hotel, 1717 S. Disneyland Dr., Anaheim, CA 92802; 714-956-6425 (reservations) or 714-999-0990 (front desk); *www.disneyland.com.*

DISNEY'S PARADISE PIER HOTEL: This property's facade reflects the cheery ambience and carefree style of the Paradise Pier district of the park, which it overlooks. The smallest of the Disneyland Resort hotels, Paradise Pier is popular with businesspeople and families alike.

The hotel's two high-rise towers—one 15 stories, the other 14 stories—are juxtaposed to create a central atrium, which cradles the lobby and a larger-than-life character sculpture. Mickey's familiar silhouette shows up in subtle ways in the hotel's beachy decor. Each of the 481 guestrooms, including 20 suites, features Disney-themed furnishings, one king-size bed

Disneyland Good Neighbor Hotels

With fewer than 2,500 rooms available at the Disneyland Resort and tens of thousands of guests pouring through the parks each day, it's no wonder that a majority of visitors stay off Disney property. To make it easier for guests to narrow down their off-property choices, the folks at Disney have selected local hotels and motels that meet their standards and anointed them Disneyland Good Neighbor hotels. Before receiving the Disney seal of approval, hotels are reportedly graded on amenities, services, decor, guest satisfaction, price, and location. Note that all Good Neighbor hotels sell Disneyland park tickets.

Ranging from national chains to smaller operations, Good Neighbor hotels proliferate along Harbor Boulevard, which flanks Disneyland resort on the east. From Harbor, it's easy to walk to the Disneyland Resort. A few hotels are on Ball Road, the Resort's northern boundary. Below Katella Avenue, which borders the resort to the south, side streets lead to the Anaheim Convention Center and the city's major convention hotels. Divided into Suite, Superior, Moderate, and Economy, there are more than 40 Good Neighbor hotels in all. In the following pages, we describe some of our favorites. For the Good Neighbor properties not detailed here, refer to The Rest of the Best on page 50.

Prices: Expect to pay $99 to $299, or more, per night for a hotel room for two adults and two children (kids usually stay in their parents' room for free), $79 to $265 for a motel room, and $50 to $80 for tent or RV camping. Prices drop a bit in winter; they are highest in the summer and over holidays. The room tax in Anaheim is 15 percent.

Additional Costs: When comparing accommodation costs, consider hidden zingers, like parking. Hotels usually charge for it ($14 to $24 a day; more for valet service). Many also charge an additional fee when more than four people occupy a room. Inquire about telephone rates when you check in—hotel surcharges are notoriously huge.

Savings: You can save money by staying in a hotel that offers complimentary breakfast and shuttle service to Disneyland. Discounts are sometimes offered to those who belong to an automobile or retirement association.

Individual Needs: What's essential for one vacationer—and worth the extra cost—might seem frivolous to another guest: room service, on-site restaurants, live music, a suite, a kitchen, concierge service and amenities, large swimming pool, exercise room, or a place that accepts pets.

Packages: The Walt Disney Travel Company offers packages in conjunction with each of the Good Neighbor hotels—representing potentially big savings for travelers. For details or to book a package, contact the Walt Disney Travel Company directly at 714-520-5060.

Note: The following establishments accept major credit cards and offer rooms for travelers with disabilities, unless otherwise indicated. Call directly to inquire about deposit requirements and cancellation policies. Rates given were correct at press time, but are subject to change and should always be confirmed by phone.

Suite Hotels

RESIDENCE INN BY MARRIOTT ANAHEIM MAINGATE: Nestled in a garden-like setting, this residential-style hotel is about a half-mile from Disneyland Resort. The well-maintained grounds are landscaped with hibiscus, bougainvillea, lemon, sweetgum, and pepper trees, plus park-style benches and, we're convinced, some of the only remaining orange trees in the city of Anaheim.

Inside the 200-suite inn, the living room-like lobby is inviting, with chairs, cocktail tables, fireplace, and TV. Facilities include a fitness center, a 24-hour swimming pool, a kiddie pool, a whirlpool, and a single court that can be adapted for tennis, basketball, or volleyball. There is also a guest laundry, a small market, a barbecue area, and a small playground.

The suites are spacious and are offered in different room configurations, including a studio suite (one queen and sofa bed, sleeps up up to 4); one-bedroom suite (2 queens in bedroom and a sofa bed in living room, sleeps up to 6); and a penthouse suite (2 queens in bedroom, a sofa bed in living room, king-size bed in a loft, and 2 bathrooms., sleeps up to 8). All have a flat-screen TV, full kitchen with stove, microwave, dishwasher, full-size fridge, and cooking utensils. Rates range from $149 to $450. Lower long-term rates are offered. Cribs and baby gates are available, but rollaway beds are not.

Complimentary amenities include a daily hot breakfast buffet, business center with free Internet access and printing services, grocery delivery (guests must pay for the groceries), daily housekeeping, Wi-Fi in all suites, and free parking—a huge perk in this neck of the woods. The hotel accepts pets for a flat fee of $100. This hotel offers a Disney planning and information desk. Anaheim Resort Transit provides bus transportation for a fee.

Residence Inn by Marriott Anaheim Maingate, 1700 S. Clementine St., Anaheim, CA 92802. 714-533-3555 or 800-331-3131; or *www.marriott.com/snaah.*

Superior Hotels

ANAHEIM MARRIOTT: Conveniently located next door to the Anaheim Convention Center, the Marriott is a favorite among conventioneers. Most of the 1,030 rooms and suites, located in two towers and two four-story wings, have balconies. Each has one king-size bed or two doubles and TV. The restaurant—nFuse Bar & Kitchen—gets busy (especially at traditional mealtimes). For a quick bite or beverage, drop by the Pizza Hut or Starbucks, both on the premises. There is a partially covered pool surrounded by lounge chairs, plus a whirlpool and a health club. Guests enjoy poolside and lobby bars, and concierge services.

PHOTO BY KEITH GROSHANS

The hotel is a couple of long blocks from the Disneyland Resort—for some, it is not within walking distance. Shuttle service to the Disney theme parks is provided by Anaheim Resort Transit for a fee; transportation to area airports may also be arranged. The hotel has a Disneyland planning desk, too.

Room rates for two start at $129 (there is no charge for children under age 18 sharing their parents' room); suites start at about $199; $20 per additional adult. Rollaway beds are $20 per stay, and cribs are free. Special packages are available. Self-parking costs $25 per day; valet parking is $30 per day. Note that pets are no longer accepted at this hotel.

Anaheim Marriott, 700 W. Convention Way, Anaheim, CA 92802; visit the hotel's website at *www.anaheimmarriott.com*, or call 714-750-8000 or 800-228-9290.

HILTON ANAHEIM: The 14-story glass exterior of this property reflects the Anaheim Convention Center, just steps away, and the newly renovated lobby area invites the outdoors (and swarms of conventioneers) inside. Hilton Anaheim, the largest hotel in the Anaheim resort area, boasts 1,572 rooms, including 93 suites, decorated in contrasting dark wood tones, with crisp white linens and warm wall coverings. Recent enhancements include larger public spaces, a Chef's Table designed by architect John Gidding, a Disney planning desk, and a Starbucks Coffee.

The hotel's outdoor recreation area, on the fifth floor, features a heated pool, 2 whirlpools, and a kids' water play activity area. Dining options include the recently revitalized Mix Restaurant & Lounge, and the Pool Grill & Bar for outdoor dining (seasonal). There is also a food court that offers Baja Fresh, Sbarro, Just Grillin' and Submarina (sandwiches).

Add to that a business center, FedEx shop, and well-appointed boutiques. The 25,000-square-foot Health Club & Spa at Hilton has state-of-the-art exercise equipment, daily fitness classes, an indoor saltwater pool, basketball court, whirlpool, steam room, sauna, spa treatments and massage.

Rates for a room with two queen beds range from $119 to $309 (there is no charge for kids under 18 when sharing their parents' room with existing bedding); suites run a bit higher. Ask about packages. There is no extra charge for cribs, but rollaway beds cost $20 a night. Self-parking costs $16 per day; valet parking, $22. Pets are not permitted.

Hilton Anaheim, 777 Convention Way, Anaheim, CA 92802; 714-750-4321 or 800-445-8667; *www.hiltonanaheimhotel.com.*

HYATT REGENCY ORANGE COUNTY: The hotel, located in Garden Grove, is one mile south of Disneyland Resort. Its dramatic, 17-story atrium encloses palm trees and greenery and houses the TusCA restaurant, Starbucks, a gift shop, Citrus Grove Deli, and OC Brewhouse. Each of the 656 guestrooms features either a king-size bed or two queen beds, and modern interior design.

Amenities include coffeemaker, hair dryer, iron with board, plus an iPod docking station. The one- and two-bedroom suites also have a living room, refrigerator, and microwave. Suites can accommodate up to 8 people.

Kids' Suites include a room for the little ones, complete with bunk beds and a TV. The parents' room has a king bed, TV, fridge, and microwave.

The hotel's impressive recreational facilities, located on the South Tower's third-story roof, include a heated swimming pool, a fitness center, basketball court, tennis court, and a fire pit. Another outdoor pool and whirlpool are on the ground floor of the North Tower. This hotel offers a Disney planning and information desk. Transportation to the Disneyland Resort is provided for a fee, and airport shuttle service is available (also for a fee).

Room rates start at about $137 (there is no additional charge for children under age 18 occupying their parents' room), plus $25 for each additional adult; $179 and higher for suites. There is no charge for cribs. Self-parking and valet parking both cost $27 per day.

Hyatt Regency Orange County, 11999 Harbor Boulevard, Garden Grove, CA 92840; *www.orangecounty.hyatt.com*; 714-750-1234 or 800-233-1234.

ANAHEIM MAJESTIC GARDEN HOTEL: With its turrets and Tudor design, this 489-room hotel looks more like a castle, surrounded by grounds that incorporate three peaceful courtyards, a rose garden, fountain, pond, and small waterfall. The lobby boasts an exotic fish tank and free Internet service in a comfortable, contemporary setting. The hotel also has a restaurant, a lively cocktail lounge, and combination deli and gift shop.

The hotel has 463 rooms and 26 suites. The rooms—all large (490 square feet on average)—have two queen- or one king-size bed, cable TV, in-room movies, voice mail, iron, fridge, hair dryer, and coffeemaker (with coffee). About 156 rooms are designed to capture the hotel's castle theme. Each of the suites has a sitting area with a sofa bed. Most rooms can be connected to accommodate large parties.

The hotel has a full-service restaurant, arcade, outdoor heated pool and whirlpool, fitness center, guest laundry, and conference rooms. It provides room service and frequent free shuttle service to the Disneyland Resort. It has a Disney planning and information desk, too. Airport transportation is available for a fee. Room rates start at $119 during off-season to $275 during peak season. Self-parking costs $14 per day. This hotel is pet-friendly. Check-out time is 1 P.M. (later than many area hotels).

Anaheim Majestic Garden Hotel, 900 S. Disneyland Dr., Anaheim, CA 92802; 714-778-1700; *www.sheraton.com/Anaheim* or *www.majesticgardenhotel.com.*

SHERATON PARK HOTEL AT THE ANAHEIM RESORT: This 14-story tower is easy to spot, and the 486 rooms and six suites have full or small balconies that have a view of the pool or the Disneyland Resort (and a view of the fireworks). Rooms offer either one king or two queen beds, refrigerator, iron, coffeemaker, and hair dryer.

The hotel has a lobby bar, Disney planning desk, a Morton's The Steakhouse restaurant, Park 55 Cafe, and a snack bar. There's also a fitness center, pool, whirlpool, and poolside bar.

Shuttle service is available (provided by Anaheim Resort Transit for a fee) to the Disneyland Resort. Room rates run $149 to $234, depending on occupancy and season; suites start at $850. Rollaways cost $15 extra; cribs are available free of charge.

Sheraton Park Hotel at the Anaheim Resort, 1855 S. Harbor Blvd., Anaheim, CA 92802; call 714-750-1811 or 800-325-3535; or visit *www.sheratonparkanaheim.com.*

Moderate Hotels

ANABELLA HOTEL: Architectural elements of this 7-acre Spanish-style property reflect the rich history of California missions. White-washed adobe walls and curved roof tiles are graced by palm trees and lush plants. Thick arches welcome guests into public areas featuring covered walkways and a fountain. Even the shape of the outdoor whirlpool echoes this theme in its rose window design.

Standard and deluxe rooms sleep up to four; Casita Suites sleep up to four, while Mission and Kids' Suites sleep up to five with an additional sleeper sofa or bunk beds. The Hacienda Suite also sleeps five. All rooms have granite baths, refrigerators, hair dryers, coffeemakers, satellite TV, and free Wi-Fi. Located in a separate building, the Club Anabella Concierge Rooms also come with robes and slippers, complimentary breakfast for two, and noon checkout.

There are two pools, one for grown-ups only. Guests can enjoy all meals indoors at the Tangerine Grill or outdoors on the Tangerine Patio (where drinks are served at the Nectarine Bar). Other amenities include a fitness center, a business center, and a guest laundry.

Rooms range from $99 to $199; suites from $149 to $299; and concierge rooms from $149 to $329. The daily charge for rollaways is $20; for cribs, $10. There is a daily fee for self-parking. Guests can walk to the Disneyland Resort in 10 to 15 minutes, but it is best to use Anaheim Resort Transit.

The Anabella Hotel, 1030 W. Katella Ave., Anaheim, CA 92802; 714-905-1050 or 800-863-4888; *www.anabellahotel.com.*

ANAHEIM CAMELOT INN & SUITES: Directly across the street—and a relatively short walk away—from the Disneyland Resort, this hotel, with its shingled roof, clock tower, turrets, and window boxes, looks like something out of a Bavarian village. Each of the 121 rooms and suites has a 36-inch TV, microwave, refrigerator, coffeemaker, in-room safe, free Wi-Fi, hair dryer, and an iron with board. It also has a fourth-floor terrace pool (with a view of Disneyland's Matterhorn), a whirlpool, a gift shop, rental scooter and stroller shop, and a guest laundry facility (fees apply). There are many family-friendly places to eat within walking distance.

Deluxe standard rooms, most with two queen-size beds, range from $129 to $159 year-round; one-bedroom suites start at about $229 and accommodate up to six people, but they have only one bath. Roll-aways are $20 plus tax; cribs are free. Adjoining rooms are usually available upon request. There is no hotel shuttle service, but it is possible to walk to the Disneyland Resort entrance via Harbor Boulevard. Of course, Anaheim Resort Transit provides transportation to Disneyland Resort (for a fee). There is a daily fee for parking.

Anaheim Camelot Inn & Suites, 1520 S. Harbor Blvd., Anaheim, CA 92802. Call 714-635-7275 or 800-828-4898, or visit *www.camelotinn-anaheim.com.*

FAIRFIELD INN BY MARRIOTT—ANAHEIM RESORT: Fronted by palms and pines, this inviting 467-room hotel is situated across from the Disneyland Resort. All of its rooms are accented with Disney artwork. The rooms are in two towers (one tower is nine stories high; the other, eight). Each room features a king-size bed or two queen beds, child-size sleeper sofa, satellite TV, free high-speed Internet, an iron and board, a hair dryer, refrigerator, and coffeemaker (with coffee).

Other facilities include a heated pool, whirlpool, gift shop, free Wi-Fi in the lobby and other public areas, video arcade, Seattle's Best Coffee, and Pizza Hut Express. The rooms may be occupied by up to five people, and rates start at about $149; cribs are available.

Anaheim Fairfield Inn by Marriott, 1460 S. Harbor Blvd., Anaheim, CA 92802. Call 714-772-6777 or 800-228-2800, or visit *www.fairfieldinnanaheimresort.com.*

COURTYARD MARRIOTT HOTEL & WATER-PARK: This newcomer, next door to Howard Johnson, is the first ever entirely "family-geared" Courtyard. All rooms sleep up to six people and feature bunk beds, two separate showers in the bathroom, and 47-inch TVs with Netflix and Pandora radio. This is a non-suite property, but the rooms start at a roomy 500 square feet. This is the only four-star hotel within true walking distance of the two theme park entrances (about five minutes' walk). Dining options include the Bistro Restaurant & Bar, Starbucks, and a lobby lounge. There is a fitness center, two laundromats, and a gift shop on the premises. Rates for a double room start at about $259.

The 20,000-square-foot Surfside Waterpark has four super slides, and two tot-friendly twin slides; a 400-gallon "drench bucket" that spills water on folks below; a 42-foot lap pool; and a hot tub perched on a sundeck. There is an observation deck for Disney fireworks viewing.

Courtyard Marriott Hotel & Waterpark, 1420 S. Harbor Blvd., Anaheim, CA 92802; call 714-254-1442, or visit the hotel's website at *www.anaheimcourtyard.com.*

BEST WESTERN PLUS STOVALL'S INN: This inn is known for its topiary garden. The property features 288 guestrooms, complimentary continental breakfast, fitness room, business center, and a pair of pools (one is heated), two whirlpools, a wading pool, and a gift shop. Room configurations include two queen, one king, or two double beds, and a bathroom with a separate sink and lots of counter space. Room service is available.

Refrigerators and microwaves are included (no charge). Room rates for up to five guests run $79 to $149. Rollaways are $15; cribs are free.

Best Western Plus Stovall's Inn, 1110 W. Katella Ave., Anaheim, CA 92802. Call 714-778-1880 or 800-854-8177, ext. 3, or visit *www.stovallshotels.com.*

CANDY CANE INN: There's a lot to like about this sweet, two-story hotel—fountain out front, relaxed ambience, wrought-iron touches, and lots of flowers. Located down the street from Disneyland Resort's main entrance (a manageable walk for adults and non-toddlers), the Candy Cane Inn is family-run and well-maintained.

Each of the 171 rooms, most of which face a courtyard, has a refrigerator, safe, dual-line phone with voice mail, coffeemaker, iron, hair dryer, and two queen beds with custom bedding. Add to that a guest laundry, pool, gazebo-covered whirlpool, and fitness center. Free continental buffet breakfast is served daily. Premium rooms also have robes, microwaves, in-room breakfast, turndown service, and 2 P.M. check-out. Sightseeing services are available, as is free shuttle service to and from the Disneyland Resort. Transportation to airports can be arranged. Parking is free.

Rates for a double room with two queen-size beds range from about $109 to $199, depending on the season. Rollaways, available in deluxe and premium rooms, are $10; cribs are free. The inn is located across the street from a shopping area with fast-food eateries.

Candy Cane Inn, 1747 S. Harbor Blvd., Anaheim, CA 92802. Call 714-774-5284 or 800-345-7057, or visit *www.candycaneinn.net.*

HOWARD JOHNSON ANAHEIM HOTEL AND WATER PLAYGROUND: This property's lush landscaping is a major reason to stay here. Flowers and trees proliferate; a central fountain

HOT TIP!

If you stay in the 1300 to 1500 block of Harbor Boulevard, you can cross the street and walk to both theme parks. Of course, once you reach Disneyland Resort property, it's another 5- to 15-minute walk to get to the parks' turnstiles.

anchors the four, two-story units. The hotel is close to Disneyland Resort and local eateries. For a fee, Anaheim Resort Transit offers shuttle service to and from Disneyland.

The 303 non-smoking rooms are divided among several buildings on 7 acres. Most have two queen beds, and all have a fridge, safe, and free high-speed Internet access. The rooms are relatively spacious, though bathrooms are a bit small. Most rooms have a full balcony. Family suites are also available.

There is one heated pool with a hot tub, plus Castaway Cove—a pirate playground featuring slides, water cannons, toddler pool, and fountains. There are two launderettes, a gift shop, and an arcade. Rates range from $149 to $229, depending on the season. There is no charge for parking. Rollaways cost $15 per day; cribs are free.

Howard Johnson Anaheim Hotel and Water Playground, 1380 S. Harbor Blvd., Anaheim, CA 92802; 714-776-6120 or 800-422-4228, or visit *www.hojoanaheim.com.*

TROPICANA INN & SUITES: This hotel is across from the pedestrian crosswalk to the Disneyland Resort (it's about a 10-minute walk). Each of its 196 rooms has a flat-screen TV, safe, coffeemaker (with coffee), fridge, small safe, microwave, hair dryer, iron, free Wi-Fi, and either a king-size bed or two queens. Guests may use a computer in the lobby free of charge. Some rooms have a view of the Disneyland fireworks.

The inn has a cafe/shop combo known as The Cove on Harbor Market and Coffee House. It carries a variety of food, beverages (including beer and wine), apparel, souvenirs, and sundries. There are many eateries in the area (some within walking distance). Anaheim Resort Transit provides shuttle service for a fee. There is a daily fee for self-parking.

The inn has a heated Junior Olympic pool, spa, and guest laundry. Room rates are about $119 to $159. Suites sleep up to 8 and range from $179 to $349. Some suites have kitchens.

Tropicana Inn & Suites, 1540 S. Harbor Blvd., Anaheim, CA 92802; 714-635-4082 or 800-828-4898; *www.tropicanainn-anaheim.com.*

The Rest of the Best

Here's a roundup of the remaining Good Neighbor hotels. They have amenities and rates similar to those described in this chapter. However, some are a bit far from the Disneyland Resort.

Note: The various properties that boast Good Neighbor status are subject to change during the year; visit *www.disneyland.com* for updates.

SUPERIOR HOTELS

★ Hyatt Place at Anaheim Resort Convention Center, 2035 S. Harbor Blvd., Anaheim; 714-750-4000

★ Red Lion Hotel Anaheim, 1850 S. Harbor Blvd., Anaheim; 714-750-2801

★ Wyndham Anaheim Garden Grove, 12021 Harbor Blvd., Garden Grove; 714-867-5555

MODERATE HOTELS

★ Best Western Plus Anaheim Inn, 1630 S. Harbor Blvd., Anaheim; 714-774-1050

★ Best Western Plus Pavilions, 1176 W. Katella Ave., Anaheim; 714-776-0140

★ Best Western Plus Raffles Inn & Suites, 2040 S. Harbor Blvd., Anaheim; 714-750-6100

★ Carousel Inn & Suites, 1530 S. Harbor Blvd., Anaheim; 714-758-0444

★ Clarion Hotel Anaheim Resort, 616 W. Convention Way, Anaheim; 714-750-3131

★ Cortona Inn & Suites, 2029 S. Harbor Blvd., Anaheim; 800-416-6819

★ Courtyard by Marriott Anaheim Resort, 2045 S. Harbor Blvd., Anaheim; 714-740-2645

★ Hampton Inn & Suites Anaheim/Garden Grove, 11747 Harbor Blvd., Garden Grove; 714-703-8800

★ Hilton Garden Inn Anaheim/Garden Grove, 11777 Harbor Blvd., Garden Grove; 714-703-9100

★ Holiday Inn–Anaheim Resort, 1915 S. Manchester Ave., Anaheim; 714-748-7777

★ Holiday Inn Hotel & Suites, 1240 S. Walnut St., Anaheim; 714-535-0300

★ Hotel Ménage Anaheim, 1221 S. Harbor Blvd., Anaheim; 714-758-0900

SUITE HOTELS

★ Anaheim Marriott Suites, 12015 Harbor Blvd., Garden Grove; 714-750-1000

★ Anaheim Portofino Inn & Suites, 1831 S. Harbor Blvd., Anaheim; 714-782-7600

★ Best Western Plus Park Place Inn & Mini Suites, 1544 S. Harbor Blvd., Anaheim; 714-776-4800

★ Desert Palms Hotel & Suites Anaheim Resort, 631 West Katella Ave., Anaheim; 714-535-1133

★ DoubleTree Suites by Hilton, 2085 S. Harbor Blvd., Anaheim; 714-750-3000

★ Embassy Suites Anaheim-North, 3100 E. Frontera St., Anaheim; 714-632-1221

★ Embassy Suites Anaheim-South, 11767 Harbor Blvd., Garden Grove; 714-539-3300

★ Homewood Suites by Hilton, 2010 S. Harbor Blvd., Anaheim; 714-750-2010

★ Homewood Suites by Hilton Anaheim–Main Gate Area, 12005 Harbor Blvd., Garden Grove; 714-740-1800

★ Residence Inn by Marriott Anaheim/Resort Area, 11931 Harbor Blvd., Garden Grove; 714-591-4000

★ SpringHill Suites Anaheim Maingate, 1160 W. Ball Road, Anaheim; 714-215-4000

★ Staybridge Suites, 1855 S. Manchester Ave., Anaheim; 714-748-7700

ECONOMY HOTELS

★ Motel 6 Anaheim Maingate, 100 W. Disney Way, Anaheim; 714-520-9696

★ Quality Inn & Suites Anaheim Resort, 1441 S. Manchester Ave., Anaheim; 714-408-9234

★ Grand Legacy–at the Park, 1650 S. Harbor Blvd., Anaheim; 714-772-0440

Disneyland Park

When you wish upon a star, your dreams come true. That's how the song goes, and it's always possible in Disneyland—Walt Disney's own dream come true. He envisioned "a place of warmth and nostalgia, of illusion and color and delight." The result: a place where imagination is given free reign, grins and giggles are encouraged, and everyone can see the world through a child's eyes.

The undisguised pleasure on the faces of park-goers reveals that they have fallen under the spell of a turreted pink castle; the oompah of a band marching down Main Street, U.S.A.; the clip-clop of a horse-drawn trolley; a close-up encounter with Mickey and Minnie; and a fireworks spectacle more fantastic than an elaborate, pyrotechnic dream.

Those who first entered Disneyland as kindergartners now return with their own kids—and grandkids—to find the park of their memories unchanged in spirit and heart. Shows and attractions have come and gone since the park opened in 1955 and whole new "lands" have been added, while many classics endure. The newest neighborhood-in-progress, Star Wars Land, promises high-flying intergalactic adventures for generations to come. (It's scheduled to open a few years in the future.) Of course, the overall enchantment that guests experience when they walk through the portals of "The Happiest Place on Earth" remains constant. That may well be Disneyland's most enduring accomplishment. Enjoy!

DISNEYLAND PARK

MAIN STREET, U.S.A.
1 Disneyland Railroad Station**
2 Main Street Cinema
3 Main Street Vehicles
4 The Disneyland Story,
  Presenting Great Moments
  with Mr. Lincoln

ADVENTURELAND
5 Enchanted Tiki Room
6 Indiana Jones™ Adventure
7 Jungle Cruise
8 Tarzan's Treehouse

CRITTER COUNTRY
9 Splash Mountain
10 The Many Adventures
   of Winnie the Pooh

MICKEY'S TOONTOWN
11 Chip 'n' Dale Treehouse
12 Disneyland Railroad Station**
13 Donald's Boat
14 Gadget's Go Coaster
15 Goofy's Playhouse
16 Mickey's House
17 Minnie's House
18 Roger Rabbit's Car Toon Spin

-------- Parade Route

FRONTIERLAND
19 Big Thunder
   Mountain Railroad
20 Golden Horseshoe Saloon
21 Mark Twain Riverboat**
22 Rafts to Tom Sawyer Island**
23 Sailing Ship Columbia**

NEW ORLEANS SQUARE
24 Disneyland Railroad Station**
25 Haunted Mansion
26 Pirates of the Caribbean

TOMORROWLAND
27 Astro Orbiter
28 Autopia
29 Disneyland Monorail
30 Disneyland Railroad Station**
31 Star Wars Launch Bay
32 Space Mountain
33 Star Tours—
   The Adventures Continue
34 Buzz Lightyear Astro Blasters
35 Finding Nemo Submarine Voyage

FANTASYLAND
36 Alice in Wonderland
37 Casey Jr. Circus Train
38 Dumbo the Flying Elephant
39 It's a Small World
40 King Arthur Carrousel
41 Mad Tea Party
42 Matterhorn Bobsleds
43 Mr. Toad's Wild Ride
44 Peter Pan's Flight
45 Pinocchio's Daring Journey
46 Sleeping Beauty Castle
47 Snow White's Scary Adventures
48 Storybook Land Canal Boats

**Attraction temporarily closed

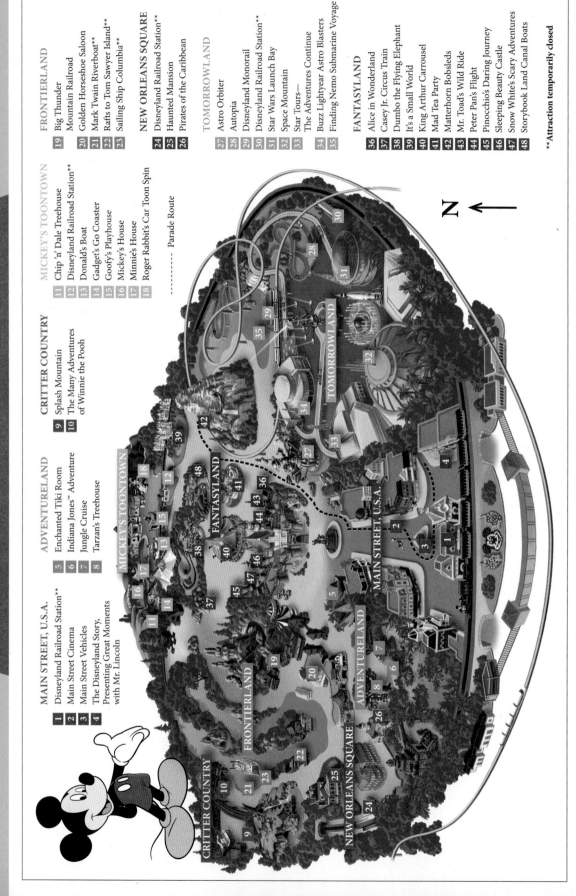

Getting Oriented

Disneyland Park's layout—a basic hub-and-spokes configuration—is simple, but it was quite innovative when the park opened in 1955. The design makes getting around easy, though it's not altogether effortless, since the numerous nooks, crannies, and alleyways can be a bit confusing at first.

The hub of the theme park's wheel is Central Plaza, which fronts Sleeping Beauty Castle. From it extend five spokes leading to eight "lands": Main Street, U.S.A.; Adventureland; Frontierland; New Orleans Square; Critter Country; Fantasyland; Mickey's Toontown; and Tomorrowland.

As you face Sleeping Beauty Castle, the first bridge to your left takes you to Adventureland; the next one, to Frontierland and New Orleans Square. To your right, the first walkway goes to Tomorrowland, and the next one—known as Matterhorn Way—leads directly into Fantasyland and on to Mickey's Toontown. If you cross the Castle's moat and walk through the archway, you'll also end up in Fantasyland. Critter Country occupies its own cul-de-sac extending north from New Orleans Square.

Study the map at left to familiarize yourself with the layout of Disneyland Park. When you arrive, ask for an Entertainment Times Guide, which includes details about the times and locations of the day's entertainment, as well as where and when to meet Disney characters.

PARKING

Guests are directed to park in Disney's Mickey and Friends parking structure or the Toy Story lot on Harbor Boulevard. If one parking area is full, a cast member will direct you to one that isn't. Courtesy tram service transports guests from the parking deck only.

Parking areas open an hour before the park does, but getting a space can take a half hour if there's a long line of park-goers, all with the same idea of getting a head start on the day. Guests using wheelchairs will be directed to a special parking area and have access to ramps in the tram-loading area.

Parking Fees: Guests arriving in regular passenger vehicles pay about $18 to park for the day. (The fee for oversize vehicles is $23, and the cost for buses and trucks with extended trailers is $28.) You may leave the lot and return later the same day at no additional charge. (Hold on to your parking stub as proof of payment.) Prices are subject to change.

Lost Cars: Even if you take careful note of where you parked, you might have trouble remembering the exact spot when you return later. Hundreds more vehicles will likely be parked around yours. If this happens, contact a cast member and tell him or her approximately when you arrived. With that information, parking lot personnel can usually figure out the car's general location pretty quickly, and someone will then comb the lanes and search for it with a scooter.

GETTING AROUND

Horse-drawn streetcars, horseless carriages, and a motorized fire engine make one-way trips up and down Main Street, U.S.A. (Disneyland Railroad's five narrow-gauge trains, which have traditionally made continuous 20-minute loops around the perimeter of the park, are temporarily out of commission to accommodate the construction of Star Wars Land.)

To travel outside Disneyland Park, consider the sleek monorail, which glides between Tomorrowland and Downtown Disney. From Downtown Disney, you can walk to any of the three on-property hotels—the Disneyland Hotel, Disney's Paradise Pier Hotel, and Disney's Grand Californian Hotel & Spa.

The Grand Californian is a short walk to the Disneyland entrance and has its own entrance to Disney California Adventure. This special gate is reserved exclusively for Disneyland Resort Hotel guests. (You'll have to flash a valid room key to use it.) Note that the theme parks require separate admission, unless you have a Park Hopper ticket; see page 55 for ticket pricing. If you plan to leave Disney property, there is an Alamo rental car location at Downtown Disney.

Park Primer

BABY FACILITIES

The Baby Care Center, on Main Street, U.S.A., by First Aid, provides changing tables, high chairs, toddlers' toilets, and a nursing area. Baby bottles can be warmed here, and baby powder, diapers, formula, and food are sold. There are no napping facilities or babysitting services.

FIRST AID

First Aid is located at the north end of Main Street, next door to the Main Street Photo Supply Co. A registered nurse is on duty during park operating hours. In case of medical emergency, notify a cast member and call 911.

GUIDED TOURS

Several tours originate from the Guided Tour Gardens, just left of City Hall. They are *Welcome to the Disneyland Resort*, *Walk in Walt's Disneyland Footsteps*, *Cultivating the Magic,* and *Discover the Magic*. There are also seasonal tours: *Disney's Happiest Haunts* for the Halloween season, and *Holiday Time at the Disneyland Resort*. Park admission is required for all tours. For details, turn to page 21.

HOURS

Disneyland is usually open daily. Monday–Thursday hours are generally from about 10 A.M. to 8 P.M., Friday and Sunday from about 9 A.M. to 10 P.M., Saturday from 8 A.M. to 11 P.M., with extended hours during the summer months

PHOTO BY JILL SAFRO

and holiday periods. For specific hours, visit *www.disneyland.com*, or call 714-781-4565.

During the busy spring break, summer, and Christmas holiday seasons, it's especially wise to arrive first thing in the morning so that you can visit the popular attractions before the lines get long. If you arrive at Disneyland too late, the parking structure and surrounding lots could be more crowded than usual; this is almost always the case in the summer months and during the last week of December.

INFORMATION

Cast members at City Hall and at Central Plaza can answer questions (or help plot your day so that you can make the most efficient use of your time and see what attractions truly interest you). Specifics on services and safety considerations have been compiled in Disneyland's guidemap; ask for it when you enter the park. There are also several services available for guests with disabilities.

Information Board: A valuable planning resource, the Main Street Information Board (aka Tip Board) is near the Jolly Holiday Bakery Cafe, it lets you know how long the waits are for most of the popular attractions, what (if anything) is not operating that day, and where and when park entertainment will take place. The board is updated every hour. Cast members can answer questions and provide information about the restaurants and hotels in the Disneyland Resort. They can help guests locate favorite Disney characters, too.

LOCKERS

Storage lockers are outside the main entrance (on the left) and on Center Street (about halfway up Main Street, on the right). Fees range from $7 to $15 per day, depending on size. Items may be stored during park hours only. There are charging lockers, too. They run about $2 per hour. (You'll need to supply the charger.)

LOST & FOUND

The theme park's Lost & Found department is on the left side of the Disneyland Park entrance. If you find a lost item, you may be asked to fill out a card with your name and address; if the object isn't claimed by its owner, you may have the option of claiming it.

MONEY MATTERS

Cash and traveler's checks are accepted at all food and merchandise locations throughout Disneyland Resort. American Express, Visa, MasterCard, JCB Card, and Discover Card are accepted at all shops, cafeterias, fast-food eateries, snack bars, and full-service establishments (cash only at some park vending carts).

Main Street's City Hall can assist with foreign currency exchange, as well as traveler's check cashing. Disneyland Resort hotel guests may charge almost any purchase made in the theme park back to their hotel bill if they gave a credit card number at check-in.

Guests may purchase Disney gift cards from many Disneyland Resort shops, Disney Stores, and from *disneygiftcard.com*. Gift cards are accepted at the Disney hotels, Downtown Disney, California Adventure, and throughout Disneyland (as are Disney Dollars). They are also valid at Walt Disney World in Florida and at U.S. Disney Store locations. Note that Disney Dollars are no longer sold.

There are several ATMs here. The first, encountered when entering the park, is near the Main Street's Disneyana shop. (Though one might expect the Bank to be, well, a bank, it is not. No financial services are offered there.)

PACKAGE CHECK

There's no need to lug bags around. You can store bulky purchases at the Newsstand at the entrance to Disneyland (on the right as you exit the park). Stashing them in a Main Street locker is also an option (for a fee).

SAME-DAY RE-ENTRY

Guests with one-day tickets who wish to leave the park and return later the same day may do so by getting their hand stamped upon exiting. The stamp will survive several hand washings. Keep in mind that both the park ticket and the hand stamp are needed for re-entry. (Guests with multi-day tickets or annual passes will have their photo taken and do not need a hand stamp for re-entry.)

SMOKING POLICY

At Disneyland Park, smoking (including e-cigarettes) is only permitted in designated smoking areas; refer to a park guidemap for specific locations. It is prohibited inside all attractions, waiting areas, shops, and indoor and outdoor dining areas. The legal smoking age in the state of California is 18.

STROLLERS & WHEELCHAIRS

Strollers ($15) and wheelchairs ($12 with a $20 refundable deposit and a credit card) may be rented outside the main entrance of Disneyland Park (on the right). Electric Conveyance Vehicles (ECVs) cost $50 for the day, with a $20 deposit and major credit card. Wheelchair and ECV supplies are limited. Lost strollers may be replaced at the park's main entrance and at The Star Trader shop in Tomorrowland.

SECURITY CHECK

All guests entering Disney theme parks are subject to a security check. Backpacks, purses, etc., are searched by security personnel before guests are permitted to enter. Guests are asked to pass through a metal detector as well.

Expect car trunks to be searched when entering Disney parking facilities.

Guests checking into Disneyland Resort hotels are asked to present a valid government-issued photo ID.

Ticket Prices

Although prices† will likely increase, the following should give you an idea of what you'll pay for tickets in 2017. For updates, call 714-781-4565, or visit *www.disneyland.com*.

	ADULTS	CHILDREN*
1-Day Ticket		
(1 park)	$95/105/119	$89/99/113
1-Day Ticket (hopper)	$155/160/169	$149/154/163
2-Day Ticket (hopper)	$235	$223
3-Day Ticket (hopper)**	$295	$283
4-Day Ticket (hopper)**	$320	$305
5-Day Ticket (hopper)**	$335	$320
2-Park Deluxe Annual Passport		$599
2-Park Signature Annual Passport		$849
2-Park Signature Plus Annual Passport		$1,049
Premier Annual Passport		$1,439

† One-day prices are quoted in Value/Regular/Peak order. For dates visit www.disneyland.com.

*3 through 9 years of age; children under 3 free

**Includes "Magic Morning" early park admission with select attractions on Tuesday, Thursday, or Saturday.

Note that there is a single price (for adults and children) for annual passports.

Main Street, U.S.A.

This pretty thoroughfare represents Main Street America in the early 1900s, complete with the gentle clip-clop of horses' hooves on pavement, melodic ringing of streetcar bells, and strains of nostalgic tunes such as "Bicycle Built for Two" and "Coney Island Baby."

The sounds of brass bands, a barbershop quartet, and ragtime piano fill the street. An old-fashioned steam train huffs into a handsome brick depot. Rows of picturesque buildings line the street. Authentic gaslights, which once lit up Baltimore and St. Louis, flicker at sundown in ornate lampposts lining the walkways, and the storefronts—painted in a palette of pastels—could not be more inviting. Walt Disney was a master of detail:

throughout Main Street, even the doorknobs are historically correct.

To make the buildings appear taller, a set designer's technique called forced perspective was employed. The first floor is seven-eighths scale (this allows guests to enter comfortably); the second story is five-eighths scale; and the third, only half size. The dimensions of the whole are small enough for the place to seem intimate and comforting, yet the proportions appear correct. (Forced perspective was also used to make the Matterhorn and Sleeping Beauty Castle seem taller than they are.)

The shops that line Main Street, U.S.A., draw guests back repeatedly during their Disneyland visit (see the Shopping section of this chapter and you'll understand why).

The following attractions are listed in the order in which you'll encounter them while walking from the main entrance up Main Street to the Central Plaza, toward Sleeping Beauty Castle.

CITY HALL: Before strolling up Main Street, stop briefly at the Information Center at City Hall, on the west side of Town Square, to find entertainment schedules, make dining reservations, or get advice to help you plan your Disneyland day. City Hall is also a great meeting place if members of your party separate and plan to regroup later in the day.

Birnbaum's Best

Stamps like this one indicate the attractions that we find superlative in one (and usually more) of the following ways: state-of-the-art technology, theming, beauty, novelty, thrills and spills (make that splashes), and overall whimsy. Each "Birnbaum's Best" promises to deliver a dynamite Disneyland experience!

FIRE STATION: Next door to City Hall, this was Walt Disney's home away from home during the construction of Disneyland. His apartment, on the top floor, is decorated just as he left it, but it's not open to the public. A light burns in the window in his memory. Kids love—and are welcome—to climb on the fire wagon parked inside the firehouse. It's a realistic copy of a truck from the early 1900s and provides a great photo opportunity.

DISNEYANA: This treasure-chest of a shop has wares representing creative efforts from throughout the Walt Disney Company, often including never-before-seen art, displayed in an ever-changing exhibit area. Disney artists and imagineers make appearances here, too.

DISNEYLAND RAILROAD: Walt Disney loved trains so much he actually built a one-eighth-scale model of one, the Lilly Belle, in the backyard of his home. So it was only natural that his first theme park include a railroad—five narrow-gauge steam trains have circled Disneyland Park since 1955. Two of the locomotives were built at the Walt Disney Studios, while three had other lives before coming to Disneyland.

While the trains are not operating this year due to the ongoing construction of Star Wars Land, guests may visit the train stations on Main Street and in New Orleans Square. Note that Star Wars Land will likely take several years to complete. When the Force finally awakens in Disneyland Park, the classic Disneyland Railroad trains will resume their 20-minute grand circle tours of the park. For updates, visit *www.disneyland.com*.

THE DISNEYLAND STORY, PRESENTING GREAT MOMENTS WITH MR. LINCOLN: The Disneyland Opera House makes the perfect backdrop for a tribute to the "Happiest Place on Earth," and the man who created it, one Walter Elias Disney. A unique collection of art, models, and mementos—as well as a film—marks more than 60 years of Disneyland magic. After taking a walk down Disney memory lane, guests may pay a visit to the 16th President of the United States. Yes, Abraham Lincoln is back! (In realistic, Audio-Animatronics form.) After a brief presentation about the Civil War, "Mr. Lincoln" stands and delivers a stirring discourse about liberty, the American spirit, and the challenges facing the nation. It's exceptionally *au courant* for an 18th-century allocution.

MAIN STREET VEHICLES: Main Street's motorized fire wagon, horseless carriages, and horse-drawn streetcars lend the thoroughfare a real touch of nostalgia, while at the same time giving guests a lift from one end of the street to the other. The fire truck is modeled after those that might have been discovered on an American Main Street in the early 1900s, except that it has seats where the hose was meant to be carried.

The horse-drawn streetcars, inspired by those in 19th-century photographs, carry up to 30 passengers each. Most of the horses that pull the cars are Belgians (characterized by white manes and tails and lightly feathered legs) and Percheron draft horses.

DISNEYLAND PARK

Save Time in Line!

For those of us who'd prefer not to waste time standing in line for theme park shows and attractions, Disneyland's Fastpass is nothing short of a miracle. Basically, the free system lets guests forgo the task of waiting in an actual line for a number of theme park shows and attractions.

How? Simply by walking up to the Fastpass booth (located near the entrance of participating attractions) and slipping their park ticket into the Fastpass machine.

In return, guests get a slip of paper with a time printed on it (in addition to the safe return of their park ticket). That time—for example, 4:05 P.M. to 5:05 P.M.—represents the "window" in which guests are invited to return to the attraction and practically walk right on—without standing in a long line! Note that latecomers will not be accommodated.

Once you use your Fastpass to enter an attraction (or the time on it has passed), you can get a new Fastpass time for another attraction. It's also possible to get a Fastpass for a second attraction two hours after the first one is issued.

For example, if one pass was issued at 2 P.M., you can get a Fastpass for another attraction at 4 P.M. Sound confusing? It won't be once you've tried it.

Disney's Fastpass service is free and available to everyone bearing a valid theme park ticket. It should be available during peak times of the day and all peak seasons. We've placed the Fastpass logo (FP) beside the listings for all of the attractions that were participating at press time. However, since more attractions are scheduled for inclusion, check a park map for an up-to-the-minute listing of Fastpass attractions.

Note that Fastpass service may be offered on a seasonal basis, and some attractions may stop offering Fastpass in 2017. For updates, call 714-781-4565 or visit *www.disneyland.com*. If Fastpass is offered during your visit, by all means, use it!

MAIN STREET CINEMA: This small, standing-room-only theater features classic, early Mickey Mouse cartoons.

PENNY ARCADE: This place is more of a candy shop than an arcade, but the air of nostalgia remains. Those who have frequented it in the past will be happy to find Esmeralda front and center, ready as always to tell your fortune. The arcade still has Mutascopes, machines that feature hand-cranked moving pictures and require a penny to operate.

PHOTO BY JILL SAFRO

Save some change for the arcade's penny presses. You insert a penny (plus a few other coins to pay for the service), and the penny will be flattened and imprinted with the image of Sleeping Beauty Castle or the face of one of the Disney characters.

CENTRAL PLAZA: Main Street, U.S.A., ends at Central Plaza, the hub of the park, and four of the park's lands are directly accessible from here. At its center stands the Walt and Mickey Partners statue. It's one of the park's most popular picture spots.

One of Disneyland's two Information Centers is located here, near the entrance to Adventureland. Besides the information desk, there is a handy Information Board, updated hourly, that posts wait times for many attractions, which attractions offer Fastpass, what (if anything) is not operating that day, and where and when park entertainment will take place. They offer park guidemaps, too.

Adventureland

For someone who grew up in Marceline, Missouri, around the turn of the 20th century, as Walt Disney did, the far-flung regions of the world must have seemed most exotic and exciting. So it's not surprising that when he was planning his new park, he designated one area, called Adventureland, to represent all the (then) remote and mysterious corners of the world.

The original South Seas–island ambience all but disappeared with the opening of the Indiana Jones Adventure in 1995, and Adventureland became a 1930s jungle outpost. Today, the entrance to the Jungle Cruise is a walk-through headquarters, with old photographs and radios playing big band music interrupted by news flashes about Professor Jones's latest exploits and discoveries. Shops here sell wares that are meant to appeal to modern-day adventurers.

WALT DISNEY'S ENCHANTED TIKI ROOM: Introduced in 1963, this was the first of the park's Audio-Animatronics attractions and the precursor of more elaborate variations, such as "Great Moments with Mr. Lincoln" and the above-mentioned Dr. Jones. Housed in a vaguely Polynesian complex situated at the entrance to Adventureland, the 15-minute show has been given a spiffy face-lift.

The stars are four feathered emcees (José, Michael, Pierre, and Fritz), backed up by a sextet of pastel-plumed, long-eyelashed parrots, and an eclectic chorus of orchids, carved wooden tiki poles, tiki drummers, singing masks, bird-of-paradise flowers, macaws, Amazon parrots, toucans, fork-tailed birds, cockatoos, and several other species.

The 225 performers all sing and drum up a tropical storm with so much animation that it's hard to resist a smile. Their repertoire includes "In the Tiki, Tiki, Tiki Room," "Let's All Sing," and "Aloha to You."

JUNGLE CRUISE: The spiel delivered by the skipper on this seven-minute river adventure has its share of corny jokes, but your navigator

may turn out to be a natural comic with a funny delivery. Just remember that the cornball humor is part of the fun.

As jungle cruises go, this one is as much like the real thing as Main Street, U.S.A., is like life in a real small town—long on loveliness and short on the visual distractions and minor annoyances that constitute the bulk of human experience. There are no mosquitoes and no Montezuma's revenge. And the Bengal tiger and king cobras at the ancient Cambodian ruins, and the great apes, gorillas, crocodiles, alligators, elephants, hippos, and lions in the water and along the shores represent no threat to passersby—though according to maintenance crews, they are almost as much trouble as real ones. Of course, there's no telling how guests will take the attraction's newest residents: a pack of peeved piranhas. Or vice versa. Good luck with that!

Movie buffs should note that Bob Mattey, who helped develop these jungle creatures, also worked on the giant squid for the Disney film *20,000 Leagues Under the Sea*, the man-eating plants in many Tarzan movies, and the menacing mechanical shark in *Jaws*.

The large-leafed upright tree in the Cambodian ruins section of the attraction is a Sacred Fig (*Ficus religiosa*), the same species of tree under which Buddha received enlightenment in India many centuries ago.

TARZAN'S TREEHOUSE: The 70-foot-high *Disneyodendron semperflorens grandis*, or "large, ever-blooming Disney tree," which cradled the Swiss Family Treehouse from 1962 to mid-1999, now embraces another lofty dwelling: Tarzan's Treehouse, inspired by the book by Edgar Rice Burroughs and Disney's 1999 animated feature *Tarzan*. Overlooking the Jungle Cruise and the Temple of the Forbidden Eye (the setting for the Indiana Jones attraction), this moss-and-vine-covered "high-rise apartment" shelters Tarzan, his adoptive mom, Kala (the ape), and Jane.

An interactive play area at the base of the tree has been designed around the scientific equipment that Jane and her father brought to the jungle. (Guests are welcome to experiment with some of it.) Nearby, a makeshift wooden staircase crafted from shipwreck salvage and a weathered suspension bridge provide easy access to the treehouse itself.

Jane's drawings, displayed throughout the compound, reveal the story of Tarzan's survival and coming-of-age in the wild. (But could there be trouble in paradise? That lout of a leopard, Sabor, is lurking in the tree!) By the time guests plant their feet on terra firma once more, they will have hit new heights—not unlike a certain high-flying hero himself—and gotten acquainted with some of the characters (both human and animal) who have shared in his notorious exploits.

Note: Tarzan's Treehouse requires guests to climb quite a few stairs. Just a heads-up.

BIRNBAUM'S BEST ★ INDIANA JONES™ ADVENTURE: FP

Hidden deep within the dense jungles of India, the Temple of the Forbidden Eye was built long ago to honor the powerful deity Mara. According to legend, Mara could "look into your very soul" and grant the "pure of heart" one of three gifts: unlimited wealth, eternal youth, or future knowledge. But legend also issues a rather stern warning: "A terrible fate awaits those who gaze upon the eyes of Mara!" Dr. Jones would only comment, "Records indicate that many have come, but few have returned."

Now *you* can take an expedition through the ancient temple ruins in this attraction based on the George Lucas/Steven Spielberg films. The experience, including the pre-show and queue area, can take more than an hour (without a Fastpass), though the ride itself lasts about 3½ minutes. You follow the jungle path through Dr. Jones's cluttered encampment, then enter the temple via the path marked by his original team. In the queue area, a newsreel tells of Jones's latest expedition. What it doesn't reveal is that he has entered the temple and disappeared.

Following in his footsteps, you will see warning signs that indicate there still may be booby traps that have not yet been disarmed. (The fun is in paying no heed to the warnings and letting the spikes fall where they may.) Inside the temple, guests board 12-passenger vehicles reminiscent of 1930s troop transports. One person takes the wheel and serves as the expedition driver, but not until all are securely fastened in their seats for the twists and turns ahead. Hold on to your hat!

The search for Indiana Jones is on, and an encounter with the fearsome Mara is unavoidable. The trip reveals a world of mummies, glowing fires, falling lava, worrisome snakes, and poisonous darts.

Surprises lurk around every bend, and escape is only temporary (just as in the movies), as you suffer an avalanche of creepy crawlies, traverse a quaking suspension bridge, and, best of all, find yourself face-to-face with a gigantic rolling ball that threatens to flatten everyone in its path. At the end of the ride, Indy himself is waiting for you, with a flippant parting remark, such as "That wasn't so bad," or "Next time you're on your own."

Thanks to the creative wizardry of Disney Imagineers, no two rides are exactly the same, so each time you enter the Temple of the Forbidden Eye, the overall experience may be slightly different.

Note: Pregnant women and guests who suffer from heart conditions, motion sickness, weak backs, and other limitations should not ride this attraction. Kids must be at least 3 years old and at least 46 inches tall to board; those under 7 must be accompanied by an adult. Spooked by snakes? There are more than a few in here. They're not real, but still rather creepy. Just a warning.

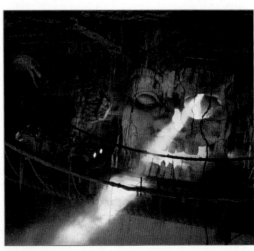

New Orleans Square

Though New Orleans Square did not figure in the Disneyland layout until 1966, it's certainly among the park's most evocative areas. This would be true even if it were home to just the superb Haunted Mansion and Pirates of the Caribbean. But there's also its picturesque site on the shores of the Rivers of America, and its architecture, a pastiche of wrought iron, pastel stucco, French doors, and beckoning verandas.

Not to be missed are the pleasant open-air dining spots; the romantic Blue Bayou restaurant overlooking the moonlit lagoon stretch of Pirates of the Caribbean; the unique assortment of shops; and the music—lively jazz and Dixieland, performed in traditional New Orleans style.

As you relax on a warm evening, snacking on beignets and New Orleans mint juleps, images of Disneyland-as-amusement-park may evaporate. Just as Main Street, U.S.A., makes

the theme park a great place to shop, New Orleans Square makes it a fine spot to spend a few relaxing hours. Those click-click sounds emanating from the railroad station are the Morse code version of the actual dedication speech Walt Disney gave on the opening day of Disneyland back in 1955.

The attractions that are described on the following pages are listed in the order in which you would encounter them while strolling from east to west in Disneyland's festive New Orleans Square.

BIRNBAUM'S ★BEST★ PIRATES OF THE CARIBBEAN: The most swashbuckling adventure you'll find at Disneyland, this 16-minute boat ride transports guests through a series of sets portraying a rowdy pirate raid on a Caribbean village. Bursting with cannon fire, stolen loot, a gluttonous feast, and a raucous band of unruly mercenaries, Pirates of the Caribbean has entertained more people than any theme park attraction in history. It was the last attraction built under Walt Disney's direct creative supervision.

The experience begins with a short excursion through a bayou, where will-o'-the-wisps glow just above the grasses. Fireflies twinkle nearby, while stars spangle the twilight-blue sky overhead. The attention to detail nearly boggles the mind. The Audio-Animatronics cast includes plastered pigs whose legs actually twitch in their soporific contentment, singing

marauders, and wily wenches. The observant will note a couple of new rapscallion residents. Yep, that beloved scallywag Captain Jack Sparrow has dropped anchor here, as has his nefarious nemesis, Captain Barbossa.

While it's by no means the most politically correct attraction (far from it, actually), the theme song, "Yo-Ho, Yo-Ho (A Pirate's Life for Me)," manages to transform what is actually a picture of some blatant buccaneering into a rousing time for all. A must—again and again.

BIRNBAUM'S ★BEST★ HAUNTED MANSION: FP

In a British radio interview, Walt Disney once explained how sorry he felt for those homeless ghosts whose hauntable mansions had fallen to the wrecker's ball. Feeling that these lost souls sorely needed a place of their own, he offered this Haunted Mansion, unquestionably one of Disneyland's top attractions. From its stately portico to the exit corridor, the special effects are piled on to create an eerie, but never terrifying, mood. Just frightfully funny.

Judicious applications of paint and expert lighting effects heighten the shadows that play ghoulishly on the walls outside. The jumble of trunks, chairs, dress forms, and other assorted knickknacks in the attic are left appropriately dirty, and extra cobwebs, which come in convenient liquid form, are strung with abandon. The eerie music and the slightly spooky tones of the Ghost Host often set small children to whimpering, and soon their Mickey Mouse ears have been pulled tightly over their eyes. Still, the spirits that inhabit this house

on the hill—999 in all—are a tame lot for the most part, though they are always looking for occupant number 1,000. Any volunteers?

What makes the seven-minute attraction so special is the attention to, and abundance of, details—so many that it's next to impossible

HOT TIP!

Haunted Mansion Holiday kicks off in late September and runs through the New Year. It features Jack Skellington from Tim Burton's *The Nightmare Before Christmas*, as well as holiday decor galore. Silly, seasonal sight gags abound.

to take them all in during the first, or even the second or third, time around. In the Portrait Chamber—a roomful of fearsome-looking gargoyles that adjoins the chandeliered and lace-curtain-adorned foyer—it's fun to speculate on whether the ceiling moves up or the room moves down. (It's one way here and the opposite way at the mansion's counterpart at Walt Disney World's Magic Kingdom.)

Once in your Doom Buggy, look for the bats' eyes on the wallpaper, the tomb-sweet-tomb plaque, and the rattling suit of armor in the Corridor of Doors. Can you spot a Hidden Mickey in the haunted dining room? And keep your eyes peeled for the infamous "Hatbox Ghost" in the attic scene. Absent from the manse since 1969, he's made a creepy comeback!

Then there are the dead plants and flowers and broken glass in the Conservatory, where a hand reaches out of a half-open casket; the terrified cemetery watchman and his mangy mutt in the Graveyard; the ghostly teapot that pours spectral tea; the ectoplasmic king and queen on the teeter-totter; the bicycle-riding spirits; the transparent musicians; and the headless knight and his supernatural Brunhilde. Nice stuff all.

The mansion was constructed in 1963, based on studies of houses around Baltimore; the attraction itself opened in 1969. The song "Grim Grinning Ghosts" was composed especially for the Haunted Mansion attraction.

PHOTO BY KEITH GROSHANS

Frontierland

PHOTO BY JILL SAFRO

This is the America experienced by the pioneers as they pushed westward: rough wilderness outposts and dense forests, and rugged mountains delineating the skyline.

The sights in Frontierland are just about as pleasant as they come in Disneyland, and the atmosphere as relaxing. The following Frontierland attractions are described in the order in which visitors encounter them while moving counter-clockwise from the Central Plaza gateway toward Big Thunder Mountain.

Note: Parts of The Rivers of America are temporarily dry while Imagineers build Star Wars Land. Also closed for 2017: *Sailing Ship Columbia*, Tom Sawyer Island, Davy Crockett Explorer Canoes, the Disneyland Railroad, and Fantasmic! The *Mark Twain Riverboat* does not leave its dock, but it may welcome visitors throughout the year.

FRONTIERLAND SHOOTIN' EXPOSITION:

This shooting gallery, set in an 1850s town in the Southwest Territory, is completely electronic. Eighteen rifles are trained on Boothill, a mining town complete with a bank, jail, hotel, and stables. They fire infrared beams that trigger silly results whenever they strike the red, reactive targets. The most challenging target is the moving shovel, which, when struck, causes a skeleton to pop out of a grave.

Note: Disneyland tickets do not include use of the arcade. Pay about 50 cents for 20 shots— then fire away (price subject to change).

BIRNBAUM'S ★BEST **BIG THUNDER MOUNTAIN RAILROAD:** FP Hold on to your hats and glasses, because this here's the wildest ride in the wilderness. Inspired by peaks in Utah's Bryce Canyon and Arizona's Sedona, Big Thunder Mountain is entirely a Disney creation. The name comes from an old Indian legend about a sacred mountain in Wyoming that thundered whenever men tried to excavate its gold. The attraction took five years of planning and two years of construction, and it cost about as much to build as the rest of the original Disneyland attractions put together.

As roller coasters go, this one is relatively tame. It's short on steep climbs and precipitous drops that put hearts in throats and make stomachs protest, but long on tight curves that provoke giggles of glee. Adding to the appeal of this thrill ride is the scenery that the runaway mine train passes along the way: a pitch-black bat cave, giant stalactites and stalagmites, a waterfall, a natural-arch bridge that affords fine views over the Big Thunder landscape, and mine walls ready to cave in.

The queue area sets the scene of the quaint mining town, with two hotels, a newspaper office, dance hall, saloon, and general store. If you listen closely, you may hear a local barmaid flirting with a miner to the tune of "Red River Valley" or "Listen to the Mockingbird."

As you proceed toward the loading area, notice the brownish stone walls on each side of you. They were created from a hundred tons of real gold ore from the former mining town of Rosamond, California, which also yielded the ten-foot-tall stamp mill designated "Big Thunder Mine 1880."

For the best of both worlds, ride twice — once by day, to see the scenery, and again after dark, for the pleasure of hurtling through the cool night.

Note: Pregnant women and guests who have heart conditions, motion sickness, weak backs, and other limitations should not ride. Children must be at least 3 years old and a minimum of 40 inches tall to board. Kids under 7 years old must be accompanied by an adult.

PHOTO BY JILL SAFRO

HOT TIP!

Due to the ongoing construction of the park's Star Wars Land, the following Frontierland attractions are temporarily closed: *The Sailing Ship Columbia*, Tom Sawyer Island, Davy Crockett Explorer Canoes, the Disneyland Railroad, and Fantasmic! *The Mark Twain Riverboat* is not touring the Rivers of America this year, but it is docked in its usual spot. Guests are welcome to explore the ship. Disney characters and musicians may come and go throughout the day. For updates on possible re-opening dates visit *www.disneyland.com*.

Walt Disney kept a private box here, just to the left of the stage, on the upper level.

Performance times vary. Check Disneyland's Entertainment Times Guide for the schedule or pay a visit to City Hall when you arrive at the park.

There is no assigned seating inside; all of the seats are good, though those up front or on the balcony are perhaps the best.

PHOTO BY JILL SAFRO

GOLDEN HORSESHOE SALOON: Tongue-in-cheek humor and Western flair are the key ingredients in the musical and specialty acts featured at this entertainment venue. The hall itself is resplendent with chandeliers, polished floors and banisters, and a long brass railing.

Critter Country

PHOTO BY JILL SAFRO

In 1989, the zone welcomed foxes, frogs, geese, rabbits, crocodiles, and many of the other critters that make up the Audio-Animatronics cast of Splash Mountain. To make the new furry residents feel at home, Disney Imagineers rechristened the area Critter Country. Observant guests will spot scaled-down houses, lairs, and nests tucked into hillsides and along the river.

Lush, shady forests of pines, locusts, white birches, coastal redwoods, and evergreen elms surround Critter Country, one of the most pleasant corners of Disneyland. In 1972, this land debuted as Bear Country, the backwoods home of the since-departed Country Bear Playhouse. From 1956 through 1971, the area was called the Indian Village, complete with teepees and a dance circle, and was considered part of Frontierland.

BIRNBAUM'S
★BEST★

SPLASH MOUNTAIN: FP The fourth peak in Disneyland's mountain range of thrill rides—along with Big Thunder Mountain, the Matterhorn, and Space Mountain—Splash Mountain is unlike the other three attractions, where passengers ride roller-coaster-style cars down tubular steel tracks. In this nine-minute ride, they board hollowed-out logs and drift on a waterborne journey through backwoods swamps and bayous, down waterfalls, and finally (here's where the speed picks up) over the top of a super-steep spillway at the peak of the mountain into a briar-laced pond five stories below.

PHOTO BY KEITH GROSHANS

DISNEYLAND PARK

FP = Fastpass attraction (see page 58)

Splash Mountain is based on the animated sequences in Walt Disney's 1946 film *Song of the South*, and the principal characters from the movie—Brer Rabbit, Brer Fox, and Brer Bear—appear in the attraction courtesy of Audio-Animatronics technology. In fact, Splash Mountain's stars and supporting cast of 103 performers number almost as many as those in Pirates of the Caribbean, which has 119 Audio-Animatronics characters.

Comparisons to Pirates of the Caribbean are particularly apt, as Splash Mountain was consciously designed to be a "How do we top this?" response to the popular, long-running pirate adventure. Splash Mountain broke new ground on several counts. Besides its impressive number of animated characters, it also boasts one of the world's tallest and sharpest flume drops (52½ feet at a 47-degree angle). It's one of the fastest rides ever operated at Disneyland Park.

One other twist makes Splash Mountain unique in the annals of flumedom: After hurtling down Chickapin Hill, the seven-passenger log boats hit the pond below with a giant splash—and then promptly sink underwater (or seem to), with just a trace of bubbles left in their wake.

Splash Mountain's designers didn't only borrow the attraction's characters and color-saturated settings from *Song of the South*, they also included quite a bit of the film's Academy Award–winning music. In fact, the song in the attraction's finale, "Zip-a-Dee-Doo-Dah," has become something of a Disney anthem over the years. The voice of Brer Bear is performed by none other than Nick Stewart, the same actor who spoke the part in the film when it was released in 1946.

Keep in mind: The hotter the day, the longer the lines, so go early or late.

Note: You must be at least 40 inches tall and 3 years old to ride the Splash Mountain attraction. Children under age 8 must be accompanied by an adult.

BIRNBAUM'S ★BEST★ THE MANY ADVENTURES OF WINNIE THE POOH: There's a cuddly critter in town, and he goes by the name of Winnie the Pooh. In this colorful attraction, everyone's favorite honey-lovin' cub treats Disneyland guests to a wild and whimsical 3½-minute tour of his home turf.

The attraction features a most unlikely form of transportation: beehives. They whisk (and bounce) guests through the Hundred Acre Wood, where the weather's most blustery. The wind is really ruffling the feathers of one of the locals. It seems Owl's treehouse has been shaken loose and just may topple to the ground—and onto the beehives below.

Similar sight gags abound, from a bubble-blowing Heffalump (hey, this is Disneyland) to a treacherous flood that threatens to sweep Tigger, Piglet, and the rest of the gang away. When the Pooh bear saves the day, it's time to celebrate—and everyone is invited to the party.

Note that, like many of the Fantasyland attractions, this Critter Country ride has a few scenes that take place in near darkness. Some youngsters may find these moments a bit unsettling. (If they can handle the likes of Mr. Toad's Wild Ride and Pinocchio's Daring Journey, they should be fine in the Hundred Acre Wood.)

Fantasyland

Walt Disney called Fantasyland a timeless land of enchantment. We couldn't agree more. The skyline, dominated by the peak of the Matterhorn, bristles with chimneys and weather vanes, turrets and towers. At the center of it all, as if deposited here by an itinerant carnival, is the regal King Arthur Carrousel.

Note: Parents of young children should be aware that many of Fantasyland's attractions have moments that take place in the dark. These include Peter Pan's Flight, Mr. Toad's Wild Ride, Alice in Wonderland, Snow White's Scary Adventures, Pinocchio's Daring Journey, and Storybook Land Canal Boats.

PHOTO BY JILL SAFRO

SLEEPING BEAUTY CASTLE: Rising above the treetops at the end of Main Street, U.S.A., it could be a figment of your imagination or a mirage created by Tinker Bell's pixie dust. Closer inspection proves this architectural confection is as real as the swans in the moat surrounding it. A composite of medieval European castles, primarily in the French and Bavarian styles, Sleeping Beauty Castle, the gateway to Fantasyland, is constructed of concrete, with towers that rise 77 feet above the moat. Trimmed in 22-karat gold leaf and draped in celebratory jewels, it appears shiny even on gray days. The structure seems larger

than it really is due to the use of forced perspective, down to the bricks.

From the Central Plaza, you're actually looking at the back of the castle; Walt Disney decided it was prettier that way and had the builders turn it around. The drawbridge, lowered when the park first opened in 1955, is like a real one—though it's been raised (and lowered again) only once since then. That historic event took place in 1983, at the rededication ceremony for Fantasyland.

Outside the castle, juniper is planted around the water's edge; it's one of the few green plants that the swans won't eat. One of the two graceful trees to the right of the drawbridge bears hundreds of tiny yellow flowers in spring, and the other is covered with fragile lavender flowers for several weeks in early summer.

CASTLE WALK-THROUGH: This classic Disney experience has "re-awakened" with additional scenes and enhanced special effects. The show, which features a series of dioramas, tells the story of *Sleeping Beauty*—including the magic of fairies Flora, Fauna, and Merryweather and the sinister spells of the evil Maleficent.

Guests enter the walk-through from the right, on the Fantasyland side of the castle. Note that it is rather dark inside (which may spook tots) and there are some stairs to climb. Guests who are unable to do stairs or navigate the narrow passageways of the castle may experience the walk-through "virtually" in a special room on the ground floor.

FANTASY FAIRE: Once upon a time . . . in a storybook village nestled beside Sleeping Beauty Castle, folks of all ages were invited to mix and mingle with Disney characters and enjoy a live (and lively!) stage show. That time is now, and the guest list includes *you*. The Royal Hall and The Royal Theatre are the highlights of Fantasyland's newest neighborhood (located in the spot formerly occupied by Carnation Gardens).

THE ROYAL HALL: Behind the richly detailed facade of this regal residence, you'll find a gorgeous gothic interior fit for a princess. A rotating group of royals is always on hand to greet guests. Expect favorites such as Belle, Cinderella, Snow White, and more.

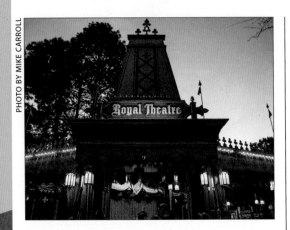
PHOTO BY MIKE CARROLL

THE ROYAL THEATRE: Bring your funny bone to this theatre—the antics on stage are meant to make you chuckle. The show features a madcap and original retelling of a classic and beloved Disney tale. Recently, the story was a little-known tale set in a place called Arendelle. (We kid! It was the ever-popular *Frozen*.) The theatrical yarns are presented by Mr. Smythe and Mr. Jones, Renaissance bards with vastly vaudevillian vigor, and a multitasking supporting cast. Tales change periodically. It's fun for the whole family.

PIXIE HOLLOW: Where do Disney fairies live? In Pixie Hollow! Disneyland guests may enter the world of Tinker Bell and her friends. As guests walk along the garden path, they feel as though they are shrinking down to fairy size as the landscape gets larger and larger. Open daily, this miniature realm is extra sparkly on summer nights, when it glows with the "magic" of pixie dust. You'll find Pixie Hollow between the Castle and the entrance to Tomorrowland.

SNOW WHITE WISHING WELL & GROTTO: Tucked off Matterhorn Way, at the eastern end of the moat around Sleeping Beauty Castle, this is one of those quiet corners of the park easily overlooked by guests. If you stand by the wishing well, you might hear Adriana Caselotti, the original voice of Snow White, singing the lovely melody "I'm Wishing," written for Walt Disney's Oscar-winning 1937 film.

Any coins tossed into the well go to charity. FYI: This is a very popular spot for guests to "pop the question."

BIRNBAUM'S ★BEST★ PETER PAN'S FLIGHT: "Come on everybody, here we go! Off to Never Land!" This attraction is one of the park's loveliest—and consistently one of the most popular. Based on the story by Sir James M. Barrie about a boy with an immunity to maturity and an affinity for flying—by way of Disney's 1953 animated feature—the ride's effects soar to celestial heights. Pirate ships embark from a newly re-imagined nursery scene and carry travelers through the clouds and into a starry sky.

Water ripples and gleams softly in the moonlight; the lava on the sides of a volcano glows with almost the intensity of the real thing. After an ephemeral few minutes, the ships drift back into reality, an unloading area that is all the more jarring after the magic of the trip through Never Land.

Of the approximately 350 miles of fiber optics found throughout Fantasyland, the majority is used in this ride. The twinkling London scene is an enlarged model of an authentic map of the city.

This attraction is atop the popularity list with guests of all ages and usually has a line consistent with its status. Head here first thing in the morning, or late in the day (after little ones have gone go bed).

BIRNBAUM'S ★BEST★ MR. TOAD'S WILD RIDE: Based on the 1949 Disney film *The Adventures of Ichabod and Mr. Toad*—which was inspired by Kenneth Grahame's classic novel *The Wind in the Willows*—this simple, zany attraction is housed in an English manor bristling with ornate chimneys that really smoke. The wild, low-tech ride is experienced from the perspective of the eccentric but lovable Mr. Toad.

Of course, he is as inept a driver as you'd expect a toad to be. During the excursion, you crash through the fireplace in his library, burst through a wall full of windows, careen through the countryside, charge headlong into a warehouse full of TNT, lurch through the streets of London, then ram into a pub and veer out again. During the 2-minute journey, you'll also be berated by a judge in court, nearly collide head-on with a railroad train, and be banished to a fiery inferno. (The darkness, near-crash, and train blast may be too intense for some youngsters.)

Did You Know?
There is a shadow of Sherlock Holmes (complete with pipe and cap) in the second-story window of the manor that houses Mr. Toad's Wild Ride.

ALICE IN WONDERLAND: This Fantasyland staple has been revamped and revitalized. It features a new Alice figure, animated flowers, and a rolling hedgehog. This is Alice in *Wonderland*, after all!

Traveling in oversize caterpillars, visitors fall down the rabbit hole and embark upon a bizarre adventure in that strange world known as Wonderland. They come face-to-face with Tweedledum and Tweedledee, a garden filled with singing roses, the Cheshire Cat, the Queen of Hearts and her playing-card soldiers, the White Rabbit, and other characters from Lewis Carroll's beloved story *Alice in Wonderland*.

At the end of the nearly four-minute ride, a giant un-birthday cake explodes (thanks to a dynamite "candle"), providing a suitable finish to this sweet interlude. It's understandably popular with the under-age-7 set.

PHOTO BY MIKE CARROLL

MAD TEA PARTY: The sequence in Walt Disney's 1951 release *Alice in Wonderland* in which the Mad Hatter hosts a tea party for his "un-birthday" is the theme for this ride—a group of colorful oversize teacups whirling wildly on a spinning tea table. Festive Japanese lanterns hang overhead. One of the park's original attractions, this ride lasts only 1½ minutes, so if the line is long, come back later.

Note: The teacups may look mild, but it's a good idea to let a reasonable interval pass after eating before you take one for a spin.

BIRNBAUM'S ★BEST★ **MATTERHORN BOBSLEDS:** Though it's 100 times smaller than the actual peak, Disney's version of the Matterhorn is still a credible reproduction. The use of forced perspective makes the snowy summit look much loftier than the approximately 147 feet it does reach. Even the trees and shrubs help create the illusion. Those at the timberline are far smaller than the ones at the bottom.

The ride itself, like the Space Mountain and Big Thunder Mountain Railroad attractions, has to be counted among the most thrilling at Disneyland. At the time the Matterhorn Bobsleds were dedicated, in 1959, they were considered an engineering novelty because their dispatch system allowed more than one car to be in action at once. The ride was also the world's first tubular steel roller coaster. This classic is also considered Disney's first thrill ride. The old favorite has enhanced snowcaps, lighting, and visual effects.

The wild adventure begins with a climb into the frosty innards of the mountain, then makes a speeding, twisting, turning descent through a cloud of fog and past giant icicles and ice crystals. The wind howls as you hurtle toward a brief encounter with the Abominable Snowman (take note of the new effects!). The speed of

Star Wars Land

The Force is strong in these parts—and it's getting stronger every day. Disney Imagineers are hard at work creating a whole new neighborhood in Disneyland Park: Star Wars Land! While this highly anticipated adventure zone is constructed (it broke ground in 2016 and will take several years to complete), Disneyland guests can get their Star Wars fix over in Tomorrowland. For details, turn to page 78.

the downhill flight away from the creature seems greater than it really is because much of the journey takes place inside tunnels. Splash-down is in an alpine lake.

Note: Pregnant women, children under 3, and guests who suffer from weak backs (the seats are hard and the ride is bumpy), heart conditions, motion sickness, or other physical limitations should not take the ride. Guests must be at least 40 inches tall.

PHOTO BY JILL SAFRO

STORYBOOK LAND CANAL BOATS: This 7-minute cruise through Monstro the Whale and past miniature scenes from Disney's animated films is not one of Disneyland's major attractions, yet few who take the trip deny that the journey is one of the park's sweetest. No detail was spared, from the homes of the Three Little Pigs to the Old English village of Alice

in Wonderland (where the White Rabbit boasts his very own mailbox) to the London park that Peter Pan and Tinker Bell flew over with Wendy, John, and Michael Darling on their way to Never Land.

Other storybook locales include the marketplace where Aladdin met Princess Jasmine, the Seven Dwarfs' home and jewel mine, and Cinderella's castle. At the end of the cruise, the boat drifts past Geppetto's village, Prince Eric and Ariel's castle, King Triton's castle—and *Frozen*'s Kingdom of Arendelle.

BIRNBAUM'S ★BEST★ IT'S A SMALL WORLD: The background music for this attraction is cheerful and singsong, sometimes maddeningly so. It does grab your attention, starting with the cheery facade, embellished with stylized representations of the Eiffel Tower, the Leaning Tower of Pisa, Big Ben, the Taj Mahal, and other landmarks. The 30-foot-tall clock with the loud ticktock and the syncopated swing is frosting on the architectural cake. The whirring of gears that marks every quarter hour alone warrants a trip to the attraction's plaza.

Boats carry guests into a land filled with more than 300 Audio-Animatronics dolls representing children (and recently added Disney characters) from 100 regions of the world. It's a pageant for the eyes, even if the ears grow weary. (If you find yourself humming "It's a Small World" for the next several hours, you can blame Richard M. and Robert B. Sherman, the Academy Award–winning composers of the music for *Mary*

PHOTO BY MIKE CARROLL

Poppins, among many other Disney scores.)

Topiary figures in the shapes of a giraffe, elephant, rhinoceros, lion, horse, and other friendly beasts bid guests farewell at ride's end.

Note that It's a Small World is transformed inside and out between Thanksgiving and New Year's to become as close to a winter wonderland as you're likely to find in Southern California. The dolls even sing "Jingle Bells" along with "It's a Small World."

CASEY JR. CIRCUS TRAIN: One of the key sequences in the movie *Dumbo*, in which an engine named Casey Jr. pulls a circus train up a steep hill, became the inspiration for this 3½-minute train ride that circles Storybook Land. The Storybook Land Canal Boats are better for viewing the landscaping and miniature details there, but it's worth a ride inside one of the wild-animal cage cars. Each train has two of them—plus a real caboose. Listen as the engine chugs, "I think I can" and then, "I thought I could" as it negotiates the hill.

DUMBO THE FLYING ELEPHANT: As beloved a symbol of Fantasyland as Sleeping Beauty Castle, this ride reminds all who see it of the baby elephant immortalized in Disney's 1941 feature film. In it, Dumbo discovers that his large ears actually enable him to fly.

PHOTO BY JILL SAFRO

A mechanical marvel, Dumbo the Flying Elephant is full of filigreed metalwork, with cogs, gears, and pulleys. Brass pipes spew water from the base, and music is supplied by a vintage band organ housed in a small, ornate structure nearby. That figure atop the ride is Dumbo's trusty sidekick, Timothy Mouse.

SNOW WHITE'S SCARY ADVENTURES: Ornamental stone ravens perch on carved stone skulls atop a stone tower, and hearts

PHOTO BY KEITH GROSHANS

pierced through with swords lie at the base of the twisted pillars that support this brooding building. The two-minute ride inside includes several fairly jarring scenes. In one, the Queen changes into a scary old hag before your eyes; in another, this wicked witch has the nerve to tempt you with a poisoned apple.

After passing a brief and joyful scene in the Seven Dwarfs' cottage, the cars travel through a creepy dungeon, visit a workshop where the Queen labors over her bubbling cauldron, and then venture into the Frightening Forest, where moss-draped trees point talon-like branches at passersby. The visit to the jewel mines, where the Seven Dwarfs work, is more beautiful than scary because of the emeralds, rubies, and sapphires glowing in the darkness.

It all ends in true storybook fashion: As the evil Queen attempts to roll a stone down the side of a mountain to crush the dwarfs below, she gets struck by lightning (via a strobe effect) and tumbles over the edge of a cliff, leaving Snow White, her Prince, and their seven sidekicks to live happily ever after, as depicted in the mural near the exit. The music is taken from rare recordings used to create the film's original soundtrack.

Note: This attraction can be too intense for many small children. Snow White's adventures really *are* scary!

PINOCCHIO'S DARING JOURNEY: Based on Disney's 1940 animated feature, this is a three-minute morality play of sorts, with Jiminy Cricket serving as host and guide. Pinocchio, who is the creation of the toymaker Geppetto, pays a visit to Pleasure Island and then discovers the right way to live.

As the ride vehicles move from the cheerful land of popcorn and Ferris wheels to the

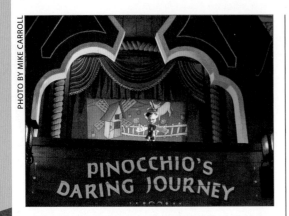

PHOTO BY MIKE CARROLL

seamy world of Tobacco Road, Pleasure Island hues are replaced by drab shades of brown and gray. Here, little boys are turned into donkeys and sold to work in the salt mines.

Pinocchio escapes that fate, nearly becomes supper for Monstro the Whale, and winds up back home in the care of Geppetto—another happily-ever-after ending. The final scene, in which the Blue Fairy turns into a cloud of sparkles and then disappears, leaving a smattering of pixie dust on the floor, is partially accomplished via fiber optics.

Note: This attraction may be a bit frightening to some toddlers (not to mention those of us who may be spooked by the concept of turning into a donkey).

KING ARTHUR CARROUSEL: Guests come upon this graceful park landmark as they stroll toward the Sleeping Beauty Castle passageway into Fantasyland. One of the few attractions in the park that is an original rather than a Disney adaptation, the carrousel contains 68 horses—all movable, as Walt Disney wished. Carved in Germany over a century ago, no two alike, they are as pampered as the live Belgian horses on Main Street. The ornamentation on them is gold, silver, and copper leaf. The nine hand-painted panels on top of the carrousel's main face tell the story of Sleeping Beauty.

PHOTO BY JILL SAFRO

Disneyland Park Fastpass Attractions

Long lines got you down? Not to worry—some of the major Disneyland attractions offer Fastpass. (For an explanation of this time-saving, line-skipping system, turn to page 58.) Here's a list of those "E-ticket" crowd-pleasers. (Note that attractions listed here may change and that Fastpass may not be offered at all times throughout the year. All admission tickets must be activated at the front gate before they can be used to obtain Fastpass tickets inside the park.)

ADVENTURELAND
Indiana Jones Adventure

CRITTER COUNTRY
Splash Mountain

FRONTIERLAND
Big Thunder Mountain Railroad

MICKEY'S TOONTOWN
Roger Rabbit's Car Toon Spin

NEW ORLEANS SQUARE
Haunted Mansion (late September through December only)

TOMORROWLAND
Autopia; Space Mountain;

Star Tours—The Adventures Continue;

Buzz Lightyear Astro Blasters

Mickey's Toontown

PHOTO BY JILL SAFRO

Disneyland lore tells us that when Mickey Mouse burst onto the movie scene in 1928 in *Steamboat Willie*, the first synchronized-sound cartoon, his success was so great that his busy schedule demanded he practically live at the Walt Disney Studios. Thirty cartoons later, in the early 1930s, he was one tired mouse, so he moved into a quiet residence in a "toon only" community south of Hollywood. Over the years, many toon stars gravitated to Mickey's Toontown, as it quickly became known. Minnie Mouse, Pluto, Goofy, Roger Rabbit, Chip, Dale, and Gadget all live here, and Donald Duck docks his boat, the *Miss Daisy*, on Toon Lake.

> ## HOT TIP!
> There are no full-service restaurants in Toontown, just a few fast-food places with window service, and limited outdoor seating. So don't plan on having a big meal here.

One afternoon in the early 1950s, while Mickey and his close friend Walt Disney were relaxing on Mickey's front porch, Walt revealed his idea for a theme park that would appeal to "youngsters of all ages." Mickey suggested that he build it next to the secret entrance to Toontown, and the rest is history. Disneyland opened to the public in 1955, but little did anyone realize when they were drifting through It's a Small World that they were right next door to Mickey's Toontown.

In 1990, Mickey and his friends decided to open up their neighborhood and their homes to non-toons, and, in preparation, all of Toontown received a new coat of ink and paint. The grand opening took place in January 1993, marking the first new "land" to debut at Disneyland since Critter (originally Bear) Country opened in 1972.

Legend aside, the development of Toontown was a real challenge: to create a three-dimensional cartoon environment without a single straight line. Yet, as topsy-turvy as it is, Mickey's Toontown is a complete community, with a downtown area, including a commercial center and an industrial zone, plus a suburban neighborhood. The best part is that everything is meant to be touched, pushed, and jumped on. Kids do just that, while adults relish the attention to detail and the assortment of gags. Much of what's here is interactive, from the mousehole covers to the public mailboxes.

This booming toontropolis is home to ten attractions, two shops, and three fast-food eateries. The attractions are described in the neighborhood sections that follow; the shops, in the Shopping section later in this chapter; and the quick-service eateries, in the *Good Meals, Great Times* chapter of this book.

Guests enter this colorful land by walking under the Toontown train depot. The attractions are listed as they are encountered when strolling counterclockwise.

Downtown Toontown

In Toontown's "business" zone, an animated taxi teeters off the second-floor balcony of the Cab Co. A runaway safe has crashed into the sidewalk, and crates of rib-ticklers, ripsnorters, slapsticks, and wisecracks wait for passersby to lift the lids. At the Fireworks Factory, a plunger sets off quite a response when pressed; it's a good thing the Toontown Fire Department is located right next door.

Lift the receiver of the police phone outside the Power House (home to all sorts of electrifying gizmos—open the door at your own risk), and you might hear a voice over the toon police car radio, announcing, "Someone put mail in the box, and the box doesn't like it. Please respond post haste." Or step on the mouse-hole cover near the post office, and you might hear, "How's the weather up there?" or "Is it time to come out now?"

You never know what to expect once inside Toontown—but it's all bound to be "goofy."

ROGER RABBIT'S CAR TOON SPIN: FP This chaotic, rollicking ride combines the technology of the Mad Tea Party teacups (cars here spin a full 360 degrees) and the tracks of Fantasyland attractions, such as Mr. Toad's Wild Ride. Benny the Cab and Roger Rabbit join the dizzying chase, which takes

guests through the back alleys of the toon underworld made famous in the film *Who Framed Roger Rabbit*. The mission of each car is to save Jessica Rabbit from the evil weasels while avoiding the dreaded Dip.

ROGER'S FOUNTAIN: In this funny fountain, a statue of Roger Rabbit is suspended in midair, afloat on a column of water erupting from a broken fire hydrant that he has seemingly crashed into. He's still holding the steering wheel from the cab he was driving. Surrounding the hydrant, four floating taxicab tires serve as inner tubes for fish spouting arcs of water into the air.

POST OFFICE: Each kooky mailbox actually speaks in the voice of the character whose mail it receives—Mickey Mouse, Minnie Mouse, Roger Rabbit, Jessica Rabbit, Donald Duck, and Goofy. It can be quite a cacophony.

Outside, the letter box pipes in with chucklesome comments like, "Don't just stand there— mail something!"

Toon Square

Located between the downtown area and the residential section of Toontown, this district is home to local businesses and institutions, including the Toontown Skool, the Department of Ink & Paint, and the 3rd Little Piggy Bank. Toontown's three eateries—Clarabelle's Frozen Yogurt, Pluto's Dog House, and Daisy's Diner—stand side by side on the square.

TOWN HALL: Toon residents emerge from this municipal building and proceed to the bandstand out front to greet guests, entertain with their antics, and provide more relaxing photo opportunities than are often available elsewhere in Disneyland.

When a character is about to arrive, the "Clockenspiel" above City Hall may spring to life: Mallets ring bells, toon hands pull whistles, and figures of Roger Rabbit and Mickey Mouse pop out of cannons, blowing horns that, in turn, produce bouquets of flowers.

GOOFY'S GAS: From the looks of it, any traveler would think twice about refueling at this station. On the other hand, it does house Toontown's public restrooms and telephones, and that's an important location to know (though we don't recommend making any important business calls here).

PHOTO BY JILL SAFRO

Pedestrians can refuel here, too. A fruit stand, called Toontown Fruit Market (open seasonally), offers fruit and other snacks. It's also a convenient locale to purchase souvenirs. The funny water fountain beside the station dispenses refreshing H_2O.

Mickey's Neighborhood

The homes in this district sit at the base of the 40-foot-tall Toon Hills, which have their own version of the famous Hollywood sign. The attractions are described as a guest would pass them while walking counter–clockwise from Mickey's Fountain.

MICKEY'S FOUNTAIN: A statue of the world's most famous mouse stands at the center of a pool surrounded by toon-style musical instruments, creating a whimsical centerpiece for the Toontown residential area.

MINNIE'S HOUSE: It's hard to miss Minnie's House. This lavender-and-pink creation has a sweetheart theme for the sweetheart inside. Here guests can peek at Minnie's living room with its chintz sofa and sophisticated magazines (*Cosmousepolitan* and *Mademouselle*) on the coffee table.

There are messages from Goofy and Mickey on the answering machine in the hallway. Guests are invited to create new fashions for Minnie on the computer in her dressing room.

In Minnie's kitchen, a cake in the oven rises when a knob is turned, pots and pans clank out a melody when the stove is switched on, and the dishwasher churns when a button is pushed. The Cheesemore refrigerator is stocked with an assortment of dairy products, including Golly Cheeze Whiz, and the shopping list left on the outside of the fridge hints at this mouse's cheeses of choice. Be sure to check out the cookies on her kitchen table (and be prepared for a little trick, courtesy of Ms. Mouse).

As you leave Minnie's House, you'll pass the wishing well in her yard. Don't think you're hearing things: It's been known to share a few parting thoughts.

MICKEY'S HOUSE: A short path leads from Minnie's backyard to the front door of Mickey's House. The welcoming yellow dwelling with a tile roof, huge green door, and green shutters is home to the toon who started it all. Not only is Mickey's face on the mailbox out front, but his welcome mat is in the instantly recognizable shape of three circles — his head and ears.

> ## HOT TIP!
> Toontown closes one hour before the pyrotechnics on nights when the park is presenting a fireworks show.

In the living room stands a player piano and a curio cabinet filled with all manner of memorabilia, including Mickey's baby shoes and a picture of him with his friend Walt Disney, as well as some of Pluto's treasures — a huge bone and a half-eaten shoe. In the laundry room, the washing machine chugs merrily away, and laundry supplies, such as Comics Cleanser and Mouse 'n' Glo, are at the ready.

From here, make your way through the greenhouse and into Mickey's backyard, where you'll see Pluto's doghouse and a garden with mysteriously disappearing carrots. If you want to meet the Mouse, be sure to visit the movie barn out back.

MICKEY'S MOVIE BARN: Ever industrious, Mickey has transformed the old barn in back of his house into a workplace, and guests are welcome to visit him here. The first stop is the Prop Department, where costumes and props from some of his famous cartoons are stored.

In the Screening Room, a bumbling Goofy projects movie clips from a few "remakes" currently in prog-ress, among them *Steamboat Willie* and *The Sorcerer's Apprentice*. Mickey is hard at work on a soundstage, but happy to take a break. Guests enter in small groups for a photo and autograph session with the "famouse" star.

Note: You can't get to Mickey's Movie Barn without going through his house. This attraction is a must for die-hard fans of the Mouse.

CHIP 'N' DALE TREEHOUSE: Just past Mickey's House stands the home of that jolly chipmunk duo, Chip and Dale. Styled to look like a redwood tree, this high-rise accommodates guests of all ages—but it's best enjoyed by small children. A spiral staircase leads to the lofty perch, whose windows provide a fine view of Toontown.

GADGET'S GO COASTER: Gadget is the brilliant inventor from the TV cartoon *Chip 'n' Dale's Rescue Rangers*. So it's only fitting that some of her handiwork is within view of their treehouse. Gadget, the ultimate recycler, has created this coaster from an assortment of gizmos that once served other purposes.

Giant toy blocks are now support beams for the tracks; hollowed-out acorns have become the cars of the train; and bridges have been created from giant combs, pencils, paper clips, and such. The thick steel tracks give the impression of a tame ride, but there are a few thrills, right up to the final turn into the station. This experience is exciting but brief (one minute), so if the line is long, save it for later.

Note: Kids must be at least 3 years old and 35 inches tall to ride Gadget's Go Coaster. Those under age 7 must be accompanied by an adult. Pregnant women should skip the trip. It may be a small coaster, but the 51-second ride is wilder than one might expect.

DONALD'S BOAT: Donald Duck's houseboat, named for his fair-feathered friend (Daisy), is docked in Toon Lake, adjacent to Gadget's Go Coaster. Parents can relax in a small, shaded seating area near a waterfall while their children explore the boat, which looks a whole lot like its owner.

See if you can recognize Donald's eyes in the large portholes of the pilothouse, his jaunty blue sailor's cap in the roof of the cabin, and his face in the shape of the hull. Would-be sailors can climb the small rope ladder or the spiral staircase up to the pilothouse to steer the wheel that turns the compass or to toot the boat's whistle.

GOOFY'S PLAYHOUSE: Located beside the *Miss Daisy*, this playground is just for kids. The garden outside Goofy's house boasts an odd assortment of delights: giant stalks bearing popcorn guarded by a Goofy-style scarecrow, spinning flowers, a leaky garden hose, and a patch with watermelons and pumpkins. Inside, young visitors can peek into Goofy's cupboards, climb on his furniture, and tickle the keys of the piano (doing so yields "goofy" sound effects rather than musical notes). Across the street is Goofy's Gas. It's not a real filling station, but is a great place to take little ones for a pit stop (it's a restroom).

TOON PARK: This tiny soft-surface enclave next to Goofy's Playhouse supplies a safe play area for toddlers. Adjacent seating gives par-ents and other guests an inviting place to rest and enjoy the youngsters' antics.

Tomorrowland

PHOTO BY JILL SAFRO

When Walt Disney was alive, the future seemed simple: We would all dress in Mylar and travel in flying saucers. The Tomorrowland he created in the '50s was set in the distant year of 1987, part Buck Rogers and part World's Fair. The current incarnation of Tomorrowland retains that spirit and is based on a classic vision of the future, one that looks at it from the perspective of the past. The result is an innocent and hopeful place — imagine, for instance, a planet that renews itself. Visit Tomorrowland today, and you enter a realm more in keeping with the rest of Disneyland than with the sterile, less positive future world often depicted in contemporary films.

Cross the bridge into this land and enter a visually engaging terrain, where the palette of colors is not otherworldly, but still forward-thinking. Futuristic boulders and dreamlike architecture coexist with apple, orange, lemon, and pomegranate trees that line pathways created from gray, mauve, and burgundy bricks. This landscape fires up the intellect as much as the imagination.

Galileo Galilei, Leonardo da Vinci, Jules Verne, H.G. Wells, and certainly Walt Disney would have felt at home here. Aldous Huxley probably wouldn't have.

Several of Tomorrowland's attractions are also at Walt Disney World in Florida: Space Mountain, Star Tours — The Adventures Continue, Astro Orbitor, and Buzz Lightyear Astro Blasters (known in Walt Disney World as Buzz Lightyear's Space Ranger Spin). Other well-loved Tomorrowland classic attractions remain, among them: the Monorail and Autopia.

A replica of the Moonliner, a Tomorrowland icon from 1955 to 1966, sits on the site of its predecessor. Sleek monorail trains glide to and from the Downtown Disney district, while traditional Disneyland Railroad trains may occupy the Tomorrowland station, a vibrant reminder that the past is indeed prologue. (Trains are temporarily closed due to construction of Star Wars Land.)

The following attractions were all operating at press time, but some may not be open during your visit to the park. Check *www.disneyland.com* for updates.

PHOTO BY JILL SAFRO

ASTRO ORBITOR: Towering high above the entrance to Tomorrowland, this big whirligig with spinning orbs and speeding starships is a fitting symbol for Tomorrowland. Astro Orbitor, modeled on a drawing made by Leonardo da Vinci almost five centuries ago, is the successor to Rocket Jets, which gave Disneyland guests a lift for 30 years. Each ride vehicle accommodates two passengers (or two adults and one small child), who can maneuver it up and down while spinning clockwise for 1½ minutes, reveling in sweeping views of Tomorrowland, Central Plaza, and Sleeping Beauty Castle.

Note: The minimum age to ride is one year. Young children have to be in the company of an adult.

BIRNBAUM'S ★BEST★ BUZZ LIGHTYEAR ASTRO BLASTERS: FP The evil Emperor Zurg is up to no good—and it's up to that Space Ranger extra-ordinaire Buzz Lightyear and his Junior Space Rangers (that means you) to save the day.

So goes the story line of Tomorrowland's video game–inspired spin through toyland. The adventure is experienced from a toy's point of view. Guests begin their 4½-minute tour of duty as Space Rangers at Star Command Action Center. This is where Buzz gives his team a briefing on the mission that lies ahead.

PHOTO BY JILL SAFRO

Then it's off to the Launch Bay to board the ride vehicles. The ships feature dual laser cannons, glowing lights, and a piloting joystick.

In addition to Buzz and the evil Emperor, you may recognize some other toy faces swirling about—the little green, multi-eyed alien squeaky toys, best known for their awe of "the claw." The squeakies have been enlisted to help in the fight against Zurg.

Once Junior Space Rangers blast off, they find themselves surrounded by Zurg's robots, who are mercilessly ripping batteries from toys. As Rangers fire at targets, beams of light fill the air. For every target hit, you will be rewarded with sight gags, sound effects, and points. The points, which are tallied automatically, are accumulated throughout the

journey. Although the vehicles follow a rigid "flight" path (they're on a track), the joystick allows riders to maneuver the ships, arcing from side to side or spinning in circles while taking aim at their surroundings.

When the star cruiser arrives at Zurg's spaceship, it's showdown time. Will good prevail over evil? Or has time run out for the toy universe? And will you score enough points to be a Galactic Hero? (Most people improve their scores with a little practice.)

BIRNBAUM'S ★BEST★ STAR TOURS— THE ADVENTURES CONTINUE: FP Inspired by George Lucas's blockbuster series of Star Wars films, this is one of the most exciting attractions at Disney-land. It offers guests the opportunity to ride on

droid-piloted StarSpeeders, the exact same type of flight simulator used by military and commercial airlines to train pilots—and explore the galaxy in a 3-D adventure. The action here takes place throughout the time period covered by the major Star Wars movies. The best part? There are dozens of different adventures to experience here—multiple visits yield multiple surprises. And several of those surprises involve scenes from the recent blockbuster and instant classic *Star Wars: The Force Awakens*.

This is a rather turbulent trip—seat belts are definitely required. Passengers must be free of back problems, heart conditions, motion sickness, and other physical limitations to ride. Guests under 40 inches tall and kids younger than 3 may not ride. Pregnant women must skip this one. If you have a young child, make sure he or she understands the significance of wearing 3-D glasses (and keeping them on) before you board the attraction—it's a concept lost on most tots.

STAR WARS LAUNCH BAY: Guests don't have to wait for Star Wars Land to be completed to get a fix of the Force—Star Wars Launch Bay offers an immersive atmosphere in which to experience both the Light and Dark side. Housed in the space formerly occupied by Innovations, Launch Bay features props and movie memorabilia celebrating Star Wars and the recently reawakened Force. In addition to Light and Dark galleries, guests may meet characters such as Chewbacca and Darth Vader. The Launch Bay may not be open in all of 2017.

JEDI TRAINING—TRIALS OF THE TEMPLE: Jedi Padawans can learn to harness the Force and properly wield a lightsaber right here in Tomorrowland. The 30-minute training program is offered several times a day (earlier runnings tend to be most popular). To sign up, potential participants (ages 4 to 12) should head to the exit for Star Wars Launch Bay as early as possible (during regular park hours). Kids who make the cut (determined on a first-come, first-served basis) receive a receipt complete with a time to return.

Arrive about 30 minutes before showtime to receive a loaner cloak. When the Jedi master arrives, kids receive lightsabers (strictly for use in the show) and start the training session. Instruct kids to pay attention to the lesson—they'll need their new skill set to search for a hidden temple and face their fears, not to mention simulate a lightsaber battle against Kylo Ren and other representatives of the dark side. Shows run throughout the day. Check a park Times Guide for the schedule.

BIRNBAUM'S ★BEST **SPACE MOUNTAIN:** FP When Space Mountain first opened in 1977, it quickly rocketed to the top of just about everyone's list of favorite attractions—where it remains to this day. While the classic facade and essence of Space Mountain remain intact, the experience is decidedly 21st century. Brave voyagers board new vehicles in a realistic launch port. After shooting through a disorienting tunnel, riders will have a close encounter with a meteorite. After that, it's all about screeching through the darkness, past spinning stars and whirling galaxies. Add to that an edgy soundtrack (which is synchronized to each car), and you've got one out-of-this-world attraction.

If your courage fails you, just ask an attendant to direct you to the nearest escape route (aka "the chicken exit").

Note: Pregnant women and guests who have weak backs, heart conditions, motion sickness, or other physical limitations must sit this one out. Children younger than 8 years old must be accompanied by an adult (kids under 3 are not permitted to ride). Guests must be at least 40 inches tall to experience Space Mountain.

AUTOPIA: FP The only attraction from the original Tomorrowland, Autopia was dubbed "The Freeway of the Future" back in 1955. Kids have always loved guiding the small sports cars around the twisting roadways (for them, a top speed of seven miles per hour is thrilling). The Tomorrowland and Fantasyland roadways now comprise a single attraction (yes, there were two Autopias; the one in Fantasyland opened in 1959 to accommodate spillover crowds). Guests enter through a single boarding area in Tomorrowland and watch an entertaining pre-show on a large video screen that presents the world from a car's point of view. Drivers (and one passenger per vehicle) travel in restyled cars through 21st-century terrain, experiencing a series of happy roadside surprises along the way. At the ride's end, they may receive a commemorative driver's license as a memento. A shop proffers auto-related toys and assorted souvenirs. This attraction is quite popular with those who've not yet reached Driver's Ed age.

Note: Kids must be at least 52 inches tall and at least 7 years old to drive alone. Pregnant women and guests with back or neck problems should not ride.

DISNEYLAND MONORAIL: Who doesn't love the monorail? The first daily operating monorail in the Western Hemisphere was a novelty when it was introduced at Disneyland in 1959. Today, it's still a thrill to watch them glide through the park. The sleek, Mark VII trains were designed to evoke images of their 1959 predecessors. Straddling a concrete beamway, the monorail has rubber tires—which enable it to glide quietly—as well as braking wheels atop the beam and guiding and stabilizing wheels on either side.

The 2½-mile-long "highway in the sky" is a distinctive and integral part of Tomorrowland. The electrically powered ride takes guests around the periphery of Tomorrowland, over to Downtown Disney and its diverting activities, and then back to Tomorrowland.

FP = Fastpass attraction (see page 58)

PHOTO BY MIKE CARROLL

For a special experience, inform the cast member on the boarding ramp that you'd like to sit up front in the pilot's cabin. It can usually accommodate up to five passengers. If all the seats are taken, you can always wait for the next monorail and try your luck again.

Note that by boarding the monorail in Tomorrowland, you are actually leaving Disneyland Park. If you get off at the Downtown Disney station, be sure to get your hand stamped. You'll need to show it and a valid ticket to reboard the monorail or pass through the park's turnstiles. Know that walking is also an option—as Disneyland is about a 5-minute stroll from the station.

PHOTO BY JILL SAFRO

Tomorrowland Icon

MOONLINER: Beside Redd Rockett's Pizza Port, this two-thirds-scale, 53-foot-high replica of an early Tomorrowland icon stands 50 feet from the site of the original rocket. It is set on a 12-foot pedestal. A fine mist cools guests in the warm weeks of summer.

HOT TIP!
A trip on the monorail yields panoramic views of the Disney California Adventure theme park and its neighbor, the Grand Californian resort. However, it does not stop at either place.

The monorail is considered more of an attraction than a mode of transportation. It takes about the same amount of time (maybe less) to walk from the Downtown Disney station to the Disneyland Park.

BIRNBAUM'S BEST **FINDING NEMO SUBMARINE VOYAGE:** Uh-oh. It seems that curious little clownfish has wandered off again. And this time he's done so in Tomorrowland's submarine lagoon. The good news is the subs that used to take guests to the North Pole now provide the perfect means for monitoring the fin-challenged fish and his high-spirited underwater hijinks.

The submarine adventure begins as a quiet expedition to observe an undersea volcano. But faster than you can say, "All drains lead to the ocean," our frisky friends from *Finding Nemo* start floating and fluttering in front of a personal porthole. The whole gang's here, including Nemo's overprotective dad, Marlin, the faithful-if-forgetful royal blue tang, Dory, that totally awesome turtle dude, Crush, and more. They're on a quest to catch up with their buddy Nemo, and you're invited along for the slightly frenetic, completely kinetic undersea search. Oh, and remember that volcano you were going to observe? It erupts.

Will you survive the sub-shaking volcanic quaking and find Nemo? Yep. They don't call this "the happiest place on earth" for nothing.

This whimsical experience is appropriate for guests of all ages, provided that the guests are claustrophobia-free. Some moments may be too intense for some tots.

81

Shopping

Until you get to know Disneyland, you might not expect that anyone would visit just to go shopping. But among Southern Californians, it's a top draw for the Disney-themed merchandise and gift items. Mickey Mouse paraphernalia, such as key chains, mugs, T-shirts, hats, and other such souvenirs, is found here in abundance, of course, but there are some surprises, such as character-inspired costumes for kids, wireless phone accessories and items for the office, plus upscale items, such as art collectibles, jewelry, and products for the home.

Main Street, U.S.A.

CANDY PALACE: An old-fashioned pageant in pink and white, this shop is alluring at any time of day, but never more than when the candy-makers are at work in the glass-walled kitchen confecting candy canes, chocolate-covered strawberries, caramel apples, toffee, fudge, and other temptations for anyone with a sweet tooth. The products made on the premises are available for purchase, along with a bounty of chocolates, licorice, and taffy.

CHINA CLOSET: If you're in the market for figurines, picture frames, or snow globes, this is the place to go.

CRYSTAL ARTS: Glasses and pitchers, trays, and other mementos can be engraved (for free) and monogrammed while you wait, or you can get them unornamented. The shop also sells glass miniatures, bells, and paperweights. To save ten percent off your purchase, use the Arribas Brothers coupon at the back of this book.

DISNEY CLOTHIERS, LTD.: Disney character merchandise has always been popular, but if you want something a little more stylish, this is where to find it. The spot caters to fashion-conscious shoppers with a love for Disney gear. Almost every item in the selection of men's, women's, and children's clothing and accessories sold here incorporates Disney characters in some way.

DISNEY SHOWCASE: Featuring the latest seasonal merchandise (Disney style), this shop also offers hats, shirts, key chains, park logo merchandise and assorted souvenirs. Personalization is offered (for a fee).

DISNEYANA: Collectors and the simply curious alike will discover rare and unusual Disney merchandise here, such as limited-edition art and hand-painted cels inspired by Disney animated classics. Popular pieces have included sculptures from the Walt Disney Classics Collection. This shop recently moved from its longtime location to a new home in The Bank of Main Street building.

   Note: Disney Imagineers and artists often drop by the shop to sign reproduction artwork, sculptures, or recently published books.

EMPORIUM: Much like an old-time variety store, this large and bustling shop offers an incredible assortment of wares, and it is home to Disneyland logo selections. Decorative figurines, mugs, home decor, clothing, plush toys, character hats, jewelry, and a variety of souvenirs make up the bulk of the stock.

PHOTO BY JILL SAFRO

FORTUOSITY SHOP: Merchandise in all shapes and sizes, including trendy fashions and accessories like Mickey Mouse watches and character-laden novelty clocks, beckons from this unique emporium.

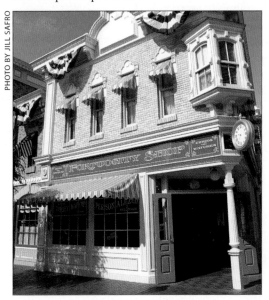

PHOTO BY JILL SAFRO

MAD HATTER: This hat shop stocks Mickey Mouse ears in black and various colors and designs. You can even get your name stitched on the back.

MAIN STREET MAGIC SHOP: Small but well stocked with gags and tricks—and books about how to pull them off—this shop has the wherewithal to inspire budding illusionists. In the market for an invisible pooch? A magic wand? An ice cube with a bug in it? This place has them all.

MAIN STREET PHOTO SUPPLY CO.: Should a roving Disneyland photographer snap your mug, this is the place to pick up the print. You can also find memory cards, batteries, film, frames, and photo albums.

MARKET HOUSE: This Disney version of an old-fashioned general store is actually a cleverly themed Starbucks coffee shop. Stop here for fresh-brewed coffee and specialty drinks, plus cookies, cake pops, savory snacks, and much more.

NEW CENTURY JEWELRY: Among the delicate offerings here are 14-karat-gold charms of Tinker Bell, Donald Duck, and Minnie Mouse. The marcasite character jewelry is subtle and somewhat sophisticated.

NEWSSTAND: While no actual news is offered here (No news is good news, right?), this stand stocks postcards and souvenir items. The Newsstand offers personalization and embroidery on hats, shirts, and other merchandise (for a small fee).

PENNY ARCADE: Adjacent to the Gibson Girl Ice Cream Parlor is a virtual Coney Island of food and fun. Fresh-made treats fill ornate shelves, and scrumptious saltwater taffy is available in an array of flavors. To add to the carnival atmosphere, old-fashioned arcade games that still cost a penny to play and a Welte Orchestrion line the walls.

SILHOUETTE STUDIO: Working at the rate of about 60 seconds per portrait, Disneyland's silhouette artists truly are a wonder to behold. Individual and group portraits are available.

20TH CENTURY MUSIC COMPANY: This little place carries a selection of collector pins, plus classic Disney music and DVDs.

PHOTO BY JILL SAFRO

New Orleans Square

CRISTAL D'ORLEANS: Glasses and chandeliers, decanters and ashtrays, pitchers and paperweights are typical treasures here. All engraving (and some monogramming) is done free of charge. To save ten percent off your purchase, use the Arribas Brothers coupon at the back of this book.

LE BAT EN ROUGE: Need to cross a few Minnie Mouse–related items off your shopping list? You've come to the right place. Expect clothing, jewelry, and other accessories featuring Ms. Mouse. Also lining the shelves are tchotchkes and thingamabobs with a Disney theme.

LA MASCARADE D'ORLEANS: A compact and brightly lit showcase for Pandora products, this shop has a variety of its signature items: necklaces, rings, earrings, and charm bracelets—many with a Disney theme. In fact, some items are Disney-parks exclusives.

MLLE. ANTOINETTE'S PARFUMERIE: This fragrant boutique carries a variety of classic and chic fragrances for men and women. The parfumerie "blends the essence of French-style elegance with American-style spontaneity." It's located in the heart of New Orleans Square.

PIECES OF EIGHT: Wares with a pirate theme are purveyed at this shop beside the Pirates of the Caribbean exit. There are pirate rings, ships' lanterns, stocking caps, and fake knives and skulls in plastic and rubber. You will also discover T-shirts, key chains, glasses, and other souvenir items imprinted with the Pirates of the Caribbean logo. In the market for a pirate sword? Look no further. And, for the right price, you may be able to fill a bag with colorful pirate booty. Arrrrrr!

PORT ROYAL CURIOS AND CURIOSITIES: Ready to give your treasured Mickey Mouse T-shirt a day off? Stop at this boutique to augment your Disney-oriented closet. Expect to find a large assortment of merchandise featuring the nearby Haunted Mansion

Get Your Ears Done Here

Since Disneyland first opened in 1955, there has been no more coveted souvenir than a pair of Mickey Mouse ears personalized with the lucky owner's name—or that of a family member. And never have there been more styles to choose from. Most can be embroidered for a nominal fee at both locations of the Mad Hatter (in Fantasyland and on Main Street), the Gag Factory in Toontown, Tomorrowlanding in Tomorrowland, and other select locations. The shops will not embroider company names on hats.

attraction: shirts, hats, coasters, and more. Also on hand: items with a *Nightmare Before Christmas* theme (cups, bags, dolls, dresses, pajamas, shirts, hats, etc.).

PORTRAIT ARTISTS: Sit for a portrait—done in pastel or watercolor—amidst the quaint charm of a New Orleans *rue* (street). Individual and group portraits are offered.

ROYAL STREET SWEETS: Satisfy your sweet tooth (or teeth) at this stand that specializes in sugary treats.

Frontierland

BONANZA OUTFITTERS: Oozing rustic ambience, this cozy-yet-quaint shop offers traditional frontier-wear with a trendy twist. Look for denim jackets, cowboy hats, plaid shirts, and coonskin caps. They sell pins, too.

PIONEER MERCANTILE: Inspired by the paraphernalia of the pioneer period in American history, this shop is home to some of *Toy Story*'s ever-popular characters and sidekicks. Expect to find plush toys, hats, shirts, books, and more. There is a "penny press" machine here, too, which allows you to convert a penny into a souvenir for a fee.

WESTWARD HO TRADING COMPANY: This rustic store stocks something for the whole pin-trading frontier family, including pins, lanyards, and other pin-collecting accoutrements.

Critter Country

BRIAR PATCH: Situated near Splash Mountain, this small shop offers hats, character merchandise, and sundry souvenirs.

POOH CORNER: This *hunny* of a spot is home to a candy kitchen filled with sweet treats. Lining its many shelves are other Disneyland logo merchandise and items with a Winnie the Pooh theme. Pooh's pals from the Hundred Acre Wood are also well represented. All kinds of Pooh products await, including plush toys, watches, infants' apparel, children's clothing, sleep shirts, and bedroom slippers. There is also a substantial selection of freshly made cookies and chocolates.

POOH & YOU PHOTOS: Pooh and his pals from the Hundred Acre Wood can be found in Critter Country. You can take photos with your own camera or purchase any of the shots taken by one of Disneyland's photographers via Disney's PhotoPass program. For specifics regarding PhotoPass, refer to the box at right.

Adventureland

ADVENTURELAND BAZAAR: The plush jungle animals corralled here include lions, tigers, and panda bears (oh, my!).

INDIANA JONES ADVENTURE OUTPOST: This outfitter can supply the most daring expeditions with all manner of safari apparel, notably Indy's trademark headgear, as well as other rough-and-ready wear and "artifacts" related to the ever-popular archaeologist and adventurer, Indiana Jones.

SOUTH SEAS TRADERS: This is the spot to browse for surf- and safari-themed items, such as T-shirts, shorts, jackets, windbreakers, bags, belts, and a selection of hats.

Fantasyland

BIBBIDI BOBBIDI BOUTIQUE: Tucked inside Sleeping Beauty Castle, this shop offers young guests the opportunity to be transformed into "little princesses" and princely "cool knights." Makeovers are available daily. Prices vary.

ENCHANTED CHAMBER: Sparkly crowns dazzle the eyes of every young princess who enters this royal boutique, tucked inside Sleeping Beauty Castle, just to the left of the entrance to Fantasyland. From toys and jewelry and other courtly keepsakes, this little shop has made more than a few special dreams come true.

Disney's PhotoPass

As you wander the theme parks, Disney cast members will be happy to snap your picture (with your camera and/or theirs). After mugging for the camera, you'll get a PhotoPass card. It'll link all such photos together for viewing on the Internet. You can ogle the low-res images for free (with watermarks) or purchase favorites for up to 45 days after they are taken. Another option is a Photopass+ One Day Package: $39 for unlimited downloads of any photos taken on one particular day. High-quality prints, plus mugs, shirts, and other items, are for sale. To buy or just peruse, visit *www.disneyland.com*. Each theme park has a spot for photo-viewing and purchasing. Check a park guidemap for locations. We were skeptical at first, but PhotoPass really is a great way to get shots of your whole party. And it includes photos taken on park attractions—a nice bonus.

FAIRYTALE ARTS: Here guests are turned into princesses, among other things, via the magic of face painting (for a fee).

FANTASY FAIRE GIFTS: On Disneyland's parade route, near the entrance to the Fantasyland Theatre, this open-air stand stocks special souvenirs and yummy treats spun from the colorful tales and sights in Fantasyland.

FAIRYTALE TREASURES: Conveniently situated next to the Royal Theater, this spot is all princesses all the time.

IT'S A SMALL WORLD TOY SHOP: The whimsical structure near the entrance to It's a Small World stocks an assortment of Disney-themed toys, dolls, pins, and plush toys featuring the Disney characters.

LE PETIT CHALET GIFTS: As cozy as a warm cup of cocoa on a winter evening, this small Swiss shop, nestled at the base of the Matterhorn, is the repository of traditional Disneyland gifts and souvenirs.

MAD HATTER: Always a great place for hats and plush character caps—and Mouse ears, of course (they'll embroider them for you for a small fee). The selection of novelty headgear includes items such as Donald's sailor cap, a hat sporting Goofy's ears, and more.

STROMBOLI'S WAGON: Located near the Village Haus restaurant, this stand offers a wagonful of wares—everything from Disney plush toys to Mickey Mouse sunglasses. Some of the smaller items available here include character key chains, pens, buttons, and candy. The shop is named after one of the villains from *Pinocchio*.

PHOTO BY JILL SAFRO

Mickey's Toontown

GAG FACTORY: A Laugh-O-Meter outside this shop gives some indication of the fun to be found inside, along with an assortment of character merchandise—plush toys, stationery, souvenirs, T-shirts, novelty headwear, and candy—all featuring the Fab Five (Mickey, Minnie, Pluto, Donald, and Goofy) and their friends. Take a moment to admire the toon architecture, especially the pillars at the back of the store. The Gag Factory will stitch your name on mouse ears for a small fee.

MICKEY & ME PHOTOS: Trying to get your photo taken with Mickey on busy days can be challenging, but if you follow this tip, it's a piece of cake: Mickey can often be found working in the Movie Barn behind his house in Toontown, and he's always happy to stop what he's doing to greet his guests and pose for pictures. You can take as many photos as you like with your own camera (at no charge) or purchase any of the shots taken by a Disneyland photographer via Disney's PhotoPass program. (For details on PhotoPass, see page 85.) Note that the line to meet the Mouse is often a long one. But to his legions of loyal fans, it's well worth the wait.

Tomorrowland

AUTOPIA WINNER'S CIRCLE: Racing enthusiasts will enjoy the Autopia-inspired souvenirs and toys offered at this small shop.

LITTLE GREEN MEN STORE COMMAND: "Sharp" traders know they can find an excellent selection of pins and Vinylmation collectibles at this spot. The ultimate pin destination at Disneyland offers open and limited-edition pins, lanyards, and pin-trading accessories, as well as souvenirs and toys featuring Disney•Pixar characters.

THE STAR TRADER: The Star Trader is the repository of everything from T-shirts and jewelry to novelty headwear, mugs, key chains, candy, and more—many emblazoned with the likenesses of Disney pals and characters from the Star Wars universe. Yes, this is the place where Star Wars legends have come to collectible life. It's even possible to customize and build your own lightsaber. Toys featuring Buzz Lightyear, Woody, and the gang from Toy Story can also be found here, along with hundreds of stuffed animals.

TOMORROWLANDING: Whether it's the Jedi Force that draws you to Tomorrowland or a desire to help find Nemo, what you'll actually find here is a super-sized assortment of headwear.

Pin Trading, Disney Style

It's one of the biggest collectible crazes to sweep through Disney's land—pin trading. These small enamel pins (there are hundreds of different styles) can be purchased all over the property, but buying them is only half the fun. The real joy comes when you encounter another pin trader with a worthy swap. To get a head start, bring pins from home (Disney Stores carry pins, too). Once on-property, keep an eye out for cast members sporting a good selection of pins—they tend to be agreeable to almost any trade. And when negotiating a trade with a Disneyland cast member, always remember these rules: (1) only Disney pins may be traded, and (2) every trade must be an even pin-for-pin exchange.

Entertainment

Together with Walt Disney World, Disneyland presents more live entertainment than any other organization in the world. What follows is typical of the variety you can expect. Check a park Times Guide for daily offerings.

Performers & Live Shows

Performers stroll, march, croon, and pluck their way through Disneyland every day— so frequently that all you usually have to do to find them is follow your ears.

Fantasyland

MICKEY AND THE MAGICAL MAP: Mickey Mouse reprises his classic role of sorcerer's apprentice in this kid-pleasin', toe-tappin', and eye-poppin' performance. What's magic about the map? It transports dreamers to all the places they can imagine. But the massive map has an empty spot—and Mickey takes it upon himself to fill it. Dozens of singers and dancers join him, making this musical fun for all ages. For the best views, don't sit up front. The 22-minute show is usually presented several times a day.

Main Street, U.S.A.

ATMOSPHERE BANDS: Look and listen for the musical groups that performs near the Fire House and the Castle on select days.

DAPPER DANS OF DISNEYLAND: The official greeters of Main Street, U.S.A., this classic barbershop quartet performs standards in perfect four-part harmony. The colorfully clad

performers may be found strolling on the sidewalk, planted by a storefront, or whizzing by on a trolley or a bicycle built for four.

DISNEYLAND BAND: A presence in the park since opening day in 1955, Disneyland's signature musical group specializes in turn-of-the-century band music and Disney tunes, but it can play just about anything. The band performs inside the main entrance when the park opens, in Town Square (at the South end of Main Street), and at other locations.

The Disneyland Band's first performance of the day often takes place in front of the train station, just inside the turnstiles. It's an interactive and magical way to start the day. Kids of all ages simply love it.

FLAG RETREAT: The flag at Town Square is lowered just before sunset each day (times vary). The ceremony is often highlighted by a performance by the Disneyland Band or the Dapper Dans. The band has been known to perform several rousing marches per show. On the band's day off, the Dapper Dans perform a capella renditions of American classics. "The Star-Spangled Banner" makes for a stirring finale. (We always get choked up during this touching ceremony.) It is a rewarding experience that captures the essence of what Walt Disney hoped guests would feel as they experienced Main Street, U.S.A. It is usually presented daily.

MAIN STREET PIANO PLAYER: Piano players are often on hand to tickle the ivories on the snow-white upright piano at the Corner Café. Presented daily.

New Orleans Square

THE BOOTSTRAPPERS: Yo, ho! Yo, ho! A Pirate Band for you! These musical buccaneers wander about New Orleans Square and perform on Tom Sawyer Island.

JAMBALAYA JAZZ: This group plays down-home New Orleans jazz with plenty of soul. Fetch yourself a mint julep (sans alcohol) or a bowl of gumbo, and let the music wash over you like the mighty Mississippi.

ROYAL STREET BACHELORS: Their style is early traditional jazz and blues, with a mellow four-beat sound similar to that once commonly heard in the Storyville section of the Crescent City. The Bachelors can be found performing throughout the Square.

Frontierland

GOLDEN HORSESHOE: Dishing up a "rootin', tootin' good time," this place never takes itself—or its guests—too seriously. The entertainment varies, but it always pairs nicely with the frontier-style grub offered at the counter. Seating is available at the bar or at tables, on a first-come, first-served basis.

LAUGHING STOCK CO.: Sheriff Clem Clodhopper has no desire to marry Mayor McGillicuddy's daughter, Sally Mae, but neither of them will take no for an answer. An old-time serial in three parts is played out as the dysfunctional trio finagles to get Sally Mae hitched to someone (anyone), even an unsuspecting park guest. Check a park Times Guide for the performance schedule.

HOT TIP!

The Entertainment Times Guide provides a current listing of entertainment offerings and schedules. Pick up a copy at the main entrance, City Hall, or at the Tip Board on Main Street. It's free. Note that custodial cast members tend to carry extra copies of park guidemaps and Times Guides, too. Just ask.

Tomorrowland

JEDI TRAINING: TRIALS OF THE TEMPLE: Star Wars fans and Jedi-wannabes can learn the ways of The Force right here in Disneyland. A Jedi Master is on hand to teach guests dos and don'ts of using a lightsaber, as well as help them fend off an unexpected march of Stormtroopers. Expect a special appearance by one notable Dark Lord who will attempt to lure you over to the dark side.

Parades

No Main Street is complete without a parade, and Disneyland has plenty. The usual route runs between Town Square and the promenade in front of It's a Small World—or vice versa. The direction and route can vary, so it's wise to ask at the Information Center at City Hall or Central Plaza.

MICKEY'S SOUNDSATIONAL PARADE: Meant to evoke happy, musical Disney memories, this parade showcases dozens of beloved Disney characters, including the Mouse himself. It is usually presented each afternoon. Check a park Times Guide or Tip Board for current details and showtimes.

Where to Watch the Parade: The best points from which to see the parades are the platform of the Disneyland Railroad's Main Street depot, Town Square near the flagpole, and the curb on either side of Main Street. If you'd like to avoid crowds, any viewing location other than Main Street would be better.

Two other options are the terrace outside the Plaza Inn (but be aware that the seating is limited here) and the tables in the courtyard of the Carnation Cafe, where the view may be partially obstructed. Better still, plan to catch a later parade on nights when more than one is scheduled—it's usually less crowded.

You can also stand on either side of the promenade area in front of It's a Small World, whose multicolored facade provides a whimsical, only-at-Disneyland backdrop. Wherever you decide to station yourself for the parade, plan to arrive about 20 to 45 minutes beforehand to claim your piece of turf.

BIRNBAUM'S ★BEST★ PAINT THE NIGHT: Disney's first-ever fully LED-light parade, Paint the Night first opened (to glowing reviews) in Hong Kong Disneyland in 2014. And now Disneyland has its very own version of this illuminating processional.

Paint the Night continues the Disney Parks' rich tradition of nighttime parades that began with the Main Street Electrical Parade. This spirited successor pays tribute to the M.S.E.P. by incorporating its legendary theme song, "The Baroque Hoedown." (We wish even more of the beloved song was included!) Featuring nearly a million twinkling lights, the interactive parade is led by Tinker Bell and includes scenes and characters from *The Little*

Mermaid, *Monsters, Inc.*, *Cars*, *Toy Story*, *Frozen*, and a whole lot more.

For information on the Paint the Night Dining Package, turn to page 112 of this book. Note that on evenings when Paint the Night is presented twice, the latter running is generally less crowded.

Fireworks

BIRNBAUM'S ★BEST★ DISNEYLAND FOREVER FIREWORKS SPECTACULAR: An impressive fireworks show called "Disneyland Forever" celebrates Disneyland and the park's rich and colorful history. The spectacle immerses guests in wondrous stories with a dazzling combo of pyrotechnics, lights, and special effects projected onto Disneyland park icons.

Guests find themselves transported into the worlds of classic Disney and Disney•Pixar films, including a dance with *The Jungle Book*'s King Louie and a flight over London with the gang from *Peter Pan*. More than 200 pyrotechnic shells are fired in all, one every couple of seconds, in time to the music—including two original songs: "Live the Magic" and the closing number, "Kiss Goodnight" (written by Disney Legend Richard Sherman). Check a Times Guide for the schedule.

Where to Watch: One of the best areas is about midway down Main Street, U.S.A., near the Main Street Photo Supply Company up to the Castle hub area. Another great spot is near It's a Small World.

Special Occasions

Along with plenty of special events in the parks and hotels year-round (some require special admission tickets), Disneyland celebrates three major seasons each year: summer (including the Fourth of July), Halloween (September through October), and the winter holidays (mid-November through early January).

SUMMER: While plenty of folks are on vacation, Disney offers a full slate of atmosphere entertainment and spectaculars from Memorial Day to Labor Day. Expect longer wait times at attractions and plan to use Fastpass (see page 58) as often as possible. Past years have seen a patriotic, pyrotechnic tribute to the U.S.A. on Independence Day in a celebration known as Disney's Celebrate America! A Fourth of July Concert in the Sky.

HALLOWEEN: Halloween at the Disneyland Resort brings a palette of fall colors, pumpkins, and trick-or-treat touches, along with the extra-spooky *Nightmare Before Christmas*–themed Haunted Mansion (see page 10).

WINTER HOLIDAYS: This jolly period stretches from November through New Year's, when the entire park glows with holiday themes. (We have witnessed the Yuletide holiday decorations in place as early as October.)

The Disneyland Resort officially begins to celebrate the holidays in November, when Jingle Jangle Jamboree and the merriest attraction on Earth—It's a Small World Holiday—return for the season.

It's a Small World Holiday celebrates Yuletide customs around the world. The singing dolls add "Jingle Bells" to their repertoire in numerous languages, and the clock on the whimsical facade dons a Santa hat.

Main Street, U.S.A., is decked out in traditional red and green, including hundreds of poinsettias and a huge Christmas tree that's surrounded by oversize holiday packages.

PHOTO BY JILL SAFRO

Highlights include the chance to meet the man in the red suit, Santa himself. In Adventureland, holiday merriment presents itself as the Jingle Cruise—the ever-popular Jungle Cruise with more than a few holiday surprises (including seasonal banter by the skipper: "Indiana Jones is *not* a fan of New Year's Eve. He can't stand it when the giant ball drops").

On select December nights, a candlelight processional ending at Town Square takes place. Special music is provided by a large choir, and a holiday story is read by a well-known entertainer. (**A Christmas Fantasy Parade**, a Disney holiday favorite, takes place throughout the holiday season.)

Live entertainment and a spectacular fireworks show on **New Year's Eve** (no special ticket required) provide the grand finale for this happy holiday season.

For details about seasonal happenings in the park, visit *www.disneyland.com*.

Where to Find the Characters

Look for the Disney characters in Town Square on Main Street, U.S.A., as well as in Mickey's Toontown, where they live. Tinker Bell and her fairy friends appear at Pixie Hollow. Princesses hold court at Fantasy Faire in Fantasyland, just off Main Street. Pooh and his pals congregate in Critter Country. In Adventureland, Aladdin and Jasmine often stop to interact outside Aladdin's Oasis.

Cast members at the Information Board can help locate characters. Also refer to the *Good Meals, Great Times* chapter of this book, and your park Entertainment Times Guide.

Where in Disneyland?

All of the photos on this page were taken at Disneyland. Do you know where?
We challenge you to find all the spots where these images were shot and snap a photo for
yourself as you discover each one. Happy hunting! (For locations, turn to page 140.)

1

2

3

4

5

6

Hot Tips

❤ Tuesday, Wednesday, and Thursday are the least crowded days to visit year-round. If you must come on a weekend, choose Sunday over Saturday.

❤ Measure your child before your visit so you'll know ahead of time which attractions he or she may be too short to ride. This can prevent disappointment later.

❤ Wear comfortable walking shoes. Blisters are the most common malady reported to First Aid.

❤ Main Street, U.S.A., may open a bit before the rest of the park (usually when Disneyland opens at 9 or 10 A.M.). Take advantage of this to grab a quick snack, shop, or mingle with Disney characters.

❤ Check the daily entertainment schedule in a current Entertainment Times Guide and plan your day accordingly.

❤ Wait times posted at the attractions and on the Information Board at the north end of Main Street, U.S.A. (on the Adventureland side), are updated every hour.

❤ Break up your time in the park (unless you have only one day). Arrive early, see major attractions until things get busy, return to your hotel for a swim or a nap, then go back to the park. Remember, you must have a hand stamp and a ticket for re-entry if you entered with a one-day ticket.

❤ An attraction may reach its Fastpass limit before the end of the day, especially if the park is packed. Be sure to get yours early if you don't want to wait in the standby line.

❤ Try to stop for lunch before 11:30 A.M. or after 2 P.M., and dinner before 5 P.M. or after 8 P.M. to avoid long lines (which tend to be a bit shorter toward the left side of the fast-food counters).

❤ Due to the ongoing construction of Star Wars Land, Fantasmic! will not be presented in 2017 (or 2018).

❤ For a change of pace food-wise, head to Downtown Disney or one of the three hotels on property. They have something for almost every budget and taste—from simple to sublime, ravioli to rack of lamb—as well as buffet meals with popular Disney characters (at the Disneyland resorts only).

❤ Avoid rides such as Star Tours, Splash Mountain, the Matterhorn Bobsleds, and the Mad Tea Party immediately after meals (for obvious reasons).

❤ The monorail takes guests from Tomorrowland to the Disneyland Hotel end of Downtown Disney. All guests must disembark, but it's okay to reboard if you'd like to complete the round-trip journey.

❤ Try to visit the major attractions—Space Mountain, Star Tours, the Indiana Jones Adventure, Big Thunder Mountain Railroad, Finding Nemo Submarine Voyage, Haunted Mansion, the Matterhorn Bobsleds, and Splash Mountain—early or during parades. The lines move faster then.

❤ During the busy afternoon hours, go to the lower-key attractions, where the wait times are comparatively shorter; Tarzan's Treehouse is always a good choice. The afternoon is also prime time for shopping, enjoying outdoor musical performances, taking in a show at the Golden Horseshoe Stage, or watching the Flag Retreat on Main Street, U.S.A.

❤ Shops are a good place to escape the midday heat, but steer clear of them in late afternoon and at the end of the park's operating hours, when they tend to be the most crowded.

❤ For most attractions, if you're in line even one minute before the park closes, you'll be allowed on. It's a great tactic for Splash Mountain and the Indiana Jones Adventure.

❤ Avoid the crowds by returning your stroller before the evening's fireworks presentation comes to an end.

Disney California Adventure

Fame, fortune, and fun in the sun have lured adventurous spirits to California for centuries. But now visitors have an alternative way to enjoy the glories of the Golden State: through Disney's eyes. In February 2001, the company officially unveiled its California Adventure theme park—and it was a work-in-progress for quite some time. To that end, an amazing, billion-dollar expansion is complete. New themes and attractions have joined the landscape, while some veteran rides have been "re-imagined," and new attractions are constantly on the horizon. The result? An adventure to excite even the most devoted Disneyland Park devotees.

Disney California Adventure sits snugly in the heart of the Disneyland Resort, sharing an entrance esplanade with Disneyland, neighboring Downtown Disney District, and the Disney hotels. But once you set foot inside the park, you're in a world all its own. Districts blend into each other, and no matter where you stand, you're sure to see (or hear whoops and hollers coming from) one of the park's icons—the spooky-but-spectacular Twilight Zone™ Tower of Terror, the sierra-inspired Grizzly Peak mountain, Paradise Pier's coaster, California Screamin,' and the recent addition and instant classic, Radiator Springs Racers.

With a small vineyard, upscale restaurants, scream-inducing thrill rides, and attractions tailored for tots, the 66-acre theme park finally has something for everyone to enjoy. California, here we come!

DISNEY CALIFORNIA ADVENTURE

HOLLYWOOD LAND

1. Disney Animation
2. The Twilight Zone™ Tower of Terror
3. Frozen—Live at the Hyperion
4. Mad T Party

5. Monsters, Inc.— Mike and Sulley to the Rescue!
6. Disney Junior— Live on Stage!

A BUG'S LAND

7. It's Tough to be a Bug!
8. Flik's Fun Fair

GRIZZLY PEAK AIRFIELD

9. Soarin' Around the World

GRIZZLY PEAK

10. Grizzly River Run
11. Redwood Creek Challenge Trail

PARADISE PIER

12. The Little Mermaid— Ariel's Undersea Adventure
13. California Screamin'
14. Golden Zephyr
15. Jumpin' Jellyfish
16. Goofy's Sky School
17. Silly Symphony Swings
18. Mickey's Fun Wheel
19. Toy Story Midway Mania!
20. King Triton's Carousel
21. World of Color

CARS LAND

22. Luigi's Rollickin' Roadsters
23. Mater's Junkyard Jamboree
24. Radiator Springs Racers

94

Getting Oriented

Disney California Adventure is smaller than Disneyland Park, so guests should have no trouble covering all of it on foot—as long as they wear comfortable walking shoes.

The entrance area is known as Buena Vista Street. Several districts compose the rest of the park. East of Buena Vista Street lies Hollywood Land. It's a mock studio backlot where guests can, among other things, meet Anna and Elsa (and see them in a new *Frozen* stage show), and enjoy a lighthearted attraction known as Monsters, Inc.—Mike and Sulley to the Rescue!

West of Buena Vista Street is Grizzly Peak Airfield, home of the re-imagined Soarin' attraction. Pacific Wharf is a district dedicated to the cultures, industries, and natural beauty that shaped California, complete with a winery. The adjacent Grizzly Peak features a white-water rapids attraction known as Grizzly River Run.

The Paradise Pier neighborhood has nostalgic rides with a modern twist, located around a lagoon. (This is the place to race to first thing in the morning if you want to minimize the wait for Toy Story Midway Mania!) The World of Color light show takes place right on the lagoon.

A Bug's Land is something of a mini-park within a park—designed for mini park guests. Finally, the immersive Cars Land offers guests the opportunity to experience all the thrills of Radiator Springs. Don't miss Mater's Junkyard Jamboree, Luigi's Rollickin' Roadsters, and the park's ever-popular Radiator Springs Racers.

Guests park in either the six-level Mickey & Friends parking structure or the Toy Story lot on Harbor Boulevard, which can be accessed from the I-5 freeway.

> ## HOT TIP!
> World of Color Fastpasses operate independently of the rest of the park's Fastpass system. You can get a W.O.C. Fastpass even if you have an assignment pending for another attraction.

Parking Fees: Guests arriving in passenger vehicles pay about $18 to park. (The fee for vans and buses is $23; for trucks and buses with extended trailers, $28.) You may leave the lot during the day and return later the same day at no extra fee. Just hold on to your parking stub as proof of earlier payment.

Lost Cars: Even if you take careful note of where you parked your car, you might have trouble remembering or recognizing the exact spot when you return hours later. Hundreds more vehicles will likely be parked around yours. If this happens, tell a cast member approximately when you arrived. With that info, parking lot personnel can usually figure out the car's general location, and someone will then comb the lanes for it on a scooter.

> ## HOT TIP!
> Radiator Springs Racers is still one of the hottest tickets in town—get a Fastpass as early as possible. They are distributed near the entrance to A Bug's Land.

GETTING AROUND

You'll have to depend a lot on your feet—other than the Red Car Trolley ride, there's no transportation in this park.

Guests staying at Disney's Grand Californian hotel have their own private entry into Disney California Adventure park. (Guests with valid hotel ID may use the turnstiles near Grizzly River Run. This entrance may be used by guests staying at the Disneyland Hotel and Disney's Paradise Pier Hotel, too.) All other visitors enter and exit the park through the main entrance, across the esplanade from Disneyland's gate. From here, trams and shuttles transport guests to the resort parking areas. Since the area is pedestrian-friendly, guests may opt to walk from the park along the esplanade to the hotels and the Downtown Disney part of the property.

Park Primer

DISNEY CALIFORNIA ADVENTURE

BABY FACILITIES

Changing tables, baby-care products, and facilities for nursing can be found at the park's Baby Care Center.

DISABILITY INFORMATION

Many park attractions and nearly all shops and restaurants are accessible to guests using wheelchairs. Services are also available for those with visual or hearing disabilities. Ask about these services at Guest Relations.

FIRST AID

Minor medical problems are handled at the First Aid Center, by the park's main entrance.

GUIDED TOUR

The *Disney California Story* tour takes place at Disney California Adventure and explores the history of the Golden State as it inspired a young Walt Disney. The *Welcome to Disneyland* tour includes visits to Disneyland Park and Disney California Adventure. (See page 21.) To book a tour, call 714-781-TOUR (8687), or stop by the Chamber of Commerce.

HOURS

Disney California Adventure is generally open from 10 A.M. to 8 P.M. Monday–Thursday, and 10 A.M. to 9 P.M. Friday, Saturday, and Sunday. For the exact times during your visit, go to *www.disneyland.com* or call 714-781-4636.

INFORMATION

The Chamber of Commerce (aka Guest Relations/Visitor's Center), located near the park's main entrance, is equipped with guide-maps, Entertainment Times Guides, and a helpful staff. Maps and Times Guides are also available at many park shops. The Information Kiosk, in Carthay Circle Plaza, is an excellent resource for attraction wait times and show schedules. Information is updated every hour.

SAME-DAY RE-ENTRY

Guests using one-day passes must get a hand-stamp as they exit the park and retain their tickets to return to the park later the same day. Multi-day-ticket and Annual Passholders will have their photo taken upon entry, so a hand-stamp is not necessary.

LOST & FOUND

The Disneyland Resort's Lost & Found is on the left side of the Disneyland Park entrance. Report lost items there. If you find an item, kindly present it to the nearest cast member (a park worker wearing a name tag).

LOCKERS

Lockers, available for unlimited use during the day, are near the park's main entrance. Fees range from $7 to $15 per day, depending on size.

LOST CHILDREN

Report lost children at the Baby Care Center, or alert the closest employee to the problem.

MONEY MATTERS

There are ATMs in the park. Currency may be exchanged at Guest Relations (aka The Chamber of Commerce). Cash, credit cards, traveler's checks, Disney gift cards, and Disney Dollars are accepted for most purchases.

STROLLERS & WHEELCHAIRS

Strollers, wheelchairs, and Electric Conveyance Vehicles (ECVs) can be rented outside the main entrance to Disneyland Park. If you need a replacement, just present a receipt.

PARK RULES

To ensure a comfortable, safe and enjoyable experience for all guests, visitors are asked to comply with all Park rules, signs, and instructions including:
- All bags are subject to inspection.
- Guests are subject to screening via wand and/or metal detector.
- Proper attire is required.
- Smoking is allowed in designated areas only.
- Selfie sticks are not permitted in Disney parks.
- Weapons (including toys) are prohibited.

For additional details and a complete listing of Disney Park Rules, visit Guest Relations or go to *www.disneyland.com/ParkRules*.

SECURITY CHECK

All guests entering Disney parks are subject to a thorough security check, including a metal detector screening. Backpacks, parcels, purses, etc., will be searched by security personnel before guests may pass through the entrance.

Buena Vista Street

When a young Walt Disney took the train from Kansas City to Los Angeles in 1923, he discovered a bustling metropolis teeming with pedestrian boulevards, shops, restaurants, and shiny red trolley cars. Buena Vista Street, the new entrance to the park, sends guests back to this era—to an idealized version of a city beaming with optimism and opportunity.

Follow festive Buena Vista Street, which begins inside the turnstiles, to the Carthay Circle Restaurant—a replica of the theater where *Snow White and the Seven Dwarfs* premiered in 1937. (This version of the Carthay Circle houses a popular restaurant. For details, see page 117.) Or enjoy a trip back in time by hopping aboard a trolley.

RED CAR TROLLEY: The Red Car Trolley system revives the gone-but-not-forgotten Pacific Electric Railway right here in Disney California Adventure. This jolly trolley transports guests between Buena Vista Street

and The Twilight Zone™ Tower of Terror by way of Hollywood Land. It's also the back-drop for an entertaining musical show courtesy of the Red Car News Boys (see page 108).

Hollywood Land

Lights! Camera! Action! The spotlight is on you in the glitzy Hollywood district of Disney California Adventure, where the action unfolds all around you. No movies are actually filmed here, so you'll have to keep waiting for your big break. You can think of this as the "Hollywood that never was and always will be."

Turn onto Hollywood Boulevard and enter into Disney's version of the legendary street. And it all fits neatly into a two-block strip. Some of Disney California Adventure's most popular attractions lie within this zone, including The Twilight Zone™ Tower of Terror, Turtle Talk with Crush, and a whole lot more.

In contrast to the starstruck Hollywood Boulevard, the backlot area peels away the sparkly facade and takes a backstage look at Hollywood without its makeup. Alongside soundstage buildings, behind-the-scenes support departments do their unseen, essential work: props are put into position, klieg lights are set to shine on the scene, and the crew is busy making sure every performer is on his or her mark before the director yells "Action!"

Ticket Prices

Although prices† will likely increase, the following should give you an idea of what you'll pay for tickets in 2017. For updates, call 714-781-4565, or visit *www.disneyland.com*.

	ADULTS	CHILDREN*
1-Day Ticket (1 park)	$95/105/119	$89/99/113
1-Day Ticket (hopper)	$155/160/169	$149/154/163
2-Day Ticket (hopper)	$235	$223
3-Day Ticket (hopper)**	$295	$283
4-Day Ticket (hopper)**	$320	$305
5-Day Ticket (hopper)**	$335	$320
2-Park Deluxe Annual Passport		$599
2-Park Signature Annual Passport		$849
2-Park Signature Plus Annual Passport		$1,049
Premier Annual Passport		$1,439

† One-day prices are quoted in Value/Regular/Peak order. For dates visit *www.disneyland.com*.
*3 through 9 years of age; children under 3 free
**Includes "Magic Morning" early park admission with select attractions on Tuesday, Thursday, or Saturday.
Note that there is a single price (for adults and children) for annual passports.

BIRNBAUM'S ★BEST★ MONSTERS, INC.—MIKE AND SULLEY TO THE RESCUE!: A monster's-eye spin through Monstropolis, this colorful, slow-moving attraction was inspired by the film *Monsters, Inc.* It invites guests to follow affable monsters Mike and Sulley as they valiantly attempt to deliver Boo safely back to her room—all the while dodging trucks, helicopters, and the occasional yellow-suited member of the Child Detection Agency.

DISNEY JUNIOR—LIVE ON STAGE!: Fans of Playhouse Disney—Live on Stage (the show that used to play here) should enjoy this production. It brings back audience favorites—*Mickey Mouse Clubhouse* and *Jake and the Never Land Pirates*—and introduces elements of Disney Junior's more recent favorites *Doc McStuffins* and *Sofia the First.* (Sofia, Disney's youngest regal, shows guests that a true princess is much more than pretty dresses and sparkling jewels.) Very young guests are the most enthusiastic members of the audience for this show.

The performance space holds large crowds (of mostly tiny people) at a time. There are just a handful of seats, but there's plenty of room to sprawl out on the carpeted floor.

This show is presented daily. The park's Entertainment Times Guide lists the schedule.

BIRNBAUM'S ★BEST★ DISNEY ANIMATION: When you look around at all the attractions, themed hotels, and dozens of familiar animated faces that Disney has become famous for, it's almost impossible to remember it all started with a simple sketch of a mouse. This behind-the-scenes exploration invites guests to step into Disney's wonderful world of animation. Here visitors are given an insider's look at the process, the heritage, and, above all, the artistry of this world-renowned art form, along with a possible preview of an animated feature that is currently in progress.

Animation Courtyard: This central area makes visitors feel as if they are stepping into an animated film. Sketches and artwork from Disney and Pixar film classics are projected onto giant screens that circle the colorful atrium as familiar tunes fill the air. From this hub, guests may progress to several interactive animation attractions.

Anna & Elsa's Royal Welcome: 🅕🅟 The royal sisters welcome visitors in the Disney Animation building in Hollywood Land. The colorful experience pays tribute to Arendelle and the revered characters from the beloved animated feature *Frozen.*

Anna and Elsa are popular, to say the least. Expect very long waits to meet the regal duo. We highly recommend getting a Fastpass for this meet-and-greet experience. They run out early, so get one as early as possible. And don't forget your camera.

Animation Academy: Inspired by the animation art in the courtyard, this attraction lets guests take a crack at drawing their favorite Disney characters. Do you want to draw a snowman? With step-by-step guidance provided by a Disney animator, you will use basic shapes and simple techniques to create your own Olaf sketch, suitable for framing.

Sorcerer's Workshop: Budding animators and artists particularly get a kick out of these three rooms. They are built around interactive exhibits featuring animation special effects. At Enchanted Books, for example, you can take a personality survey (hosted by *Beauty and the Beast*'s Lumiere and Cogsworth) to determine to which Disney character or villain you are most similar.

Turtle Talk with Crush: If ever there were an attraction that left guests smiling and asking, "How do they do that?!"—this is it. The concept is simple enough: a 10-minute, animated show featuring the surfer-dude sea turtle from *Finding Nemo.* The amazing part? The cartoon critter actually interacts with the audience. In doing so, he imparts turtle-y wisdom, answers questions, and cracks more than a few jokes. Dory and friends may join in the fun. You have to see it to believe it. To do that, you'll have to wait—the show is popular with guests of all ages. It so totally rocks, dude.

🅕🅟 = Fastpass attraction (see page 58)

FROZEN—LIVE AT THE HYPERION:
The Hyperion Theater is home to a rousing new musical show inspired by the animated blockbuster hit *Frozen*. This dynamic production features all your favorites from the film, including Anna, Elsa, Olaf, Kristoff, and Sven. The peppy production premiered in 2016. The fanciful re-telling of the *Frozen* tale is presented several times a day.

Note: Check a Times Guide for the performance schedule, and plan to arrive early.

Did You Know?
The "Hyperion" name has a special Disney heritage. The Walt Disney Studios moved to 2719 Hyperion Street, Los Angeles, in 1926. It was there that Mickey Mouse was born. In 1940, Walt moved his studios to a bigger lot in Burbank, but he took some of the original Hyperion buildings with him.

BIRNBAUM'S ★BEST★ THE TWILIGHT ZONE™ TOWER OF TERROR: FP
The Hollywood Tower Hotel houses a creepy-yet-thrilling ride. On the facade of the ominous 199-foot-tall building hangs a sparking electric sign. As the legend goes, lightning struck the building on Halloween night in 1939. An entire guest wing disappeared, along with an elevator carrying five guests.

The line for the popular ride runs through the hotel lobby, where dusty furniture, cobwebs, and old newspapers add to the eerie atmosphere. As guests enter the library, they see a dark TV set suddenly brought to life by a bolt of lightning. Rod Serling invites them to enter The Twilight Zone.

Guests are led toward the boiler room to enter the ride elevator. (This is your chance to change your mind about riding. Simply ask the attendant to direct you toward the "chicken exit.") Once you take a seat, the doors close and the room begins its ascent. At the first stop, the doors open and guests have a view down a corridor. Among the effects is a ghostly visit by the hotel guests who vanished. The doors close again and you continue your trip skyward.

At the next stop, you enter another dimension, a combination of sights and sounds reminiscent of *The Twilight Zone*™ TV series. In fact, Disney Imagineers watched each of the 156 original *Twilight Zone* episodes at least twice for inspiration. This part of the ride is rather suspenseful, as you can't quite tell when you're going to take the plunge. What happens next depends entirely upon the whim of Disney Imagineers, who have programmed the ride so that the drop sequence can change.

PHOTO BY JILL SAFRO

At press time, the elevator was taking an immediate plunge (of about eight stories) before shooting up to the 13th floor. At the top (about 157 feet up), passengers can look out at the park below. Once the doors shut, you plummet 13 stories. The drop lasts about two seconds, but it seems a whole lot longer.

Just when you think it's over, the elevator launches skyward, barely stopping before it plunges again. And again. From the time you are seated, the trip takes about 5 minutes.

Note: You must be at least 40 inches tall to ride the Twilight Zone Tower of Terror. It is not recommended for pregnant women, or people with heart conditions, back and neck problems, or other medical issues. Though thrilling (and rather scary), the drops are surprisingly smooth. Still, if you are susceptible to motion sickness, skip this one. Details about this attraction may change in 2017. For updates, visit *www.disneyland.com*.

Grizzly Peak Airfield

Inspired by California's aviation history, this airfield and its display area pay tribute to famous flyers and their precious planes. A huge aircraft hangar, the focus of this site, houses the wildly popular Soarin' attraction.

BIRNBAUM'S ·BEST· **SOARIN' AROUND THE WORLD:** Up, up, and away! On this smooth, high-flying attraction, you'll be suspended in a hang glider 45 feet in the air, above a giant IMAX projection dome, and treated to an aerial tour of some of the most awe-inspiring landscapes the world has to offer. Wait? Soarin' has been here since 2005. Why the "new" stamp? Well, the beloved Soarin' experience is still here in all of its glory—but instead of hovering over one state (California), the new version treats park-goers to a broader tour. The updated experience touched down in summer of 2016.

Soarin' Around the World showcases some of the world's most glorious sights. With the wind in your hair and your legs dangling in the breeze, the hang glider feels so convincingly real that you may even be tempted to pull up your feet for fear of tapping treetops or buildings below.

In all, the airborne trip takes about five minutes and employs synchronized wind currents, scent machines, and a musical score set to a film that wraps 180 degrees around you, making this a thoroughly enveloping experience. A DCA original, there is now a version of this attraction in several Disney theme parks around the world. The re-imagined version of this attraction, which features an all-new digital screen and projection system, is a hit with all ages. Get a Fastpass if you can.

Note: You must be 40 inches tall and free of back problems, heart conditions, motion sickness, and any other physical limitations to ride. If you are afraid of heights, you should definitely skip this one.

Grizzly Peak

The centerpiece of the Grizzly Peak recreation area (which includes the Airfield) is the grizzly bear-shaped mountain peak that juts 110 feet above the park floor. The eight-acre mini wilderness surrounding the Grizzly Peak mountain pays tribute to California's grandeur and natural beauty.

FP = Fastpass attraction (see page 58)

GRIZZLY RIVER RUN:  Disney legend says that Grizzly Peak was once chock-full of gold—which made it a magnet for miners in search of riches, as is evidenced by the mining relics scattered about the mountain. But the gold rush has come and gone, and the peak has since been taken over by another enterprising group—the Grizzly Peak Rafting Company. They converted the area into a rafting expedition known as Grizzly River Run.

> ### HOT TIP!
> Don't bring cameras or other valuables that must stay dry on Grizzly River Run. They will get drenched! Leave them with a non-riding member of your party or in a nearby (free) short-term locker.

Each round raft whisks eight passengers on a drenching tour of Grizzly Peak. The trip begins with a 45-foot climb, and it's all gloriously downhill from there. Fast-moving currents send adventurers spinning and splashing along the river, bumping off boulders and rushing through an erupting geyser field. Because the raft is constantly spinning as it moves through the water, each rider's experience is slightly different, but one thing's for sure—everyone gets wet. During the expedition, rafters encounter two major drops. It's the 21-foot drop that earns Grizzly River the distinction of being the world's tallest, fastest raft ride.

Note: Passengers must be free of back and neck problems, heart conditions, motion sickness, and other physical limitations to ride. Pregnant women, guests not meeting the 42-inch height requirement, and children under age 3 will not be permitted to board. Finally, if you wish to stay dry, skip this ride.

REDWOOD CREEK CHALLENGE TRAIL: Russell and Dug, from the animated feature *Up*, want to help you earn Wilderness Explorer badges while navigating forested paths, climbing rocks, swinging on rope bridges, and zipping down slides. Russell has left hints throughout the trail to help guests get those badges. Think you're up to the challenge? Lace up your sneakers and give it a try!

Of course, even the most intrepid explorers need directions. Fortunately, there are maps available at the trail's entrance—just ask a park ranger. After consulting the detailed map, you can start the quest to earn badges in

tracking, bravery, rock climbing, wolf howling, animal spirit, and puzzle solving.

Afterward, head to the Ahwahnee Camp Circle for a special ceremony with Russell. Wilderness Explorer ceremonies take place throughout the day. For showtimes, check an Entertainment Times Guide. Need a hand to assist you through the course? Just whistle for one of the workers outfitted in ranger gear. She or he will be happy to help.

Pacific Wharf

Inspired by Monterey, California's Cannery Row, this industrial waterfront salutes the cultures, products, and industries that make California so international in nature. Guests can tour a working bakery and watch local products, such as fresh-baked San Francisco sourdough bread, being prepared. There are also many tables scattered about, making this a good place to stop and enjoy a rest or a snack.

THE BAKERY TOUR: Soft sourdough bread is featured at this working bakery. While baking tips are shared in the walk-through corridor tour, the famous Boudin-family recipe remains a well-kept secret.

> ### HOT TIP!
> Little ones love to romp in the splash zone near Flik's Flyers and under the giant, leaky hose across from Francis' Ladybug Boogie. Swim diapers are an absolute must for the area known as Princess Dot Puddle Park.

A Bug's Land

FLIK'S FUN FAIR: Guests of all ages are invited, but this area caters to the wee ones. Who better to enjoy the experience of seeing the world from the vantage point of a bug?

Somewhat of a park within a park, Flik's Fun Fair boasts a total of four honest-to-goodness, kid-pleasing attractions, plus a splash zone for tots—all of them ostensibly built by a bug:

Flik's Flyers is a hot-air "balloon" ride that Flik cleverly crafted with (giant) leaves, twigs, and old food containers. This ride is big with fans of Disneyland's Dumbo the Flying Elephant (the line here is usually shorter). The ride lasts about a minute and a half.

PHOTO BY JILL SAFRO

Francis' Ladybug Boogie: Stop here to spin yourself silly. The Francis vehicles "boogie" for about 90 seconds per ride. It's good for guests of all ages—provided they didn't just enjoy a big snack. Spinning on a full stomach is a no-no!

Heimlich's Chew Chew Train: A simple railroad ride, here Heimlich treats guests to a 2-minute gustatory sojourn—all the while clutching his precious piece of candy corn.

Princess Dot Puddle Park is a micro-water park themed around a giant lawn sprinkler. Tots must wear swim diapers here.

Tuck and Roll's Drive 'Em Buggies is an old-fashioned bumper car experience, courtesy of everyone's favorite Hungarian pill bugs. Guests must be at least 48 inches tall to drive and 42 inches tall to ride shotgun.

BIRNBAUM'S ★BEST★ IT'S TOUGH TO BE A BUG!: The underground Bug's Life Theater, just inside the entrance to A Bug's Land, features an eight-minute, animated 3-D movie augmented by some surprising "4-D" effects. The stars of the show are the world's most abundant inhabitants— insects. They creep, crawl, and demonstrate why, someday, they just might inherit the earth. It's a bug's-eye view of the trials and tribulations of their multi-legged world.

As guests enter the dark auditorium, the orchestra is warming up amid the chirps of crickets. When Flik, the emcee (and star of *A Bug's Life*), makes his first appearance, he dubs audience members honorary bugs and instructs them to don their "bug eyes" (or 3-D glasses). Then our oh-so-mild-mannered hero introduces some of his not-so-mild-mannered pals, including a Chilean tarantula, a duo of dung beetles, and "the silent but deadly member of the bug world"—the stinkbug. Hopper, Flik's nemesis and the leader of the evil grasshopper pack, crashes the show and adds to the antics. What follows is a manic, often hilarious, not-to-be-missed revue.

Note: The combination of intense special effects and frequent darkness tends to frighten toddlers and young children. In addition, anyone leery of spiders, roaches, and their ilk is advised to skip the performance, or risk being seriously bugged.

Cars Land

Ladies and gentlemen, start your engines—a real-life Radiator Springs has sprung up in the area between A Bug's Land and Paradise Pier. This 12-acre *Cars*-themed town invites guests to enjoy the following attractions:

LUIGI'S ROLLICKIN' ROADSTERS: Luigi's Flying Tires has, well, flown away. But Luigi fans, fear not! The mechanically inclined Radiator Springs resident has a brand-new, fun-filled (or is that fun-fueled?) experience for guests to enjoy. The attraction, which sits behind Luigi's Casa Della Tires, takes guests for a wild ride as Luigi's cousins demonstrate dances from their native Italy. It's a "wheel" hoot!

MATER'S JUNKYARD JAMBOREE: This attraction is a tractor-pulling dance party hosted by everyone's favorite tow truck. As baby tractors pull the junkyard cart (with you in it), the cart gets whirled and twirled in time to tunes pumped through Mater's junkyard jukebox. To ride, guests must be at least 32 inches tall. Don't ride on a full stomach.

BIRNBAUM'S BEST RADIATOR SPRINGS RACERS: FP Fasten your seat belts—this bona fide "E-Ticket" attraction will set your heart racing as you compete with other speed seekers. Using technology similar to that of Epcot's beloved Test Track attraction, Imagineers have devised a thrilling experience for guests: a high-speed tour of Ornament Valley, featuring hairpin turns, steep banks, and a head-to-head race to the finish. Sally, Luigi, Guido, Ramone, and other *Cars* friends zoom around this revved-up racetrack.

Note: Guests must be at least 40 inches tall and without health conditions. Expectant mothers must skip this race.

Paradise Pier

It's all about fun in the sun at Paradise Pier, a throwback to California seaside boardwalks of yesteryear. Like most classic amusement zones, the rides here offer simple thrills of speed and weightlessness—but don't let the nostalgic look fool you: The technology is quite current.

At night, the district undergoes a dazzling transformation. Thousands of tiny lights illuminate the rides and building facades, creating a magical display—especially as you soar past them on one of Paradise Pier's most thrilling attractions.

BIRNBAUM'S BEST CALIFORNIA SCREAMIN': FP Like many classic boardwalks, the centerpiece of Paradise Pier is a gleaming roller coaster. A steel coaster, California Screamin' is designed to look (and sound) like an old-fashioned wooden coaster, but the thrills are as modern as they get. The

ride starts at lagoon level, where the long car bursts up the track as if catapulted up by a crashing wave. The car goes from zero to 55 miles per hour in 4.7 seconds—before reaching the first hill. Several long drops are combined with an upside-down loop, plus a blasting soundtrack. The result is the longest and fastest coaster in the Disneyland Resort.

Along the way, vehicles travel through blue "scream" tubes that trap guests' yells as they test their vocal cords on the big drops, magnifying the hoots and hollers and adding to the excitement. Every time you approach a tube, you know you're in for a big thrill, so brace yourself and prepare to scream!

Daredevils should be sure to enjoy this ride after the sun goes down, when the night sky is speckled with the pier's glowing lights, and the topsy-turvy twists and turns on the roller coaster will prove even more disorientingly exciting—and scary!

Note: Passengers must be at least 48 inches tall and free of back problems, neck problems, heart conditions, motion sickness, pregnancy, and other physical limitations to ride.

HOT TIP!

A few Mickey's Fun Wheel cars remain fixed on the edge as the wheel spins. Request to sit in one of these if you'd prefer to take a more tranquil trip. They are easy to identify—just look for the cars that are marked with an image of Mickey Mouse. (Swinging gondolas are emblazoned with Minnie, Goofy, Pluto, and Donald Duck.)

MICKEY'S FUN WHEEL: A modern loop-de-loop, this gleaming Ferris wheel, centered by a huge Mickey face, takes guests on a head-spinning trip. If you think this is a run-of-the-mill Ferris wheel, you're in for quite a surprise: While the wheel turns, most of its cabins rotate in and out along the interior edges of the wheel's giant frame—which creates a dizzying effect. At 150 feet, this is one of the park's tallest attractions, and while it may wreak havoc on sensitive stomachs, thrill seekers rave over its ride within a ride. FYI: This attraction used to be called the Sun Wheel.

Note: Passengers must be free of back problems, heart conditions, motion sickness, and other physical limitations to ride. Afraid of heights? Better skip this one!

SILLY SYMPHONY SWINGS: This attraction pays tribute to some of Walt Disney's earliest animated triumphs—the *Silly Symphonies*. The specific symphony highlighted here is the 1935 cartoon called *The Band Concert*. Riders take flight in swings, while Mickey and his barnyard band serenade them with a rousing rendition of the *William Tell Overture*.

As the attraction's momentum picks up, a cyclone reveals itself as guests swirl higher and higher. Skip it if you fear heights.

Note: Riders must meet the Silly Symphony Swings height requirement of 48 inches to ride solo. (Guests between 40 and 48 inches may ride in a double swing. Those under 40 inches are not permitted to take this flight.) All guests must be free of back problems, heart conditions, motion sickness, and other physical limitations to swing here.

GOOFY'S SKY SCHOOL: FP At this mini roller coaster attraction, guests of most sizes climb into crop dusters and follow the same fluky flight path taken by the Goof himself. The planes zip through the farm and crash through a barn, causing quite a ruckus among the chickens. Don't let the size fool you. This roller coaster proves that big thrills come in small packages. Although guests as young as three are allowed to ride, it may be too turbulent for some guests.

Note: Although it's small as roller coasters go, the ride's sudden stops and herky-jerky motion during turns may prove too scary for riders not used to more strenuous coasters. Riders must be at least 42 inches tall and free of back problems, neck problems, heart conditions, motion sickness, and any other physical limitations to take this jolting ride.

PHOTO BY JILL SAFRO

JUMPIN' JELLYFISH: A dense kelp bed tops this sea-themed attraction, from which riders sitting in brightly colored jellyfish seats are lifted straight up in the air. When you reach the top, hang on to your tentacles! A parachute unfolds, and fish and friends float safely back down to the ground. While the trip is a rather gentle one with special appeal for younger riders, it might take a few minutes for guests with the most sensitive of stomachs to get their land legs back.

Note: All guests must be at least 40 inches tall and free of back problems, heart conditions, motion sickness, and any other physical limitations to ride.

THE LITTLE MERMAID—ARIEL'S UNDERSEA ADVENTURE: In the first attraction ever to feature everyone's favorite Disney mermaid, guests are invited to board (continuously moving) clam-mobiles and embark on a jolly journey above and below sea level. Along the way, they join Ariel, Flounder, and all of their aquatic acquaintances, and enjoy major musical moments and pivotal plot points from the classic animated feature. It's fun for the whole family.

GOLDEN ZEPHYR: Disney Imagineers took the rocket ride to new heights with the launch of Astro Orbitor in Disneyland. But long before those space-age ships took off, riders were taking flights in rocket-shaped swings on boardwalks and amusement piers across America. Disney pays homage to those old-fashioned attractions with rocket ships that take guests for a spin beneath the Golden Zephyr tower. As speed picks up, the rockets lift into the air and fly over the lagoon several times before touching down for a landing. The ride lasts about a minute and a half.

Note: All passengers must be free of back, neck, and heart problems, motion sickness, and other physical limitations to ride. This attraction does not run when it's windy. There is no height requirement, but youngsters must be able to ride without assistance. Afraid of heights? Sit this one out. Trust us.

GAMES OF THE BOARDWALK: The games of skill and chance that make up Paradise Pier's Midway are themed with Disney and Pixar characters. Guests can try their hand at amusements like Goofy About Fishin' (magnetic fishing game), Dumbo's Bucket Brigade (water squirting contest), Casey at the Bat (baseball toss), and Bullseye Stallion Stampede (wooden ball-propelled horse race).

Note: To play the games, you must buy a special Playcard with prepaid credits (the games do not accept cash). Playcard machines are located nearby, and the cards can be recharged with additional credits.

KING TRITON'S CAROUSEL: Take a spin on one of California's native aquatic creatures on this colorful merry-go-round, located on the boardwalk. The deep-sea theme is carried out in aquatic detail right down to the ride vehicles themselves. The only horses you'll find here are golden sea horses. They're joined by dolphins, sea otters, seals, and fish, which move to classic organ tunes as the elegant carousel revolves. Be sure to notice all of the fish and marine mammals as they float by—each one was hand-carved, and no two of the creatures are exactly alike.

BIRNBAUM'S ★BEST★ TOY STORY MIDWAY MANIA!: This beloved attraction is an energetic, interactive toybox tour with a twist: Guests wear 3-D glasses as they take aim at animated targets with spring-action shooters. The adventure is about as high-tech as they come, yet rooted in classic Midway games of skill. As points are scored, expect effusive encouragement from a colorful cast of cheerleaders—Toy Story's Woody, Buzz, Hamm, Rex the Dinosaur, and, of course, the Little Green Men.

Fans of Disneyland's Buzz Lightyear Astro Blasters will no doubt delight in this adventure, which takes the experience of the interactive attraction into a whole new dimension. As far as skill level goes, there's something for everyone—from beginners to seasoned gamers alike. (Most folks up their score with a little practice.)

Toy Story Midway Mania! is a popular destination with guests of all ages—make a beeline for it when the park first opens. You'll be glad you did!

Shopping

Buena Vista Street

ATWATER INK AND PAINT: Shoppers enjoy the quaint ambiance of a 1930s Hollywood-style market house as they peruse decorative items for the home, seasonal merchandise, kitchen gadgets, towels, dinnerware, and more.

BIG TOP TOYS: Teeming with toys, Big Top sells innovative and interactive toys and games, plus plush character merchandise. You may also find items inspired by theme park attractions, such as the Red Car Trolley.

ELIAS & CO.: Paying tribute to the opulent Art Deco–style buildings of yesteryear, this sprawling emporium features an array of fashion finery for the whole family—it rivals Disneyland Park's Emporium shop in size. It stocks clothing (hats, shirts, shoes, jackets, and more), snacks, accessories, watches, and hats. FYI: Elias was Walt's middle name and his dad's first name.

JULIUS KATZ & SONS: With its vast array of pins, this trading destination is a hot spot for collectors. The shop's name was inspired by Julius the Cat, a featured character in Walt Disney's classic *Alice in Cartoonland* shorts.

KINGSWELL CAMERA: Stop here to view and purchase photos taken by Disney's PhotoPass team of roving photographers. You'll also find memory cards, cameras, batteries, film, photo albums, and other camera-related souvenirs. The shop's name comes from Walt Disney's first California address. When he arrived in Los Angeles in 1923, he rented a room from his Uncle Robert on Kingswell Avenue. It's where the Walt Disney Company was born.

LOS FELIZ FIVE & DIME: In addition to the park attraction- and California-themed clothing and souvenirs, there is a selection of Disney character items. It's possible to have some items personalized (for a fee).

OSWALD'S: Stop here for autograph books, hats, bags, and souvenirs themed to the park, Cars Land, and Oswald the Lucky Rabbit. Note that it is often possible to meet Oswald just across the street from this shop.

TROLLEY TREATS: If the thoughts of "mountains of candy" and "rivers of fudge" make you smile, this is the shop for you. Temptations include caramel apples, toffee, chocolate-dipped strawberries, fudge, and seasonal selections such as house-made marshmallows. Choose from packaged candy or items made fresh in the display kitchen. It's fun to watch the candy makers at work—and it's even more satisfying to gobble up their creations.

Hollywood Land

GONE HOLLYWOOD: A glamorous, larger-than-life boutique, Gone Hollywood celebrates the shopping styles of Hollywood's rich and famous. Here you will find apparel and accessories—most with a Disney twist.

PHOTO BY MIKE CARROLL

OFF THE PAGE: The magic of Disney animation leaps off the page at this shop that showcases collectible Disneyana pieces. Cels, limited-edition prints, books, and figurines are sold here, as are attraction-inspired items. Guests may interact with artists as they sketch classic Disney characters.

TOWER HOTEL GIFTS: The exit lobby of the Twilight Zone Tower of Terror does double duty as a gift shop. The store sells souvenirs themed to the attraction (pins, shirts, hats, etc.), plus Tower Hotel items such as robes and bellhop bells. This is also the place to buy the photo taken on the attraction. The shot is snapped just before the big drop, so that look of horror is captured forever!

WANDERING OAKEN'S TRADING POST: This open-air shop specializes in cool items with a *Frozen* theme. Look for Anna and Elsa dolls, plush Olafs and Svens, shirts, hats, costumes, toys, snacks, and more. It's across from Monsters, Inc.—Mike and Sulley to the Rescue!

Grizzly Peak Airfield

HUMPHREY'S SERVICE & SUPPLIES: When you see the large selection here, you know this is a "beary" serious shopping spot. The grizzly-inspired merchandise includes hats, souvenirs, toys, pins, items with a Soarin' theme, and glow merchandise. This souvenir shop is across from the park's re-imagined Soarin' Around the World attraction.

Grizzly Peak

EMBARCADERO GIFTS: The mementos here are themed to nearby Ariel's Undersea Adventure attraction. Look for shirts, pins, mugs, books, and assorted playthings.

RUSHIN' RIVER OUTFITTERS: This outpost is the perfect place to gear up for an outdoor adventure. Expect to find a variety of Rushin' River apparel, headwear, towels, ponchos, plus plush toys and more.

Cars Land

RADIATOR SPRINGS CURIOS: Hit the brakes and make a quick stop at this country-style mercantile. You may be tempted to fill the trunk with the latest park logo merchandise, *Cars*-themed paraphernalia, and other accessories. There is also a substantial supply of collector pins.

RAMONE'S HOUSE OF BODY ART: Ramone stocks all manner of items with a *Cars* theme (hey, this *is* Cars Land). There are T-shirts, hats, and Radiator Springs merchandise.

SARGE'S SURPLUS HUT: Young (and young-at-heart) racers, rejoice: Sarge has a super supply of clothes and toys that were designed with you in mind. Among the wares are costumes, hats, toys, and snacks. For many *Cars* fans, it's well worth making the pit stop—even if it's just to browse.

Paradise Pier

MIDWAY MERCANTILE: This small spot features toys, games, and other merchandise inspired by characters from Toy Story films.

POINT MUGU TATTOO: Merchandise with a World of Color theme (see page 108) is the stock-in-trade at this shop. Point Mugu has apparel and accessories with a California vibe. Oddly enough, there are no tattoos for sale here. Though you can get your face painted on the boardwalk (for a fee).

SEASIDE SOUVENIRS: An open-air souvenir stand, Seaside offers character merchandise, hats, glow items, and more.

SIDESHOW SHIRTS: The spotlight here is on shirts of all sorts—tanks, tees, and sweatshirts representing Disney attractions, characters, and films. To complete the look, hats with similar logos are also available for purchase.

PHOTO BY JILL SAFRO

TREASURES IN PARADISE: Treasure awaits little princesses at this seaside location. The shop stocks princess-inspired costumes, apparel, and accessories. Other treasures include *Phineas & Ferb* T-shirts and hats, Mouse ears, watches, jewelry, and candy. This is also the place to pick up Duffy the Disney Bear and Duffy-themed souvenirs. There is a Duffy meet-and-greet location near the entrance.

HOT TIP!

Still haven't quenched your thirst for shopping? Head to the World of Disney in nearby Downtown Disney. It's teeming with Disney character merchandise and souvenirs. (And it's one of many spots to offer a discount to Annual Passholders.)

Entertainment

As Disney California Adventure evolves, new entertainment offerings emerge. For updates, go to *www.disneyland.com*. Check a park Times Guide for schedules.

FIVE & DIME: This singing group travels Buena Vista Street in their jalopy, hoping to get their big break in the music world.

MAD T PARTY: Journey down a glowing rabbit hole and enter a wonderland filled with lights, color, and music. Mad T Party is a vibrant nighttime dance party. It's offered seasonally.

OPERATION PLAYTIME: A rhythmic squad of *Toy Story*'s Green Army Men is on a mission to serve, protect, and entertain! The plastic platoon engages guests with games and percussive shenanigans.

PIXAR PLAY PARADE: This peppy, interactive processional features the colorful worlds of Disney•Pixar pals.

RED CAR NEWS BOYS: Mickey Mouse joins the fun as the boys hawk newspapers in this peppy musical show at Buena Vista Street's Red Car Trolley. They perform period tunes (and songs from Disney's *Newsies*).

RED TO THE RESCUE: Red the Fire Truck needs help watering the flowers and cleaning up Cars Land. Stop by to lend a hand. Just know that Red's firefighter buddy always has trouble with the hose. You might get spritzed.

BIRNBAUM'S ★**BEST**★ **WORLD OF COLOR:** ⓕ Arrive early and prepare to be dazzled. This 25-minute nighttime spectacular, presented on select evenings on Paradise Bay, is a kaleidoscopic journey of music, animation, water fountains, special effects, and, of course, brilliant color. The show is best viewed from the esplanade near The Little Mermaid: Ariel's Undersea Adventures attraction. Get a Fastpass if you can.

World of Color is intended for all audiences, but it does feature loud noises, fire, and other effects that may be too intense for some tykes. While not a drenching experience, guests closest to the water's edge will get spritzed by the fountains used in World of Color.

Hot Tips

❤ Disney characters (including Mickey Mouse) make appearances throughout the day. Check a park Times Guide for specifics.

❤ Take advantage of Disney's free, time-saving Fastpass system whenever possible.

❤ Check the Information Board often to get an idea of showtimes and crowds.

❤ Many attractions have height restrictions—measure the kids before you leave home.

❤ Golden Vine Winery offers wine tastings (for a fee).

❤ The line for Soarin' Around the World dwindles a bit by midday. Ride it then if you choose to forgo the Fastpass option (the experience is great any time of day).

❤ Shops on Buena Vista Street usually stay open a half hour after the park closes.

❤ On hot days, head to Grizzly River Run or Princess Dot Puddle Park. These splashy spots provide much-needed heat relief.

❤ The jarring motion of California Screamin' can wreak havoc on digital cameras. Store yours in a locker.

❤ Ready for a break from the park? Head to the Downtown Disney to shop or grab a quick bite to eat. There are more than a few (relatively) cost-efficient snacking spots to consider (i.e., Wetzel's Pretzels, Häagen-Dazs, Diggity Dogs, Napolini, Tortilla Jo's, Jamba Juice, and La Brea Bakery).

❤ Toy Story Midway Mania! has maniacally devoted fans. To minimize the time spent on line, set the alarm, get to the park before it opens, and head straight to this attraction after passing through the turnstile.

❤ Don't risk water-logging your valuables while riding Grizzly River Run. Take advantage of the complimentary lockers (located near the ride's exit). Each locker may be used for free for up to one hour.

Good Meals, Great Times

D ining at the Disneyland Resort is definitely an adventure—and not just in Adventureland. There's more to any meal in a theme park, Downtown Disney, or a Disneyland Resort hotel than just food. Disney friends such as Mickey, Minnie, Goofy, Tigger, Pooh, Chip and Dale, or Donald Duck might drop by your table to say hello. A colorful parade or a romantic paddle wheeler could drift by. Or you might find yourself surrounded by twinkling stars (in the middle of the day!) as you savor Cajun cooking in a peaceful bayou setting.

In this chapter, the Disneyland Resort restaurant section is divided by location (Disneyland Park, Disney California Adventure, the three Disney hotels, and Downtown Disney). Within the theme parks, eateries are arranged by area, and then by category—table service or fast-food and snack facilities, including food courts; individual eateries are alphabetized within each respective category.

If you're hankering for something to do after dinner, or you just need to take a break from the theme parks, you'll find plenty of suggestions at the end of the chapter. Downtown Disney, the property's dining and entertainment district, is party central. Or for a more relaxed atmosphere, chill out in a lounge at one of the Disneyland Resort hotels.

Dining
In Disneyland Park

One of the most popular foods in Disneyland is the burger, followed closely by ice cream and churros (sticks of deep-fried dough rolled in cinnamon and sugar). But healthy-minded eaters will be happy to find fish, salads, grilled chicken, and vegetable stew, plus fresh fruit and juices. Disneyland's table-service restaurants (the Blue Bayou, Cafe Orleans, River Belle Terrace, and the Carnation Cafe) provide full-course meals and lighter fare, plus a welcome break from long lines and the California sun.

Main Street, U.S.A.

TABLE SERVICE

CARNATION CAFE: On the west side of Main Street, near Town Square, this indoor/outdoor cafe is exceptionally pleasant, especially in springtime, when its planters are bursting with seasonal flowers. Stroll into the court-yard dining area filled with umbrella-shaded tables and surrounded by a cast-iron fence; from your table you'll hear the melodies from any passing parade. Breakfast choices include Mickey-shaped waffles; apple-granola pancakes; steel-cut oatmeal; eggs Benedict; ham and cheese omelet; spinach, tomato and egg white omelet; and fruit parfait, along with coffee, tea, and orange juice.

Lunch and dinner feature comfort foods, including some of Walt Disney's favorites—homemade meatloaf (with mashed potatoes and seasonal vegetables) and chicken-fried chicken. Popular items include fried pickles (with dipping sauce), salads, baked potato soup, penne pasta with shrimp, cheeseburgers, and vegan burgers. There are special selections just for kids, too. Finish off the meal with a housemade dessert (a chocolate malted, perhaps?) and specialty coffees. This cafe is one of four restaurants at Disneyland that offers table service for lunch and dinner (River Belle Terrace, Blue Bayou, and Cafe Orleans are the others). **B L D** $–$$

FAST FOOD & SNACKS

JOLLY HOLIDAY BAKERY CAFE: A festive tribute to Disney's *Mary Poppins*, the Jolly Holiday is at the far end of Main Street, in the space once occupied by the Plaza Pavilion restaurant. There is always a steady supply of

GOOD MEALS, GREAT TIMES

pastries here, including cookies, cupcakes, and Mickey macarons. Coffee drinks are available all day (hot and iced). Also on the seasonal menu (after 10:30 A.M.): soups, salads, quiches, and sandwiches. Wash it down with a soft drink—"Practically Perfect Punch," anyone? Kids' meals are available as well. **B L D S $**

GIBSON GIRL ICE CREAM PARLOR: A perennially popular place, with a polished-wood soda fountain, the parlor serves up a delightful array of scoops and toppings in paper cups, handmade waffle cups, and plain or chocolate-dipped cones. We are big fans of the "firehouse Dalmatian mint sundae" (hold the cherry). Don't be daunted by the long line; it moves rather quickly. **S $**

LITTLE RED WAGON: This wagon, near the Plaza Inn, is a throwback to the delivery trucks of the early 1900s, with ornate beveled and gilded glass panels. Step right up and order your hand-dipped corn dogs, the specialty of the wagon. A selection of soft drinks and chips is also served. **L D S $**

MAIN STREET FRUIT CART: Parked between Disney Clothiers Ltd. and Market House, this old-fashioned cart is stocked with fresh fruit and chilled juices, bottled water, and soft drinks. Other snack options include hummus, veggie cups with ranch dressing, and apple slices with caramel dipping sauce. It's the perfect pit stop for a (relatively) healthy snack. **S $**

MARKET HOUSE: Visit this Victorian-style market for a fresh-baked or brewed treat. It sells sweet and savory snacks and a cornucopia of tea and coffee concoctions, courtesy of Starbucks. Breakfast items, fresh fruit, and pastries are served all day. **B S $**

PLAZA INN: On the east side of Central Plaza, this eatery is the one Walt Disney was most proud of, and with good reason. Tufted velvet upholstery, gleaming mirrors, and a fine, ornate floral carpet elevate this cafeteria above similar eateries. Two ceilings are stained glass framed by elaborate painted moldings. Sconces of Parisian bronze and Baccarat crystal are mounted on the walls, and two dozen basket chandeliers hang from the ceiling.

The setting, including front-porch and terrace dining (with heat lamps to keep guests toasty at night), creates a lovely backdrop for the food—pasta; seasonal fish; fried chicken, served with mashed potatoes and mixed vegetables; pot roast served with fresh veggies and mashed potatoes; Cobb salad; and desserts.

A popular character breakfast is held here daily, from park opening until 11 A.M. Minnie and her pals make the rounds. A fixed-price

Where to Dine with the Characters

Character meals take place at Disneyland Park's Plaza Inn (breakfast with Minnie and friends) on Main Street; Ariel's Grotto in Disney California Adventure (princesses); Paradise Pier Hotel (breakfast with Mickey and friends); Storytellers Cafe (breakfast with Chip and Dale) in the Grand Californian Hotel; and Goofy's Kitchen in the Disneyland Hotel (brunch and dinner with Goofy and his pals).

| **B** breakfast | **L** lunch | **D** dinner | **S** snacks | **$** under $15 | **$$** $15–$29 | **$$$** $30–$50 | **$$$$** $51 and up | **111** |

buffet features omelets, eggs, French toast, Mickey waffles, sausage, bacon, yogurt, fresh fruit, pastries, cereal, and more. **B L D S** $–$$

REFRESHMENT CORNER CAFE: Better known as Coke Corner, this eatery at the northern end of Main Street is presided over by a ragtime pianist who tickles the ivories periodically throughout the day while visitors nibble hot dogs, chili cheese dogs, turkey dogs, or chili in a bread bowl. Mickey pretzels (stuffed with cream cheese), chips, soft drinks, lemonade, hot cocoa, and coffee are sold, too. **L D S** $

Adventureland

FAST FOOD & SNACKS

PHOTO BY JILL SAFRO

BENGAL BARBECUE: Opposite the entrance to Tarzan's Treehouse, this is a great place to munch on a skewered snack of bacon-wrapped asparagus (a local favorite), or chicken, beef, or veggies. Other menu items include fresh fruit yogurt parfaits, Mickey Mouse pretzels, and tiger tails (bread sticks). Cookies, chips,

Paint the Night Dining

Disneyland offers two different dining packages providing a "dinner and a show" experience—each pairing a meal with preferred viewing for Paint the Night:

1. Blue Bayou Restaurant: Includes a three-course, table-service meal (starter, entrée, and dessert). Seating begins at 4 P.M.

2. Aladdin's Oasis On-the-Go: Includes one grab-and-go meal, which may be picked up between noon and 7 P.M.

Space is limited for these experiences, so reservations are recommended. For pricing and reservations, visit *www.disneyland.com* or call 714-781-3463. All reservations require a credit card guarantee. Cancellations must be made at least 24 hours ahead to avoid a $10-per-person fee.

and soft drinks are also available. There is limited outdoor seating. If you can't find a place to park, head to the French Market seating area in New Orleans Square. This spot generally opens at 11 A.M. **L D S** $

TIKI JUICE BAR: Located at the entrance to Walt Disney's Enchanted Tiki Room, this thatched-roof kiosk sells fresh Hawaiian pineapple spears and pineapple juice, but the biggest draw here is the Dole Whip soft-serve—an extremely refreshing pineapple sorbet (it's nondairy). **S** $

TROPICAL IMPORTS FRUIT CART: A close neighbor of the Jungle Cruise, this stand offers fresh fruit, dill pickles, trail mix, chilled bottled water, and soft drinks. There is a selection of plush animal toys, too. **S** $

Critter Country

FAST FOOD & SNACKS

CRITTER COUNTRY FRUIT CART: This peddler's cart is filled with refreshing selections, including fresh fruit, trail mix, dill pickles, chilled bottled water, and soft drinks. It's handy if you need some fortification after taking the big Splash Mountain plunge. **S** $

HARBOUR GALLEY: This tiny place, tucked into the shanties that line the docking area for the *Columbia*, offers bread bowls with New England clam chowder, broccoli and cheddar cheese soup, and seasonal soup of the day; steak or shrimp salad; baked potatoes; lobster rolls; fruit plates; kids' "power packs" (snack packs with string cheese, yogurt, sliced apples, and crackers); soft drinks; and desserts. **L D S** $

HUNGRY BEAR RESTAURANT: A rustic, water-side classic, this eatery serves cheeseburgers, chili cheeseburgers, crispy chicken sandwiches, turkey wraps, french fries, and onion rings. For kids, there are chicken breast nuggets, burgers, or mac and cheese (kids' meals come with apple sauce, fruit, and a choice of milk or bottled water). Dessert options include strawberry fruit bars, ice cream sandwiches, and funnel cakes. **L D S** $

New Orleans Square

TABLE SERVICE

BLUE BAYOU: The lure of this popular dining spot is as much the enchanting atmosphere as it is the menu. Occupying a terrace alongside the bayou in the Pirates of the Caribbean attraction, the restaurant appears perpetually moonlit—stars shine through Spanish moss draped languidly over the big, old live oaks. Off in the distance, an old settler rocks away on the porch of a tumbledown shack.

> ### HOT TIP!
> A gratuity is automatically added to the bill at some Disney restaurants. Examine your tab and tip accordingly.

For lunch, choose from items such as pan-seared salmon, roasted chicken, beef short ribs, Royal Street seafood jambalaya, and New York roast. Vegetarians are drawn to the portobello mushroom and couscous *maque choux* (a rich mix of peppers and corn). Of course, the venerable Monte Cristo sandwich (turkey, ham, and Swiss cheese fried in a battered egg bread) remains a favorite. For dessert, there's chocolate cake, crème brûlée, and more.

The dinner menu features many of the lunch selections, plus panko-crusted rack of lamb, filet mignon, and the Bayou Surf & Turf combo—petite lobster tail paired with a broiled filet mignon. Kids' selections include steak, chicken breast, seared salmon, and Mickey's cheesy macaroni. Kids' meals are served with a beverage and side dish.

The busiest periods are from about noon to around 2 P.M. and from about 5 P.M. until 9 P.M. Reservations are suggested. **L D** $$–$$$

CAFE ORLEANS: An authentic Cajun-Creole spot, the Cafe offers starters such as French onion soup and New Orleans gumbo. Among the entrées, look for salmon and spinach salad, blackened chicken sandwich, vegetable ragout, two versions of the Monte Cristo sandwich, and seafood and chicken gumbo crêpes. Dessert options include Mickey-shaped beignets and berry crepes. Guests may dine inside or outside overlooking a gristmill on Tom Sawyer Island and the *Columbia* and the *Mark Twain* resting on the Rivers of America. Reservations are suggested. **L D S** $$–$$$

FAST FOOD & SNACKS

FRENCH MARKET: Situated beside the old-time train depot in New Orleans Square, this eatery is a destination in its own right. On a pleasant day, nothing beats sitting on the open-air terrace, munching on oven-roasted chicken, salmon, Cajun meatloaf, creamy corn chowder or Louisiana beef stew (both served in a bowl fashioned from a hollowed-out loaf of bread), Creole shrimp pasta, or jambalaya, the house specialty. Other lunch selections include French dip and shrimp po'boy sandwiches. Kids' portions of baked chicken, macaroni and cheese, and other dishes are available. Dinner entrées include seasonal catch of the day, red

Happy Birthday, Disney Style

For starters, it's always a good idea to inform cast members when you are celebrating a special occasion, no matter where you are at the Disneyland Resort. But it also helps to plan ahead. Birthday cakes can be delivered to any full-service theme-park restaurant. They range in price from about $34 to $137 and can be ordered from 3 to 60 days in advance. For more information or to order a cake, call 714-781-3463.

The Paradise Pier Hotel's PCH Grill has birthday celebrations, too. The cost is about $5 per person (plus the meal) and includes party favors.

For details, to order a cake, or to make reservations at the aforementioned eateries, call 714-781-3463.

Finally, be sure to pick up (and wear!) a special Happy Birthday button. They are complimentary and available at City Hall in Disneyland Park, at Chamber of Commerce in Disney California Adventure, and at some shops throughout the parks.

beans and rice with Andouille sausage, and salads. Dixieland jazz music is played periodically throughout the evening; the Royal Street Bachelors hold forth with such spirit that you could listen for hours. Lunch is served from 11 A.M. until 4 P.M. The dinner bell rings at 4 P.M. **L D S** **$–$$**

MINT JULEP BAR: Beside the New Orleans Square train station, this window-service bar serves Mickey-shaped beignets (topped with powdered sugar), hot chocolate, coffee, cappuccino, espresso, and iced coffee drinks. The (alcohol-free) mint juleps taste a bit like lemonade spiked with mint syrup (definitely an acquired taste); happily, real lemonade is also on tap, as are other soft drinks. Enjoy your snack at one of the tables on the French Market's terrace. **B S** **$**

ROYAL STREET VERANDA: Situated opposite Cafe Orleans, this snack stand has bread bowls overflowing with creamy clam chowder, steak or gumbo (each with a bit of a slightly spicy kick); fritters that come with a dipping sauce; and a variety of beverages. Check out the wrought-iron balustrade above the Royal Street Veranda's small patio. The initials at the center are those of Roy and Walt Disney (this balcony belonged to an apartment that was being constructed for Walt himself). **L D S** **$**

Frontierland

TABLE SERVICE

RIVER BELLE TERRACE: The terrace, between the Golden Horseshoe Saloon and the Pirates of the Caribbean, offers one of the best views of the Rivers of America and of the passing throng—and the food is wholesome and hearty. Walt Disney himself used to dine here most Sundays. The lunch menu features sandwiches, salads, and kids' meals. Dinner can include a starter, entrée, and dessert. (For menu specifics, visit *www.disneyland.com*.) Dinner may include a ticket for same-day, premium viewing of Paint the Night—as part of a Dining Package (see page 112). With a lovely interior, it's just as pleasant to dine inside as it is out. **L D** **$–$$**

FAST FOOD & SNACKS

RANCHO DEL ZOCALO: Big Thunder Mountain Railroad's neighbor, this Frontierland eatery features south-of-the-border specialties. Several of the usual Mexican dishes, including soft tacos and burritos, along with selections

PHOTO BY JILL SAFRO

GOOD MEALS, GREAT TIMES

such as fire-grilled citrus chicken, *carne asada*, tortilla soup, tostada salad, and Mexican-inspired Caesar salad are sure to hit the spot. Breakfast includes Mickey Mouse pancakes. For dessert, there's flan, *tres leches* cake, chocolate cake, and fresh fruit. **B L D S** **$**

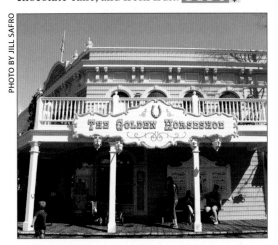

PHOTO BY JILL SAFRO

GOLDEN HORSESHOE: Head to this (dry) saloon for chicken nuggets, fish and chips, chili in a bread bowl, and chili cheese fries. Wash it down with a refreshing soft drink. Cap off your meal with an ice cream sundae. Seating is on a first-come, first-served basis. Disneyland purists may remember that the Golden Horseshoe Revue was one of Disneyland's original 18 attractions and was the world's longest-running stage show (July 17, 1955–October 12, 1986). **L D S** **$**

SHIP TO SHORE MARKETPLACE: Nestled near the shores of the Rivers of America (which are temporarily inactive, as the construction of

Sweet Treats

Sweet teeth may be satisfied at a plethora of places in Disneyland Park. After passing through the turnstiles, make a beeline for Main Street, U.S.A., and the Jolly Holiday Bakery Cafe, the Gibson Girl Ice Cream Parlor, or the Candy Palace, which has tasty saltwater taffy. And by all means, sample a churro (fried dough rolled in cinnamon and sugar) from a food cart—it's quite popular. Finally, no trip to the "happiest place on earth" is complete without savoring the classic frozen pineapple treat known simply as the Dole Whip. The line at the Tiki Juice Bar is often long, but for many a Dole Whip fan, it's well worth the wait.

Star Wars Land continues), this snack stand sells turkey legs, fresh fruit, corn on the cob, chimichangas, frozen lemonade, soft drinks, and hot cocoa. **S** **$**

STAGE DOOR CAFE: In the mood for one of Disneyland's famous hand-dipped corn dogs? Head here. This small stand, which adjoins the Golden Horseshoe Stage, also serves fish and chips, chicken nuggets, funnel cakes, and soft drinks. Grab a seat at an outdoor table. **L D S** **$**

Fantasyland

FAST FOOD & SNACKS

EDELWEISS SNACKS: Next door to the Matterhorn, this chalet-style kiosk can supply a quick post-ride pick-me-up in the form of turkey legs, chimichangas, buttered or chili-lime corn on the cob, chips, and soft drinks (including frozen beverages). **S** **$**

TROUBADOUR TAVERN: Located within the Fantasyland Theatre (home of the Mickey and the Magical Map stage show), this spot dispenses bratwurst in a garlic-and-herb brioche bun with hickory smoked sauerkraut, pretzel bites with cheese sauce, apple slices with caramel dipping sauce, frozen treats, and soft drinks. Breakfast pastries are served until 11 A.M. **B L S** **$**

VILLAGE HAUS: Near Pinocchio's Daring Journey, this house with its gables, pointy roof, and wavy-glass windows could easily have been relocated to Fantasyland from an alpine village. Inside, murals recount the story of Pinocchio. The menu features pastrami cheeseburgers, classic cheeseburgers, chicken sausage in a pretzel roll, pizza (cheese, pepperoni, or specialty flatbread such as BLT), apple and cheddar salad, chocolate cupcakes, apple strudel, and soft drinks. A children's meal is available. **L D S** **$**

Mickey's Toontown

FAST FOOD & SNACKS

CLARABELLE'S: On Toon Square, adjacent to Pluto's Dog House, Clarabelle's specializes in "udderly" tasty frozen treats, Mickey Mouse crispie treats, plus sandwiches and salads. Wet your whistle with lemonade, root beer, milk, or other soft drinks. **S** **$**

DAISY'S DINER: This walk-up window serves up individual cheese and pepperoni pizzas (served with sliced apples). Cookies, milk, juice, sodas, and lemonade round out the menu. **L D S** **$**

GOOFY'S FREE-Z-TIME: The vacation trailer parked by Goofy's House is a dispenser of large frozen slurpy drinks. **S** **$** (Seasonal)

PLUTO'S DOG HOUSE: Nestled between Clarabelle's and Daisy's Diner, this is the place to find a hot dog served with chips or sliced apples. Extras include cookies, Pluto's crispie treats, and soft drinks. The kids' meal comes with a turkey hot dog or mac and cheese with chips, and a soft drink. **L D S** **$**

Tomorrowland

FAST FOOD & SNACKS

GALACTIC GRILL: In the vicinity of Star Traders, this is one of the park's largest dining areas. (It used to be known as Tomorrowland Terrace.) All menu items have a Star Wars theme. For breakfast there's a choice of Darth Tamale, Lars Family Breakfast Platter, Bantha Blue Milk Bread, and Moisture Farm Fresh Fruit Platter. At lunch and dinner, choose from First Order Specialty Burger, Jedi Order Chicken Sandwich, Cheese-3PO Salad, Chopper Salad, Wicket's Wicked Veggie Sandwich, and more. A children's menu is available, too. **B L D** **$–$$**

REDD ROCKETT'S PIZZA PORT: Situated near the entrance to Space Mountain, this food court overlooks the Moonliner and Cosmic Waves. Separate stations serve pasta, pizza, or salads, all prepared in a display kitchen.

Menu choices include pizzas (cheese, pepperoni, veggie, and a daily special, by the slice or pie), Celestial Caesar Salad, Asian chicken salad, spaghetti and meatballs with tomato sauce, vegetarian pasta, and Count-Down Chicken Fusilli. A beverage counter and cooler supply drinks. **L D S** **$–$$**

TOMORROWLAND FRUIT CART: Fruit may not sound very futuristic, but it is a healthy way to snack today. Stop here for apple slices with caramel dipping sauce, oranges, grapes, bananas, watermelon, pineapple spears, pickles, soft drinks, trail mix, and more. **S** **$**

In Disney California Adventure

With a winery and an elegant bayside eatery, the tastes at Disney California Adventure are clearly grown-up. But several fast-food spots and snack stands supply theme park fare with an entertaining flair—retro Hollywood decor or a seaside boardwalk setting. Just remember: Don't gorge before experiencing thrill rides.

The full-service eateries here—including Ariel's Grotto, Carthay Circle Restaurant, and Wine Country Trattoria—accept reservations. Call 714-781-3463 to book a table. For updates, visit *www.disneyland.com*.

Buena Vista Street

TABLE SERVICE

CARTHAY CIRCLE RESTAURANT: The original Carthay Circle Theatre was one of the best known and revered movie palaces in Hollywood history. It also happens to be where Walt Disney's *Snow White and the Seven Dwarfs* made its dazzling debut. The theatre has been painstakingly re-created here at Disney California Adventure. But don't go expecting to catch a flick—this version of Carthay Circle Restaurant is actually a popular signature restaurant. Menu items such as fried cheddar biscuits, firecracker duck wings, ceviche of blue cobia, summer garden risotto, and sustainable fish earn rave reviews. Reservations are recommended. **L D** $$$

FAST FOOD & SNACKS

CLARABELLE'S HAND-SCOOPED ICE CREAM: Cones, shakes, and sundaes are the chilly treats served here. The specialty of the house is hand-dipped ice cream bars. Simply choose your bar flavor, milk or dark chocolate for dipping, and a topping (Mickey-shaped candy confetti, chocolate chips, blue raspberry bursts, and more). Sweet! **S** $

FIDDLER, FIFER & PRACTICAL CAFE: Named for everyone's favorite trio of little pigs, this is a great spot to quell hunger pangs and enjoy your favorite Starbucks beverage. Breakfast items, fresh-baked pastries, and other snacks are served all day. **L D S** $

MORTIMER'S MARKET: Stop here for "the freshest fruit in town." In addition to produce, there are other healthy snacks and soft drinks from which to choose. FYI: The Mouse was almost named Mortimer. Lillian Disney talked her husband into naming him Mickey! **S** $

Hollywood Land

FAST FOOD & SNACKS

AWARD WIENERS: Hot and heaping cheese and chili dogs—with the occasional autograph request or two—are the specialties here. Sausages round out the menu. A nearby seating area provides plenty of shaded tables (by the For the First Time in Forever attraction). **S** $

FAIRFAX MARKET: Inspired by the historic Farmers Market in Los Angeles, this stand serves up whole fresh fruits, sliced mango, pineapple, and watermelon, and apple slices with caramel dipping sauce. Also on the menu? Fresh, cut vegetables with ranch dip, hummus, dill pickles, chips, and soft drinks. **L D S** $

SCHMOOZIES: Yogurt-and-fruit smoothies are the specialty of the house. For some, these chilly drinks are a meal unto themselves. Lattes, cappuccinos, and other coffees are also available. **S** $

Grizzly Peak Airfield

FAST FOOD & SNACKS

SMOKEJUMPERS GRILL: Paying tribute to the brave souls who parachute into forest fires, this spot serves items such as cheeseburgers, bacon cheeseburgers, veggie burgers, grilled chicken and Jack sandwiches, grilled chicken and feta salad, fries, chili-cheese fries, and onion rings for lunch and dinner. For dessert there's chocolate and vanilla shakes topped with whipped cream. `L D S` `$`

Pacific Wharf

TABLE SERVICE

GHIRARDELLI SODA FOUNTAIN: San Francisco's famous sweet-maker also calls Disney California Adventure home. Stop by this soda fountain for a chocolaty treat, root beer float, or a malt. There's no better place to please a sweet tooth. (And there's always the possibility of a free sample.) The coffee is tops, too—both the hot and iced varieties. `S` `$–$$`

PHOTO BY JILL SAFRO

WINE COUNTRY TRATTORIA: Located on the lower level of the mission house at the Golden Vine Winery, this family-friendly spot offers creative Mediterranean fare that blends nicely with the international wine list. Favorites include "pasta your way," braised lamb shank, and sustainable fish with citrus pesto. Wines are available by the glass or the bottle (of course). Wine flights with three tastings are also offered. There is a children's menu for the little ones.

Outdoor dining in the plaza features a fountain surrounded by herbs and flowers, conjuring images of Napa Valley. Inside, the dining room is reminiscent of a hacienda, with plastered walls, terra cotta tiles, and arched doorways. Reservations are recommended. `L D S` `$–$$$`

FAST FOOD & SNACKS

ALFRESCO LOUNGE: One flight up from Wine Country Trattoria is an inviting lounge with a full bar and light appetizers. On the menu: Wine Country Shrimp served on polenta cake with lemon caper butter sauce, fried calamari, and beef tenderloin panini. Pair your food with red or white sangria or wine flights from California or Italy. There is a full bar, and soft drinks are served. The Lounge offers guests a great view of Cars Land—which is exceptionally lovely at night. `L S` `$$–$$$`

COCINA CUCAMONGA MEXICAN GRILL: Tasty tortillas are the house specialties and serve as the foundation for most menu items. Among the choices are soft tacos, wet burritos, tamales, fire-grilled citrus chicken, *carne asada*, and chicken tamales. Kids' meals include a bean and cheese burrito, chicken taco, and chicken with rice. `L D` `$–$$`

LUCKY FORTUNE COOKERY: This walk-up eatery serves hearty Asian creations: beef, chicken, or tofu with vegetables, rice, and a choice of four sauces (Mandarin orange, spicy Korean, Thai coconut curry, or teriyaki). Sides include mango slices and edamame. There's a special selection for children, too: teriyaki chicken and rice. `L D` `$–$$`

MENDOCINO TERRACE WINE TASTING: Take a break beside a hand-carved stone fountain and sip local varietals in this alfresco lounge at the Golden Vine Winery. Cheese platters complement the vino nicely. Included in each $15 platter are three types of cheese, grapes, olives, and crackers. Wines are available by the glass or bottle, and in sets of three sampling flights. Sparkling apple cider and other soft drinks round out the menu. `S` `$$–$$$`

PACIFIC WHARF CAFE: Guests at this extension of Boudin's display bakery have the chance to sample some of the country's finest sourdough bread (from a secret family recipe dating back to 1850). Hearty soups such as New England clam chowder or broccoli and cheese, plus salads are served up in thick bread bowls for lunch and dinner. Pastries are offered throughout the day. `B L D S` `$–$$`

Paradise Pier

TABLE SERVICE

ARIEL'S GROTTO: A character-laden dining spot, Ariel's Grotto offers views of Paradise Pier's amusements and overlooks the lagoon (dinner is especially festive when the boardwalk is aglow with twinkling lights). What's more, Disney princesses mingle with diners during breakfast and lunch. Guests pay one price and select an item for each course. Expect the usual breakfast favorites, plus Belgian waffles. For lunch, the menu offers fish, salads, pastas, and lobster tail salad. At dinnertime, the eatery transforms into a World of Color dining experience. After the meal, guests receive tickets to World of Color (see page 108 for show details). Menu items include steak, lobster tail, pasta, fish, and homemade desserts. Reservations are an absolute must. **B L D** **$$$**

THE COVE BAR: This waterside, open-air lounge offers a light menu with items such as tenderloin sliders, lobster nachos, spinach and artichoke dip, and more. A full bar is available. Guests may sit at a table or the bar (provided they are 21 years old and willing to wait in line for an available seat). **L D S** **$–$$**

FAST FOOD & SNACKS

BOARDWALK PIZZA AND PASTA: Near the Jumpin' Jellyfish, this restaurant serves Italian dishes, including pizzas, pastas, and freshly tossed salads. For dessert, there's tiramasu, brownies, and more. Meals may be enjoyed alfresco, on the shaded patio. Live entertainment from the Paradise Garden Bandstand is an added treat. **L D S** **$**

HOT TIP!
In the mood for dinner and a show? Visit www.disneyland.com to reserve a World of Color Dinner Package at a table-service eatery. Call 714-781-DINE for information and to make reservations.

CORN DOG CASTLE: Juicy corn dogs, deep-fried to a golden brown and served on a handy stick, reign supreme. **L D S** **$**

DON TOMÁS: Step up to this window for turkey legs, chimichangas, chips, and drinks. **L D S** **$**

HOT DOG HUT: Head here for hot dogs, corn on the cob (buttered or chili-lime), and bags of chips. **L D S** **$**

PARADISE GARDEN GRILL: True to its name, this spot specializes in grilled items, including marinated skewers of beef and chicken. The menu also includes Greek salad, strawberry brownie, and baklava. Kids may choose from meatball slider or peanut butter pita. **L D S** **$**

PARADISE PIER ICE CREAM CO.: Refreshing soft-serve ice cream (chocolate, vanilla, and twist) helps guests cool off after a long day of fun in the sun. The "beachfront floats" are quite satisfying. **S** **$**

Cars Land

FAST FOOD & SNACKS

COZY CONE MOTEL: Sally's cozy motel has been converted to a colorful eatery in the park's Radiator Springs. Here guests may find items such as bacon mac and cheese cones, soft-serve ice cream cones, pop "cone," and chili "cone" carne. Soft drinks of note include "Ramone's Pear of Dice Soda" and "Red's Apple Freeze." **L D S** **$**

FILLMORE'S TASTE-IN: Guests here fuel up on healthy snacks like fresh fruit and crunchy veggies, chips, and soft drinks. It's the perfect place for a quick and refreshing pit stop. **S** **$**

FLO'S V8 CAFE: Inspired by classic roadside diners, Flo serves rotisserie beef and cheddar or hot turkey sandwiches, BBQ ribs, milk shakes, and pie. There is ample indoor and outdoor seating. **L D S** **$–$$**

In the Disneyland Resort Hotels

Disneyland Hotel

The diverse dining possibilities here range from grand to Goofy. For reservations or information, call 714-781-3463.

THE COFFEE HOUSE: Order bagels, muffins, pastries, fruit, yogurt, cold cereal, cookies, and coffee in this small shop. Sandwiches are added to the menu at lunchtime. As the name indicates, this place specializes in fresh-brewed coffee—with everything from a simple cup of decaf to a cafe mocha and ice-blended latte. Outside seating only. Expect long lines in the morning. **B L S** $

GOOFY'S KITCHEN: This whimsical dining room features popular meals and personal encounters with Goofy and other Disney characters. Service here is buffet style, so fill your plate as high and as often as you please. Just be sure to clean that plate!

Highlights at brunch include Mickey Mouse–shaped waffles and made-to-order omelets. Dinner offers roasted strip steak,

HOT TIP!
You may encounter a very long line at The Coffee House in the morning. If so, head to Downtown Disney's Earl of Sandwich, La Brea Bakery, or Starbucks for breakfast and/or a cup of coffee.

pasta, chicken dishes, macaroni and cheese, pizzas (including peanut-butter-and-jelly pizza, a favorite with youngsters and Birnbaum editors alike), salads, breads, fruit, and desserts. Don't forget your camera—characters provide prime photo opportunities. Reservations are required. (Same-day reservations may be secured via *www.disneyland.com* up to 20 minutes ahead, based on availability.) **Brunch D** $$–$$$

STEAKHOUSE 55: An upscale dining establishment, Steakhouse 55 is decorated with oak paneling and etched glass and has a nostalgic Hollywood motif featuring pictures of the matinee idols of yesteryear. But the real stars here are the steaks, all cooked to perfection. The menu also boasts lamb, chicken, and seafood selections. Specialties of the house include a bone-in rib eye with the signature Steakhouse 55 rub, and Maryland crab cakes. The impressive wine list touts several fine California vintages. Reservations are required. Menu selections are subject to change. **B D** $$$$

TANGAROA TERRACE: Visit this eatery and travel back in time. The retro-tiki design was inspired by the Tahitian Terrace restaurant—a longtime Adventureland staple. The fare at this casual counter-service restaurant, however, is decidedly modern. The breakfast menu includes an egg white, veggie, and tofu bake; French toast with bacon and warm banana-caramel sauce; grilled cinnamon-spiced oatmeal cakes with island fruit compote; and

GOOD MEALS, GREAT TIMES

a whole wheat breakfast wrap with scrambled eggs, ham, and avocado. Items available all day include Hawaiian cheeseburgers (with teriyaki sauce, bacon, and grilled pineapple); Asian chicken salad; and Kahlua pulled-pork flatbread. For dinner, consider miso-crusted salmon, teriyaki-glazed New York strip steak, or panko-crusted chicken. The kids' menu includes chicken breast nuggets, grilled salmon, and burgers. There is a small grab-and-go selection, too. Choose from items such as a yogurt parfait with tropical fruit and housemade granola, tropical fresh fruit plate, pastries, sandwiches, and a variety of frozen treats. **B L D S** $–$$

Disney's Paradise Pier Hotel

The eatery here has all the bases covered—from creamy mushroom bisque to wood-fired pizza. And wait till you see what Mickey Mouse has cooked up for breakfast! For reservations at PCH Grill, call 714-781-3463.

> ## HOT TIP!
> Any full-service dining location at a Disneyland Resort hotel will validate your parking at that hotel; remember to get your parking pass stamped before you leave.

> ## HOT TIP!
> Napa Rose's adjoining lounge offers the restaurant's full menu, as well as its impressive wine list.

DISNEY'S PCH GRILL: Besides the Surf's Up! Breakfast with Mickey & Friends (which offers a buffet meal), Disney's PCH Grill—the initials stand for Pacific Coast Highway—reflects classic California tastes. Family favorites are offered at the omelet station and kids' buffet, plus specialties that include breakfast flatbreads from the wood-burning oven, and caramel banana French toast. Dinner—a character-free, buffet affair—offers smoked barbecue ribs, pizza, shrimp alfredo, mini tacos, salmon, build-your-own-salads, and more. The kids' section has mac and cheese, mini hot dogs, and cheeseburger sliders. For dessert, the s'mores bar is quite the temptation—as are the strawberry shortcake and ice cream cones. Reservations are suggested. **B L D** $$

Disney's Grand Californian Hotel & Spa

The restaurants here offer a taste of (and a twist on) California cuisine. For reservations, call 714-781-3463.

NAPA ROSE: This popular, nationally recognized, award-winning restaurant features a creative menu of market-fresh, wine country-inspired dishes flavored by fruits of the sea and vine (the eatery is named after California's most famous valley of vineyards). A striking, 20-foot, stained-glass window offers views of Disney California Adventure, while the open kitchen gives insight into California cooking.

The offerings evolve as new items are introduced, but favorites include pan-roasted scallops with a sauce of lobster and lemon accented with vanilla, mushroom risotto, and braised Alaskan halibut. Slowly braised Angus beef short rib is a signature dish, but the Napa Rose best seller is the shared appetizer known as Seven Sparkling Sins. The dessert tray offers delectable creations from artisanal ice cream to a Wine Country Fuji apple crisp and Cordillera chocolate pave. The California wine list is one of the most extensive on-property. Reservations are suggested. **D** $$$–$$$$

HEARTHSTONE LOUNGE: Though primarily a drinking spot, this lounge offers appetizers and is open in the morning for early risers in search of coffee and the day's paper. Continental breakfast items—including specialty coffees—are also available. **B S** $

STORYTELLERS CAFE: It's hard to imagine a time before computers and television (especially for the youngest members of the group), when children were exposed to new cultures and histories only through the stories of others. This restaurant salutes tales set in the state of California, like "The Celebrated Jumping Frog of Calaveras County" and *Island of the Blue*

Dolphins, through murals that act as backdrops to the chefs at work in the exhibition kitchen. In the morning, the stage is set for a festive, character-hosted buffet. Chip, Dale, and other Disney characters entertain guests, while the buffet offers a bounty of breakfast options, from pancakes and waffles to eggs, sausage, and a selection of fresh fruit. Lunch and dinner offer such pleasers as Nebraska corn chowder, spare ribs, flatbreads, pastas, steak, salads, seafood, and chicken. Reservations are strongly suggested. **B L D** $$–$$$

WHITE WATER SNACKS: The splish-splash of the waterfall and kids soaring down the slide at the Redwood pool set the mood for this ultra-casual dining spot. Open for breakfast, lunch, and dinner (though hours vary), the snack bar serves coffee, muffins, bagels, sweet rolls, French toast sticks, buttermilk biscuit egg sandwiches, Mickey waffles, oatmeal with berries and brown sugar, and breakfast burritos in the morning. Salads, deli sandwiches, burgers, veggie burgers, hot dogs, personal pizzas, chicken or beef nachos, and grilled chicken are lunch and dinner options. Other items that may be offered: candy, crackers, whole fruit, yogurt, cereal, soft drinks, beer, and wine. **B L D S** $

In Downtown Disney

CATAL RESTAURANT & UVA BAR: A sun-kissed balcony, outdoor tapas bar, and villa-style dining room set the Mediterranean mood at this restaurant. The menu focuses on grilled seafood, chicken, and vegetables, infused with olive oil and citrus accents. With pastas and salads available, vegetarians have much to choose from here. Reservations are suggested; 714-774-4442. **B L D** $$$

DIGGITY DOGS: A handy spot for a portable bite, Diggity Dogs can be found near Downtown Disney's World of Disney shop. Like the idea of buying two dogs and getting one for free? Use the coupon at the back of this book. You're welcome! **L D S** $

EARL OF SANDWICH: This spot celebrates the history of the sandwich and the family credited with its creation. It features deli cuisine, with sandwiches and salads. Snacks and beverages are sold, too. The coupon at the back of this book will net you a 20 percent discount on your food and beverage purchase. **B L D S** $

ESPN ZONE: This place is heaven on earth for sports fans. In addition to ballpark fare, it offers items like sirloin steak, fettuccine Alfredo, grilled salmon, and salads. **L D S** $$

HÄAGEN-DAZS: The dessert specialist has ice cream, frozen yogurt, sorbet, and gelato—as well as baked goods and coffee. **S** $

JAMBA JUICE: In the mood for a tropical smoothie? Perhaps one with protein or a berry blast? They've got that and more. **S** $

LA BREA BAKERY: Many offerings at this destination—breakfast treats, panini sandwiches, and classic sandwiches—are built on La Brea's legendary, freshly made bread. Also available are salads (with organic greens), soups, and coffees. There is counter service and a covered patio with table service. **B L D S** $-$$

NAPLES RISTORANTE E PIZZERIA: Dine inside or alfresco at this contemporary Italian trattoria. A large outdoor terrace provides perfect views of the Disney landscape, plus a peaceful and romantic setting for lunch or dinner. Pizzas are served in individual portions or *al metro* (one meter long and perfect for a hungry family to share). The menu also includes *piccoli piatti* (salads served tapas style), pastas, and seafood. For reservations, call 714-776-6200. **L D** $$$

NAPOLINI: Adjacent to the popular Naples Ristorante e Pizzeria, this quick-serve spot also offers Italian fare, but on the simpler side than that served by its neighbor. There is a selection of grab-and-go items, too. **L D** $$

RAINFOREST CAFE: Greenery, misty waterfalls, tropical storms, mechanical animals, and real-life creatures create a sometimes hectic, always colorful atmosphere in this spot. The menu features environmentally themed appetizers and entrées, including pastas, burgers, and sandwiches. Reservations, available up to one year in advance, are recommended; call 714-772-0413 at least two weeks ahead. **B L D S** $$-$$$

RALPH BRENNAN'S JAZZ KITCHEN: Sample some home-style New Orleans specialties at this comfy cafe while listening to jazz. Gumbo, jambalaya, chicken, and fresh pasta dishes are house favorites. Reservations are suggested; 714-776-5200. **L D S** $$-$$$

STARBUCKS: This sleek coffeehouse neighbors the World of Disney store. In addition to a full menu of coffee drinks, stop here for teas, smoothies, pastries, breakfast sandwiches, snacks, packaged coffee, and more. Guests of all ages dig the interactive digital "chalk board." The line is generally the most manageable in the afternoon hours. **B L D S** $

TORTILLA JO'S: A colorful Mexican restaurant and open-air cantina, this spot offers culinary traditions including freshly prepared tamales, carnitas, and fajitas, made-to-order guacamole, and lime-marinated ceviches. Reservations are suggested; 714-535-5000. The adjacent Taqueria serves classic Mexican quick-service selections. **L D S** $$-$$$

WETZEL'S PRETZELS: Whether you prefer pretzels salty or sweet, Wetzel's can satisfy. Ambitious snackers enjoy the Sinful Cinnamon and the Cheese Meltdown. Buy two, get one free with the coupon at the back of this book. **S** $

BIRNBAUM'S BEST

RESTAURANT ROUNDUP

There are more dining choices than ever before at the Disneyland Resort. We've picked our favorites, based on food quality, restaurant atmosphere, and overall value. Use these **Birnbaum's Bests** to help you decide where to grab a quick bite or have a hearty meal.

GOOD MEALS, GREAT TIMES

BEST RESTAURANTS FOR FAMILIES

TABLE SERVICE
Goofy's Kitchen ....Disneyland Hotel (p. 120)
Blue Bayou ....Disneyland Park (p. 113)
Storytellers Cafe .... Grand Californian Hotel (p. 122)
Rainforest Cafe................................Downtown Disney (p. 123)

QUICK SERVICE
Royal Street Veranda ....Disneyland Park (p. 114)
Rancho del Zocalo ....Disneyland Park (p. 114)
Refreshment Corner Cafe ....Disneyland Park (p. 112)
Pacific Wharf Cafe.......... Disney California Adventure (p. 118)
Flo's V8 Cafe .... Disney California Adventure (p. 119)

BEST PIZZA
Naples Ristorante e Pizzeria
Downtown Disney (p. 123)

BEST SANDWICHES
La Brea Bakery
Downtown Disney
(p. 123)

BEST QUICK SERVICE
Flo's V8 Cafe
Disney California Adventure
(p. 119)

BEST CHARACTER MEAL
Goofy's Kitchen ....Disneyland Hotel (p. 120)

RUNNERS-UP
Disney's PCH Grill ....Paradise Pier Hotel (p. 121)
Plaza Inn ....Disneyland Park (p. 111)
Storytellers Cafe .... Grand Californian Hotel (p. 122)

BEST RESTAURANTS FOR ADULTS
Napa Rose .... Grand Californian Hotel (p. 121)
Steakhouse 55... Disneyland Hotel (p. 120)

RUNNERS-UP
Carthay Circle Restaurant.. Disney California Adventure (p. 117)
Ralph Brennan's Jazz Kitchen ....Downtown Disney (p. 123)
Wine Country Trattoria....... Disney California Adventure (p. 118)

BEST LOUNGE
Trader Sam's Enchanted Tiki Bar
Disneyland Hotel
(p. 125)

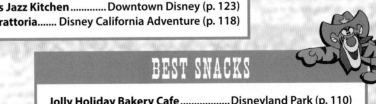

BEST SNACKS
Jolly Holiday Bakery Cafe...................Disneyland Park (p. 110)
Tiki Juice Bar..Disneyland Park (p. 112)

Entertainment
Disney Hotels

The Disneyland Resort has more to offer than thrill rides and characters. There's plenty to do at Disney's three hotels and in the Downtown Disney dining, shopping, and entertainment district. Whether you're seeking a break from the theme parks or a place to party the night away, the following options are sure to please.

Note: For additional information on evening theme park happenings, refer to the *Disneyland Park* and *Disney California Adventure* chapters of this book.

Lounges

DISNEYLAND HOTEL: The **Lounge at Steakhouse 55**, with its comfortable leather sofas, convenient conversation areas, and sophisticated decor, provides an intimate meeting place. The boisterous **Trader Sam's Enchanted Tiki Bar**, named for the infamous "head" salesman at the Jungle Cruise (he'll gladly trade you two of his heads for one of yours), mixes drinks and snacks with a bit of Disney magic.

DISNEY'S GRAND CALIFORNIAN HOTEL: The lounge adjoining the elegant **Napa Rose** restaurant offers an extensive selection of wines by the glass and a soothing atmosphere. Guests may order a savory snack here, too.

At the handsome **Hearthstone Lounge**, you can sip a cocktail or an after-dinner cordial opposite a roaring fireplace. If so inclined, you may enjoy your beverage on a comfy couch in the majestic lobby, where live piano music is always a possibility.

DISNEY'S PARADISE PIER HOTEL: The **Surfside Lounge** in the resort's lobby serves hot breakfast items in the morning and light

fare (burgers, salads, sandwiches, snacks, and more) throughout the day.

Live Entertainment

DISNEY'S GRAND CALIFORNIAN HOTEL: As a tribute to the early 1900s storytelling tradition, entertainers tell tall tales in the hotel's main lobby during the evening hours. A piano player adds to the ambience.

Arcades

DISNEY'S GRAND CALIFORNIAN HOTEL: The Grizzly Game Arcade scores high points on evenings when the parks close early.

DISNEY'S PARADISE PIER HOTEL: Youngsters have a blast at this hotel's arcade, located off the main lobby.

Spa Services

DISNEY'S GRAND CALIFORNIAN HOTEL: A relaxing escape to a spa is as welcome a diversion as they come—especially when it is a visit to the world-class pampering palace known as **Mandara Spa**. Treatments here include all manner of massage, facials, body wraps, manicures, pedicures, and more. There are services specially tailored for couples and teens. A tea pavilion allows spa guests to enjoy a meditative, Zen Buddhist tea ceremony. For a complete list of services, go to its website: *MandaraSpa.com*. To make an appointment, call 714-300-7350.

Downtown Disney

PHOTO BY JILL SAFRO

Easily accessed by foot (from the Disneyland Resort hotels or theme parks) or monorail (from Disneyland Park's Tomorrowland), this entertainment district offers a break from the theme park hustle and bustle during the day, and a busy place to mix and mingle in the evening hours. Many Downtown Disney venues serve double (or triple) duty as dining and dancing (and sometimes shopping) spots.

Shops open early and don't close until late in the evening. Club performers generally hit the stage post-dinner and wrap by midnight.

Lounges

CATAL RESTAURANT & UVA BAR: Designed to resemble the Art Nouveau style of a Paris metro station, this large wine and tapas bar tempts guests with the fruits of the vine and sea. Guests can drink under the stars at the outdoor bar or mingle indoors, and can select from the extensive wine list.

ESPN ZONE: Stop by the bar area of the Zone's Studio Grill for a tall one before heading upstairs to play arcade games at the Sports Arena. With large-screen TVs blaring from each section of the room, expect the joint to be jumping on big-game nights. If there is a big game you simply cannot miss, get there at least an hour (or more) before it begins. Reservations are not accepted.

MAGIC MUSHROOM BAR: Part of the lush Rainforest Cafe, this circular drinking hole is capped by a giant mushroom and serves up aptly named blended beverages, such as the Mongoose Mai Tai and the Cheeta Rita (non-alcoholic beverages are also available). Don't be surprised if a tot takes over a neighboring stool—this establishment is a big family spot.

OUTDOOR PERFORMERS: Downtown Disney boasts an eclectic lineup of free, live musical entertainment. From calming classical to rousing rhythm and blues, professional musicians create a party-like atmosphere every day. For up-to-the-minute entertainment schedules, text DTDNOW to DPARK (37275) to receive up to three updates via text per week, or visit *www.disneyland.disney.go.com/downtown-disney/*.

RALPH BRENNAN'S JAZZ KITCHEN—FLAMBEUX'S JAZZ CLUB: The sounds of jazz set the tone for the relaxed atmosphere at this restaurant's lounge. Bands and singers entertain with live jazz every evening. A smooth soundtrack provides music when the stage is dark. Special tickets may be required for certain performances. Call 714-776-5200 to inquire about ticket reservations.

Shopping

ANNA & ELSA'S BOUTIQUE: With a *Frozen*-inspired makeover, kids can be magically transformed into Anna, Elsa, or summer-loving snowman, Olaf. Basic packages start at about $35, plus tax. Reservations are recommended; 714-781-STYLE (7895). Makeovers are designed for guests ages 3 to 15. All kids must be accompanied by an adult. Expect each makeover to take roughly 45 minutes. (It's a good idea to arrive a few minutes before your scheduled appointment time.)

The cheery boutique doubles as a shop, featuring all manner of *Frozen* paraphernalia. There's apparel, toys, magnets, ornaments, snacks, and much more.

BUILD-A-BEAR WORKSHOP: Make your own stuffed animal, as you "choose, stuff, fluff, name, and dress" your way through a series of bear-making stations. It's a "beary" special experience for kids. Save $5 off your purchase of $25 or more by using the coupon at the back of this book.

DISNEY PIN TRADERS: Do we really need to tell you what this spot specializes in? Didn't think so.

DISNEY VAULT 28: A chic boutique, this spot showcases trendy items and apparel for men and women, some inspired by familiar Disney characters and films.

D STREET: A place where urban art–inspired products "intersect" with Disney design. This space showcases a mix of Disney-themed art created by local and underground artists. Also available are clothing, collectibles, and more.

ESPN ZONE STUDIO STORE: Sports fans will cheer for the ESPN, SportsCenter, and Monday Night Football–branded apparel and other stuff at this shop in ESPN Zone.

FOSSIL: Got the time? They do! Stop here for watches galore, plus fashionable leather goods, accessories, and jewelry.

BEST BUY GADGET MAGIC: This self-serve kiosk (think oversized vending machine) dispenses items such as digital cameras, memory cards, earbuds, computer accessories, and other gadgety goodness.

THE LEGO STORE: Hundreds of the world's most famous building brick sets and products are for sale here. There's a play area, too.

LITTLE MISSMATCHED: Tired of trying to match up stray socks? This place is your dream come true. None of the socks here match. Also on the shelves are boots, flip-flops, jammies, dresses, and more. Most of the items are meant for young girls, but there are some selections for boys, babies, and grown-ups, too.

MARCELINE'S CONFECTIONERY: Named after Walt Disney's childhood hometown, this shop offers candies, pastries and other sweet treats.

It's fun to watch the candymakers at work.

QUIKSILVER: Surfwear and accessories help guests dress as beachcomber/adventurer.

RAINFOREST SHOP: Adjacent to the Rainforest Cafe, this shop offers plush animals, environmentally themed toys, Rainforest Cafe logo items, and snacks.

RIDEMAKERZ™: Guests can build and customize their own freewheeling or radio-controlled vehicle at this interactive store. Trick out real-world and concept cars—Ford Mustangs, Dodge Vipers, Chevy Corvettes, hot rods, pickups, and more—including character cars such as Mater and Lightning McQueen. Net a $10 savings off a $40 purchase with the coupon at the back of this book.

SANUK: Retire those pinchy old shoes and replace them with cool and comfy footwear at Sanuk. In addition to "sidewalk surfers" for kids and grown-ups, this shop sells hats, hoodies, T-shirts, and more. FYI: *Sanuk* is the Thai word for fun. By the way, if we could wear Sanuks every day of the year, we would.

SEPHORA: A black-and-white motif provides a perfect backdrop for the colorful palette of products in this cosmetics mecca. Sephora's own line of makeup is complemented by a selection of popular beauty products and designer fragrances.

SOMETHING SILVER: Perfect for celebrating a 25th anniversary, or just creating a look, the jewelry here is simple and stylish. Note that there are many lovely non-silver selections to choose from, too.

SUNGLASS ICON: Custom-fit shades are the stock-in-trade at this shop. All the big-name designers are represented here.

WORLD OF DISNEY: Shelves are stacked sky-high at this souvenir shopper's dream come true. Each overflowing room features a different theme and type of merchandise, from men's and women's apparel to watches and accessories, plus a lot in between. With areas dedicated to plush toys, dolls, home decor, DVDs, clothing, mugs, and collectibles, everyone is bound to find something here. The place is busy most evenings and on weekends—especially after the parks close.

WONDERGROUND GALLERY: Distinctive and eclectic, Wonderground is a work of art in and of itself. The contemporary venue showcases unique art collections and works from a new generation of artists, interpreted through different mediums, styles, and forms.

Fun & Games

AMC MOVIE THEATRES: Moviegoers enjoy wall-to-wall movie screens and comfy stadium seating at each of the 12 cinemas located inside this megaplex (including IMAX). Current releases are shown throughout the day, with special matinee and late-night screenings. The first showing of the day usually comes at a discounted price.

ESPN ZONE: This sports complex offers dining options and a lounge area, plus two distinct fun zones. In the Screening Room, sports fans can cheer their teams to victory, as games from around the world are televised on one central 16-foot screen and a dozen 42-inch monitors.

The Sports Arena challenges guests with sports-themed games that put your skills, strength, and smarts to the test. Game cards (necessary to play the arena's games) can be purchased in $5 increments.

Arrive early when a big game is scheduled.

HOT TIP!

Want to save a little money at Downtown Disney? Visit *www.disneyland.com* to see if there are any special offers available for the day you plan to visit—and use the coupons at the back of this book!

Sports

Southern California's appealing combination of warm, sunny weather and invigorating ocean breezes has created a population of outdoors and exercise enthusiasts. Athletes flex their muscles on golf courses and tennis courts; atop surfboards, bicycles, and in-line skates; on hiking and jogging trails; or 15 feet underwater, mingling with schools of fish.

As part of Orange County, California, Anaheim is within easy distance of the county's 35,000-plus acres of parkland and several hundred miles of bike trails. Hiking paths and fishing streams crisscross 460,000 acres of mountain terrain in Cleveland National Forest. Just 15 miles south of Anaheim, prime Pacific Ocean beaches—perfect for basking in the sun or catching the ultimate wave—await the wayfarer. In fact, 42 miles of glistening sand and sleepy seaside communities are within an hour's drive of Anaheim.

Those who delight in spying on Mother Nature can catch glimpses of California's gray whales as they migrate to Mexico for the winter, or ospreys, blue herons, and swallows returning to the area in the spring. A team of Orange County's most entertaining creatures, hockey-playing Ducks, can be spotted from September through April (and later, if they make a run for the Stanley Cup). Even Angels have been sighted, gracing the bases at Angel Stadium, April through September (and possibly October).

No question, the sporting opportunities in and around the city of Anaheim are quite bountiful.

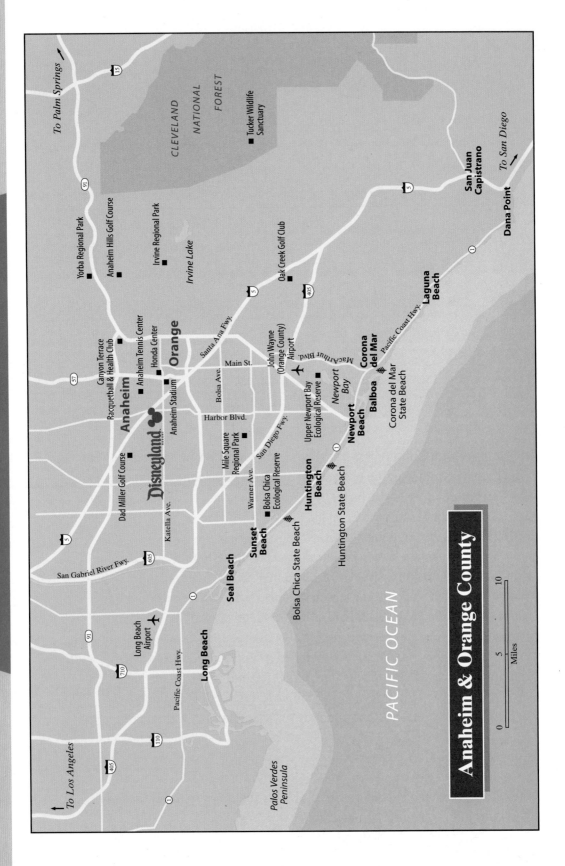

Anaheim & Orange County

PACIFIC OCEAN

To Los Angeles

To Palm Springs

To San Diego

CLEVELAND NATIONAL FOREST

Tucker Wildlife Sanctuary

San Juan Capistrano

Dana Point

Laguna Beach

Yorba Regional Park

Anaheim Hills Golf Course

Irvine Regional Park

Irvine Lake

Oak Creek Golf Club

Canyon Terrace Racquetball & Health Club

Anaheim Tennis Center

Honda Center

Orange

Anaheim

Main St.

John Wayne (Orange County) Airport

MacArthur Blvd.

Corona del Mar

Balboa

Anaheim Stadium

Bolsa Ave.

Santa Ana Fwy.

Newport Bay

Newport Beach

Corona del Mar State Beach

Disneyland

Harbor Blvd.

Upper Newport Bay Ecological Reserve

Dad Miller Golf Course

Mile Square Regional Park

San Diego Fwy.

Huntington Beach

Katella Ave.

Warner Ave.

Bolsa Chica Ecological Reserve

Huntington State Beach

Sunset Beach

Bolsa Chica State Beach

San Gabriel River Fwy.

Seal Beach

Long Beach Airport

Long Beach

Pacific Coast Hwy.

Palos Verdes Peninsula

Pacific Coast Hwy.

Miles

0   5   10

Eye on the Ball

Golf

ANAHEIM HILLS GOLF COURSE: This challenging championship course is a hilly, par-71, 6,245-yard layout nestled in the valleys and slopes of the scenic Anaheim Hills. Greens fees (cart included) are $52 Monday through Thursday, $59 on Friday, and $70 on weekends and holidays. Guests age 55 and older can play Monday through Friday for $41. Clubs can be rented for $30. Reservations are recommended (call seven days ahead for both weekend and weekday play). The Anaheim Hills Golf Course is open 365 days a year, from dawn till dusk. 6501 E. Nohl Ranch Rd., Anaheim; 714-998-3041; *www.anaheimhillsgc.com.*

DAD MILLER GOLF COURSE: "Dad" Miller made a hole-in-one on this course (on the 116-yard 11th hole) when he was 93 years old, and it's still a favorite with older guests, who appreciate the flat, walkable terrain and park-like setting. But if you're a tad on the younger side, don't let that keep you from playing here. This par-71, 6,025-yard golf course is one of the busiest in California—partly

HOT TIP!

To get additional information about these and other Orange County area golf courses and tournaments, visit *www.playocgolf.com.*

because of its convenient location in the northwest corner of the city, but also because it's just right for the strictly recreational golfer. The cost to play here is $29 Monday through Thursday, $36 on Friday, and $41 on Saturday, Sunday, and holidays. Guests 62 and older can play standby for $19 Monday through Friday. Golf carts cost about $13 for 18 holes, $8.50 for nine holes.

Reservations are suggested and may be made up to a week in advance. The course is open 365 days a year, dawn till dusk. 430 N. Gilbert St., Anaheim; 714-765-3481 (pro shop and reservations); *www.dadmillergc.com.*

Tennis & Racquetball

ANAHEIM TENNIS CENTER: This public facility has all the perks of a private tennis club—an inviting clubhouse, a well-stocked pro shop, computerized practice machines, lockers, and showers. The staff will make an effort to pair you with a suitable partner, as long as you make your request in advance.

There are 12 fast, hard-surface courts, all lighted for night play. Singles and doubles rates range from about $5 to $12 per person, per hour (depending on time of day). Use of a ball machine is about $25 per hour; they are separated from the courts, but this area is still a good place to practice forehand and backhand strokes.

Playing hours begin at 7 A.M. and end at 10 P.M. Monday through Friday, and start at 7 A.M. and end at 6 P.M. weekends and holidays. Racquets are free for those taking lessons. Locker and shower facilities are free (you must supply towels). A half-hour private lesson with the resident pro costs about $38; call for rates for semiprivate or group lessons.

SPORTS

131

Reservations (which are bookable up to three days in advance for nonmembers) are suggested, especially for court times after 5 P.M. It's approximately three miles from the Disneyland resort. 975 S. State College Boulevard, Anaheim; 714-991-9090; *www.anaheimtenniscenter.com.*

CANYON TERRACE RACQUETBALL & FITNESS CLUB: A real find for visitors, this facility has five air-conditioned racquetball courts and low court fees—$9 per person on weekends or before 4 P.M. Monday through Friday. After 4 P.M., it is $10 per person. The club rents racquets for $2 to $4 and offers its full-size weight room to nonmembers for $7. Towels may also be rented for a small fee. (All prices are subject to change.) There is a pro shop, too. Hours are 6 A.M. to 10 P.M. Monday through Thursday, 6 A.M. to 9 P.M. on Friday, 7 A.M. to 7 P.M. on Saturday, and 7 A.M. to 5 P.M. on Sunday. 100 N. Tustin Ave., Anaheim; 714-974-0280; *www.canyonterraceracquetball.com.*

Spectator Sports

BASEBALL
Los Angeles Angels of Anaheim (April–October): Angel Stadium of Anaheim, 2000 E. Gene Autry Way, Anaheim; call 714-634-2000 (information) or 714-663-9000 (tickets); *www.angelsbaseball.com*

Los Angeles Dodgers (April–October): Dodger Stadium, 1000 Elysian Park Ave., Los Angeles; call 866-363-4377; or visit *www.dodgers.com*

BASKETBALL
Los Angeles Clippers (October–April): Staples Center, 1111 S. Figueroa St., Los Angeles; 800-462-2849; *www.nba.com/clippers*

Los Angeles Lakers (October–April): Staples Center, 1111 S. Figueroa St., Los Angeles; 800-462-2849; *www.nba.com/lakers*

Los Angeles Sparks (May–September): Staples Center, 1111 S. Figueroa St., Los Angeles; 877-447-7275; *www.wnba.com/sparks*

HOCKEY
Los Angeles Kings (October–April): Staples Center, 1111 S. Figueroa St., Los Angeles; 800-745-3000 (Ticketmaster); *www.lakings.com*

Anaheim Ducks (October–April): Honda Center, 2695 E. Katella Ave., Anaheim; 877-945-3946 (info) or 800-745-3000 (Ticketmaster); *www.anaheimducks.com*

SPORTS

Surf & Sun

Beaches

Orange County's public beaches cover 42 miles of coastline—some dramatic, with high cliffs and crashing waves; others tranquil, with sheltered coves and tide pools. In summer, the water temperature averages 64 degrees but can get as high as 70; in winter, it's a nippy 57 to 60 degrees.

Beaches are open from around 6 A.M. to 10 P.M., with lifeguards on duty in the summer. Bicycles, in-line skates, and roller skates are available for rent in some locations. Access is free, but there is usually a fee to park. For additional beach information, go to the Surf and Sand section of *www.orangecounty.net*.

BALBOA/NEWPORT BEACH: The Balboa Peninsula juts into the Pacific Ocean, creating beaches—Newport on the mainland, Balboa on the peninsula—that are long and horseshoe-shaped, pleasant and sandy, and popular with families, surfers, and sightseers alike. Visit *www.ocbeachinfo.com* for water quality and environmental information.

The largest small-craft harbor in the world, Newport Harbor shelters more than 9,000 boats. For the best view, drive south along the peninsula on Newport Boulevard to Balboa Boulevard; turn right on Palm Street, and you'll find parking for the Balboa Pier and Fun Zone; *www.thebalboafunzone.com*.

> ### HOT TIP!
> For a scenic 45-minute walk, follow the harbor-hugging pathway around Balboa Island. For a mini-expedition, head to Little Balboa Island—it can be easily circumnavigated in about 20 minutes.

Throughout the fall and winter, the 1,000-acre Upper Newport Bay Nature Preserve and Ecological Reserve teems with great blue herons, ospreys, and many other winged creatures. The park's partially subterranean Peter and Mary Muth Interpretive Center, at 2301 University Drive (at Irvine Avenue), has exhibits on bird life, the watershed, and the history of Newport Bay (closed Mondays).

During migratory season (October through March), the Newport Bay Conservancy leads free walking tours (once a month, on a Saturday), pointing out birds, as well as fossils, marsh plants, and fish. Every Saturday and Sunday morning, year-round, the conservancy also offers a 2-hour guided kayak tour of the Back Bay for $25 per person, age 8 and above.

The reserve is open daily 7 A.M. to sunset. To obtain updated information about guided tours and various special events year-round, as well as directions to specific parts of the reserve, contact Newport Bay Conservancy: 949-640-1751 or *www.newportbay.org*.

CORONA DEL MAR STATE BEACH: Secluded Corona del Mar State Beach is a favorite for swimming and snorkeling; and the lookout point above the beach is a great place to watch the sun set. There are picnic tables, grills, fire rings, a snack bar, and showers. For information, visit *www.orangecounty.net* (Surf and Sand section) or call 949-644-3151.

HUNTINGTON BEACH: The self-proclaimed "Surf City, U.S.A." (and home to the International Surfing Museum) hosts competitions year-round (winter is best for wave height). Surfboards and wet suits may be rented or purchased; *www.surfcityusa.com*.

Huntington City Beach is a 3.5-mile stretch of sand fronting the town and is a popular place for swimming, bodysurfing, and beach volleyball. The pier provides an ideal spot for fishing and a good vantage point for observing the passing scene. For surf information, call 714-536-9303; *www.hbonline.com*.

Bolsa Chica Wetlands, 1,449 acres of Pacific Ocean marshland a mile north of Huntington Beach pier on Pacific Coast Highway, harbors fish and wetland birds. To get there, cross the bridge from the beach parking lot and follow a trail through the marsh; 714-846-1114; *www.bolsachica.org*.

LAGUNA BEACH: More than 20 different beaches and coves line this seven-mile coastline, popular with surfers, kayakers, body boarders, and snorkelers. Laguna is one of the best spots in Orange County to scuba dive, though you need a wet suit year-round.

Laguna Sea Sports (925 N. Coast Hwy.; 949-494-6965; *www.beachcitiesscuba.com*) offers full rentals, guided beach dives, classes, general information, and more; there's a pool on the premises, and it's only approximately one block from the beach. Main Beach (which is located in the middle of town) offers basketball and volleyball.

A short walk away, Heisler Park has picnic areas, beaches, cliff-top lookout points, and charcoal grills; stairs lead to tide pools. Serious hikers like to head for Crystal Cove State Park (*www.crystalcovestatepark.com*), Aliso and Wood Canyons Wilderness Park (*www.ocparks.com*), or Laguna Coast Wilderness Park. Watch the sun set from Laguna Art Museum or from Laguna Village; *www.lblg.org* or *www.lagunabeach.com*.

Fishing

In Orange County, you can cast for bass, catfish, and trout in tranquil lakes; troll the Pacific for bonitos, barracuda, halibut, and more; and hand-scoop grunions (license required) off the beach.

GRUNION ALERT: One place to try your hand—literally—at catching grunion (provided that you have a license) is at Cabrillo Beach in March, June, July, and August, when the tiny fish come ashore to lay eggs in the sand and then head back out to sea on outgoing waves. (Grunion catching is illegal—even with a license—in April and May.)

Know that grunion are notoriously slippery, and you are required to catch them exclusively with your hands; fortunately, they also shimmer in the moonlight, so they're fairly easy to spot. The best time to go grunion fishing is about an hour or two after high tide on the second through fifth nights after a new or full moon. The park closes at 10 P.M.; gates close at 9 P.M. For additional information, visit *www.wildlife.ca.gov* or call 831-649-2870.

SPORTFISHING: Fishing boats set out from Davey's Locker at Balboa Pavilion in Newport Beach (949-673-1434; *www.daveyslocker.com*) and from Dana Wharf Sportfishing at Dana Point Harbor (*www.danawharf.com*; 888-224-0603). Reservations are suggested. Licenses, which are legally necessary for deep-sea sportfishing, must be purchased in advance via *www.ca.wildlifelicense.com*. Fishing licenses cost about $16 per day.

Parks

IRVINE REGIONAL PARK: Located in Santiago Canyon, near Irvine Lake, this peaceful place has hiking and equestrian trails that wind through 477 hilly acres and centuries-old sycamores and oaks. The oldest county park in California, it offers bike trails, the Orange County Zoo, playgrounds, and a small waterfall, creek, and picnic facilities. Zoo admission is $2 for guests age 3 and up. There is a $3 to $5 parking fee per vehicle year-round (the parking fee is usually $7 to $10 on major holidays). 1 Irvine Park Rd., Orange; 714-973-6835; *www.ocparks.com/irvinepark*.

MILE SQUARE REGIONAL PARK: It's one square mile in area—hence the name. Besides five miles of winding bike trails, the park has a walking course, a nature area, and picnic areas and shelters. Bicycles may be rented here on weekends and holidays. 16801 Euclid Ave., Fountain Valley; 714-973-6600; *www.ocparks.com/milesquare*.

TUCKER WILDLIFE SANCTUARY: This 12-acre sanctuary in the Santa Ana Mountains' Modjeska Canyon is an oasis of flora and fauna. Naturalists answer questions, and there are hiking trails, a small natural history museum, and a children's garden. A donation is suggested. 29322 Modjeska Canyon Rd., Modjeska Canyon; 714-649-2760; *www.tuckerwildlife.org*.

YORBA REGIONAL PARK: These 175 acres in the Santa Ana Canyon cradle four lakes, picnic areas, playgrounds, and hiking trails, equestrian activities, horseshoe pits, model sailboating, volleyball courts, baseball fields, and biking trails (bike rentals on weekends). Visitors can walk or ride a bicycle into the park without charge; parking costs $3 to $5 ($7 to $10 on holidays). 7600 E. La Palma Ave., Anaheim; 714-973-6615; *www.ocparks.com/parks/yorba*.

Index

INDEX

Index

Where in Disneyland?
(from page 91)

1. **Sleeping Beauty Castle
   (Fantasyland)**
2. **Storybook Land Canal Boats
   (Fantasyland)**
3. **Adventureland's Jungle Cruise**
4. **Peter Pan's Flight attraction
   (Fantasyland)**
5. **Mark Twain Riverboat
   (Frontierland)**
6. **The Disneyland Monorail
   (Tomorrowland)**

Coupons

FREE UPGRADE

Book at **www.alamo.com**
Or call 1-800-462-5266
Reference coupon code **AU526WEF8**
at the time of reservation

Subject to terms and conditions on reverse side.

10% OFF
ENTIRE PURCHASE

Offering authentic Disney collectibles,
exquisite crystal mementos,
and sparkling hand-blown glass gifts.

Subject to terms and conditions on reverse side.

$5 OFF
YOUR PURCHASE OF $25 OR MORE

Make your own furry friend!
Personalize it with outfits,
sounds, scents, and more.

Subject to terms and conditions on reverse side.

Free Hot Dog

When you purchase 2 hot dogs
of equal or greater value

Subject to terms and conditions on reverse side.

Rent a compact through midsize vehicle, now through December 31, 2017. One-car-class upgrade applied at the time of reservation. One coupon per Alamo rental and void once redeemed. Offer is subject to standard rental conditions. Blackout dates may apply. 24-hour advance reservation required. Not valid with any other discount or promotional rate. Subject to availability and valid only at these participating Southern California Locations: Los Angeles Airport, Orange County/John Wayne Airport, San Diego Airport, Long Beach Airport, Ontario Airport, Burbank Bob Hope Airport, Palm Springs Airport, Downtown Disney and Anaheim. Taxes, other governmentally-authorized or imposed surcharges (including GST/VAT), license and concession recoupment fees, airport and airport facility fees, fuel, one-way rental charge and optional items (such as CDW up to US $30 per day) are extra. In the U.S. check your insurance and/or credit card for rental vehicle coverage. Renter and additional driver(s) must meet standard age, driver and credit requirements. 24-hour advance reservation required. Availability is limited. Subject to change without notice. Void where prohibited. Coupon VOID if bought, bartered, or sold for cash. Must present original coupon at time of rental. ©2016 Alamo Rent A Car. All rights reserved.

Valid only at Build-A-Bear Workshop® in DOWNTOWN DISNEY® Anaheim District. Valid on all Build-A-Bear Workshop® furry friends, clothing and accessories. Not valid on prior purchases, a Build-A-Party® celebration, Bear Bucks® cards. Coupons may not be combined and cannot be bought, sold or exchanged for cash or coupons. Not valid with any other offer. Local and state taxes, as applicable, are payable by bearer. Must present original coupon at time of purchase. Photocopies prohibited. Valid for coupon recipient only. Limit one coupon per person, per visit. Nontransferable. Offer good while supplies last. Void where prohibited or restricted. Where required cash value 1/100 of 1 cent. Not valid at buildabear.com.

Offer valid through 12/31/17

For more information, visit
buildabear.com, or call (714) 776-5980.

Valid at the Arribas Brothers stores at Disneyland® Park at Crystal Arts on Main Street, U.S.A. and at Cristal D' Orleans in New Orleans Square (Park admission is required) and at the kiosk in the Downtown Disney District.

Coupon excludes: C.D Thailand/Crystela, Glassblowing Custom/Special Orders (torch and furnace work), Herend, Hummel, Liuli, Lladró, Moser, Nao Collection by Lladró, Starlite Collection (acrylic), Swarovski, Wendt & Kuhn, shipping charges and online purchases.

Discount cannot be combined with any other offers or discounts.

No cash value.

Coupon must be presented at time of purchase to receive discount

Reproductions not accepted.

Offer subject to change without notice.

For more information, visit *www.arribas.com*, or call 714-635-1940

Offer valid through 12/31/17

TERMS AND CONDITIONS

Redeemable at Downtown Disney
in Anaheim, California.

Coupon must be surrendered at time of purchase.

Not valid with any other offers or discounts.

Limit one per coupon.

For information, call 714-535-5994 or 626-432-6900.

Photocopies will not be accepted.

Non-transferable, non-negotiable.

Offer valid through 12/31/17

Coupons

20% OFF

ANY PURCHASE

(valid on food and beverage only)

Subject to terms and conditions on reverse side.

1 FREE PASTRY

With any purchase over $15

Subject to terms and conditions on reverse side.

60 BONUS POINTS

Purchase a $20 game card at
ESPN Zone® Restaurant
and receive 60 Bonus Points—a $15 value.
Located in the *Downtown Disney*® District

Subject to terms and conditions on reverse side.

$10 OFF

ANY RIDE PURCHASE OF $40 OR MORE

Build and customize your own
radio-controlled RIDE at this
super-charged, interactive store.

Subject to terms and conditions on reverse side.

SOMETHING SILVER®

www.somethingsilver.com

10% OFF

ENTIRE PURCHASE

Offering stylish, high-quality jewelry
from top national and international
designer collections

Subject to terms and conditions on reverse side.

Free PRETZEL

**When you purchase 2 pretzels
of equal or greater value**

Subject to terms and conditions on reverse side.